CARMEN NIEHAUS

LET'S COOK

5

This book was published in
Human & Rousseau's fiftieth
anniversary year.

First edition 2009
by Human & Rousseau
an imprint of NB Publishers
40 Heerengracht, Cape Town 8000

Commisioning editor: Daleen van der Merwe
Editor: Celia van Zyl
Design: PETAL**DESIGN**
Photography: David Briers
Styling: Bernice van der Merwe
Proof reading and index: Joy Clack

Reproduction by Resolution, Cape Town, RSA
Printing and bound by Craft Print, Singapore

ISBN 978-0-7981-5078-1

Accessories courtesy of
Mr Price Home, Clicks, Ackermans Home Comforts,
Woolworths, Game, NocNatural Affairs, Albert Carpets

CONTENTS

Acknowledgements

No author, especially not the author of a recipe book, is ever solely responsible for compiling a book. There are several people who help ensure the recipes are accurate and read well and that the pictures inspire you to try the recipes. Firstly, I would like to thank everyone at *YOU,* including publisher Willem Breytenbach and editor Esmaré Weideman who always give me free rein to delve in *YOU's* treasure trove of recipes, and Kerneels Breytenbach, head of Human & Rousseau, who always takes such good care of his authors. In the test kitchen, as has been the case for many years, everything possible is done to ensure that each recipe works and for this I would like to thank my assistants who've come and gone over the years. For the past few years Daleen van der Merwe was in charge of the test kitchen. She was also a wonderful source of knowledge and inspiration. And now, with this book, she was my publisher at Human & Rousseau. Thank you, Daleen, for your enthusiasm and thoroughness. To Bernice van der Merwe and David Briers who were responsible for the photography, thank you so much for the beautiful pictures – I wish I could explain to everyone how much time and energy goes into hunting for the props, preparation and ensuring that every little detail is just right. Thank you Leander Jewells for copying the original recipes, buying the ingredients and preparing the dishes, and Priscilla Petersen for patiently helping out in the test kitchen. Thank you Vanessa Hollies for checking that all the pictures were loaded. And to Magda Herbst, who has been inputting recipes for me for years, thank you for sacrificing your weekends and evenings to ensure this project was finished on time. To Cecilia van Zyl and Joy Clack who did the editing and proofreading, many thanks for your painstaking accuracy. To Petal Palmer of Petaldesign thank you for the book's beautiful design.

FOREWORD

YOU Let's Cook recipe books can be found in many South African homes. Over the years they've held their own alongside cookery books by well-known food authors. After selling thousands of copies the series is now a collector's item in its own right. What makes these books so unique is that they give us a glimpse into the homes of South Africans, not only through the recipes we receive, but also through our visits to many places and well-known chefs countrywide. For this book I sifted through our recipe files going back 20 years and put together a collection of recipes, revamping and adapting them and adding tips and ideas. To keep up with current trends we have over the past few years published several articles featuring cuisines from other continents, such as recipes from Asia - adapted and simplified these recipes so everyone can make and enjoy them. Many of these recipes have been included in this book, along with all the information you need to make them with ease. As with interior design where the latest trend is to combine the old and the new, my aim with *Let's Cook 5* was to put together a collection of old favourites for everyday cooking and a few slightly more sophisticated and unusual recipes with which you can impress your guests.

Enjoy the mix.

Carmen Niehaus
Food editor
YOU and *Huisgenoot*

SNACKS AND BREAD

A variety of containers (spoons, glasses and wood and glass bowls) and platters packed with an assortment of appetising finger food is the latest way to entertain rather than serving a full three-course meal. Create a fusion spread with eats from various cuisines such as spring rolls from Asia, meze from Turkey and Greece, antipasti from Italy and tapas from Spain. And don't forget the old favourites, spreads and bread.

Toasted ciabatta

Toast thin slices of ciabatta and serve them with a combination of tart ingredients to wash down with a glass of wine with a high acid content.

1 each red, yellow and green pepper, diced
1 small onion, finely chopped
100 ml wine vinegar
1 ml (pinch) salt
cherry tomatoes and gherkins
1 ciabatta, very thinly sliced and toasted
olive oil

Mix the peppers, onion, vinegar and salt and spoon into a small bowl. Put the cherry tomatoes and gherkins in separate bowls and serve with the toasted ciabatta and a drizzle of olive oil.

Makes 6.

Bruschetta with grilled tomatoes

A quick recipe from chef Nic van Wyk of Stellenbosch: grilled tomatoes served on toast.

a variety of cherry tomatoes
olive oil
brown sugar
salt and freshly ground black pepper
slices of toasted bread, such as sweet sourdough bread or ciabatta
garlic cloves, peeled

Arrange a single layer of tomatoes in an ovenproof dish, drizzle with a little olive oil and grill rapidly until just soft. Sprinkle with a little brown sugar if desired and season with salt and pepper. Rub the toast with a fresh garlic clove, spoon the tomatoes on top and serve.

Makes 4–6.

Tip
Opt for eats you can prepare in advance. Alternatively ask your guests to help you with last-minute preparations.

Bruschetta with grilled tomatoes

Bruschetta with a variety of spreads

Use interesting breads such as Italian ciabatta or sourdough bread and toast the slices on both sides until golden. Alternatively use small griddle cakes. Top with any of the following:

RICOTTA SPREAD
Mix 200 g crumbled ricotta with 1 firm peeled, chopped tomato. Finely chop 2 basil leaves and add to 30 ml (2 T) olive oil. Season to taste with salt and pepper. Drizzle toasted slices of bread with olive oil and spoon a little of the ricotta spread on top. Serve with stuffed green olives.

CHICKEN LIVER SPREAD
Fry 250 g (1 packet) chicken livers and 1 finely chopped garlic clove in heated olive oil and butter until the livers are just done. Season with 2 chopped fresh sage leaves, a little freshly squeezed lemon juice and salt and pepper to taste. Mash with a fork and mix with 125 g (½ container) cream cheese and serve on toasted bread.

TUNA SPREAD
Drain 1 can (187 g) tuna in oil, add the finely grated rind of 1 lemon and blitz in a food processor until smooth. Add about 45 ml (3 T) olive oil. Finely chop ½ onion and season with freshly ground black pepper. Add to the tuna mixture. Drizzle toasted bread with olive oil and spoon the tuna mixture on top. Garnish with capers.

Potato mini pizzas

These pizzas are made from potatoes and resemble rösti but are baked in the oven.

1 kg fairly old potatoes, peeled
80 g butter, melted
80 g ready-made basil pesto
1 can (85 g) smoked mussels
250 ml (1 c) grated mozzarella cheese
125 ml (½ c) grated Parmesan cheese
fresh basil leaves to garnish

Tip
Make the pizzas in advance but add the toppings just before serving.

Preheat the oven to 200 °C. Line a large baking sheet with baking paper and grease with butter, margarine or nonstick food spray.

Coarsely grate the potatoes and put them in a mixing bowl. Cover the potatoes with cold water and leave for 5 minutes. Drain well and squeeze out the excess liquid. Put the potatoes on a clean tea towel and pat dry. Mix the potatoes and butter in a clean mixing bowl. Put a 6 cm cookie cutter on the baking sheet and spoon 20 ml (4 t) of the potato mixture inside, pressing the mixture down firmly. Remove the cookie cutter and repeat with the remaining potato mixture, leaving a 3 cm space between each pizza. Bake the pizzas for 20 minutes, turn with a spatula and bake for another 5 minutes or until golden. Spread the pizzas with the pesto, top each with a mussel and scatter the mozzarella and Parmesan cheeses on top. Bake for about 5 minutes or until the cheese begins to melt. Garnish with basil leaves and serve immediately.

Makes 24.

Spinach flapjacks with smoked trout and sour cream dressing

Flapjacks are used instead of toast.

SOUR CREAM DRESSING
125 ml (½ c) sour cream
30 ml (2 T) thick mayonnaise
salt and freshly ground black pepper
fresh herbs, salt and pepper

SPINACH FLAPJACKS
250 ml (1 c) self-raising flour
125 ml (½ c) milk
125 ml (½ c) water
2 extra-large eggs
1 ml (pinch) salt
nutmeg
30 ml (2 T) butter, melted
150 g cooked spinach, squeezed
   to remove excess liquid and
   finely chopped
1 small onion, finely chopped
oil for frying

TO ASSEMBLE
1 packet (125 g) smoked trout
1 avocado, sliced
1 packet (250 g) Chinese rice noodles
oil for frying

SOUR CREAM DRESSING
Mix the ingredients for the dressing and chill until needed.

SPINACH FLAPJACKS
Mix all the ingredients for the flapjacks, except the spinach and onion, to make a smooth batter. Fold the spinach and onion into the batter and fry spoonfuls of the batter in a little heated oil until done. Keep warm.

Makes about 20.

TO ASSEMBLE
Put a flapjack on a plate, stack slices of trout and avocado on top, and drizzle with the dressing. Heat oil in a pot and deep-fry a handful of rice noodles. Drain on paper towels and pile on top of each flapjack.

> **Variation**
> Add ½ a can (200 g) whole sweet-corn kernels to the flapjack mixture instead of the spinach.

Oyster and litchi treats

6 tots (150 ml) vodka
crushed ice
1 litre (4 c) berry juice
6 fresh oysters, cleaned and loosened
1 red chilli, seeded and finely chopped
12 litchis, pitted and sliced into thin strips
freshly ground black pepper
fresh mint to garnish

Pour a tot of vodka into each of 6 martini glasses. Fill the glasses with crushed ice and top up with berry juice. Put an open oyster shell half on the ice and spoon the chilli and litchi strips on top of the oysters. Season with freshly ground black pepper and garnish with fresh mint leaves. Serve immediately.

Serves 6.

Calamares

In Spain calamari rings are dipped in seasoned cake flour and fried.

300 g frozen calamari rings
5 ml (1 t) paprika
2 ml (½ t) cayenne pepper
2 ml (½ t) salt
1 ml (pinch) black pepper
200 ml cake flour
2 extra-large eggs, whisked
oil for deep-frying
lemon and fresh parsley to serve
extra lemon slices for serving

Leave the calamari rings to soak in cold water to defrost. Pat dry with paper towels. Combine the paprika, cayenne pepper, salt, black pepper and flour in a large bowl. Add the calamari rings, ensuring each ring is completely coated with the flour mixture. Lift each ring from the flour mixture with a fork, dip in the whisked egg and then in the flour again. Heat sufficient oil and fry a few rings at a time until golden. Remove, drain on paper towels and sprinkle over lemon juice and finely chopped parsley. Serve immediately with extra lemon slices.

Serves 4.

> **Tip**
> Squid heads can be prepared in the same way.

Prawns in chilli sauce

The prawns are stir-fried in a chilli sauce to give them an Asian flavour.

20–24 large frozen prawns,
   heads and shells intact

CHILLI SAUCE
100 ml canola oil
10 ml (2 t) sesame oil
15 ml (1 T) finely grated lemon rind
   or crushed lemon grass
45–60 ml (3–4 T) rice vinegar or lemon
   juice
2–4 cloves garlic, crushed
2–3 small red chillies, seeded and
   finely chopped
15 ml (1 T) grated fresh ginger
2 ml (½ t) turmeric
2 ml (½ t) paprika and/or Chinese five spice
generous dash soy and fish sauces
chopped coriander leaves

TO FINISH
extra olive oil for frying
salt and freshly ground black pepper
fresh lemon slices and extra coriander
   leaves to serve

Cut open the back of each prawn and remove the alimentary canal. Do not remove the heads and shells.

Mix the ingredients for the chilli sauce and pour over the prawns in a glass or ceramic dish. Marinate for at least 1 hour, turning once or twice. Drain but reserve the marinade.

Heat a little olive oil in a wok or pan and stir-fry 7 prawns at a time over high heat until pink and very crisp – it won't take longer than 3–4 minutes. Remove the prawns from the wok and set aside. Pour the sauce into the wok and bring to the boil. Return the prawns to the boiling sauce and stir-fry for about 2 minutes. Season well with salt and freshly ground black pepper. Serve immediately with extra lemon slices and a scattering of coriander leaves.

Serves 4–6.

> **Tip**
> Calamari steaks cut into strips can be prepared in the same way.

Prawns in chilli sauce

Prawns in vinaigrette

These prawns are served chilled.

VINAIGRETTE DRESSING
75 ml (5 T) olive oil
30 ml (2 T) white wine vinegar
20 ml (4 t) sherry
1 clove garlic, crushed
10 ml (2 t) lemon juice
10 ml (2 t) soy sauce
5 ml (1 t) honey
20 ml (4 t) chopped fresh basil leaves OR
   5 ml (1 t) dried basil
salt and freshly ground black pepper

PRAWNS
250 ml (1 c) chicken stock
200 g frozen prawns, defrosted

TO FINISH
½ English cucumber, quartered
   lengthways and each quarter cut
   into thin strips
4 spring onions, sliced diagonally
12–15 small tomatoes, halved or diced
selection of salad leaves
extra basil to garnish

VINAIGRETTE DRESSING
Whisk together the dressing ingredients in a glass bowl.
Season to taste and set aside.

PRAWNS
Bring the chicken stock to the boil in a saucepan. Arrange the prawns on a steamer rack or in a metal sieve and put over the boiling stock. Cover and steam the prawns for 8–10 minutes or until just done. Remove from the heat. Put the prawns in a glass bowl and pour over half the vinaigrette. Leave to cool then chill.

TO FINISH
Mix the cucumber and spring onion strips and tomatoes with the remaining vinaigrette and chill. Remove the chilled prawns from the vinaigrette and add them to the salad ingredients. Arrange the salad and basil leaves on individual plates or in individual bowls and spoon the prawns on top.

Serves 6.

Boquerones with salsa

Rapidly fry tiny silverfish and serve with a tomato salsa.

SILVERFISH
60 ml (¼ c) cake flour
salt and freshly ground black pepper
300 g silverfish
oil for deep-frying

GARLIC AND TOMATO SALSA
2 red peppers, seeded, grilled,
   skins removed and chopped
3 large tomatoes, peeled, seeded
   and chopped
3 cloves garlic, roughly chopped
2–3 dried chillies, seeded and
   finely chopped
100 ml olive oil
15 ml (1 T) red wine vinegar
5 ml (1 t) salt
pinch sugar

SILVERFISH
Mix the flour, salt and pepper in a plastic bag, add the fish and shake until coated with the flour. Fry the fish in a pan with hot oil for 3–4 minutes. Serve with the garlic and tomato salsa.

GARLIC AND TOMATO SALSA
Blitz all the ingredients in a food processor until fairly coarse.

Serves 6.

Spring rolls with smoked snoek and piquanté peppers

These Asian bites are given a South African twist with snoek and piquanté peppers.

150 g smoked snoek, bones removed
12 round rice paper wrappers (see tip)
12 fresh coriander leaves
10 sweet piquanté peppers,
  cut into thin strips
sweet chilli sauce to serve

Cut or break the snoek into 24 thin strips. Dip a rice paper wrapper in very hot water until it just softens. Lay it on a damp tea towel. Put a coriander leaf in the middle and top with 2 strips of snoek and a few strips of piquanté pepper. Fold in the left and right sides of the wrapper and roll up. Repeat with the remaining ingredients. Serve with sweet chilli sauce. Cover the rolls with a damp tea towel until ready to serve.

Makes 12.

Tip
Rice paper wrappers are transparent sheets made of rice flour, salt and water. They are sold at Asian shops and supermarkets specialising in Asian ingredients. The rolls can be enjoyed as is or deep-fried. These wrappers bear no resemblance to the rice paper used for sweets such as nougat.

Vietnamese shrimp rolls

To make these tasty morsels, spring roll wrappers are filled with shrimps and soaked vermicelli noodles.

DIP
30 ml (2 T) satay sauce
45 ml (3 T) hoisin sauce
1 red chilli, seeded and finely chopped
15 ml (1 T) chopped toasted peanuts
15 ml (1 T) lemon juice

ROLLS
100 g mung bean vermicelli noodles
20–25 round rice paper wrappers,
  about 16 cm in diameter
40–60 fresh coriander leaves
20 large cooked shrimps, peeled
  and halved lengthways

DIP
In a small mixing bowl whisk together the ingredients for the dip and set aside until needed.

ROLLS
Soak the vermicelli in enough boiling water to cover for about 5 minutes. Drain well and cut them into shorter lengths with a scissors. Work with 1 rice paper wrapper at a time. Dip it into hot water for 30 seconds or until soft and flexible. Remove immediately, taking care as the wrappers tear easily when soft. Put the wrapper on a clean surface and spoon about 15–20 ml (3–4 t) of the noodles on the bottom third of the circle, keeping an edge clear to fold over. Put 2–3 coriander leaves and 2 shrimp halves on top of the noodles. Fold in the sides and roll up firmly. Repeat with the remaining wrappers and ingredients and put the rolls seam side down on a plate. Cover the rolls with a damp tea towel if not serving them immediately. Serve with the dip.

Makes 20.

Vietnamese salad rolls

Crisp vegetables are wrapped in lettuce leaves and then in rice paper wrappers.
These rolls are light and refreshing, making them ideal for summer.

1 iceberg lettuce, leaves separated
　　and hard sections removed
2–3 carrots, scraped and cut into
　　thin strips
1 small cucumber, peeled, seeded and
　　cut into thin strips
3 spring onions, cut into thin strips
225 g bean sprouts
1 handful fresh mint leaves
1 handful fresh coriander leaves
12 round rice paper wrappers

Put 12 lettuce leaves on a work surface. Put the carrot, cucumber and spring onion strips and sprouts in the middle of the leaves. Top with a few mint and coriander leaves and roll up each leaf. Trim the ends of each roll. Fill a large flat dish with hot water and soak the rice paper wrappers in the water one by one for about 20 seconds or until soft and sticky. Put the soaked wrappers on a damp tea towel and cover with another damp tea towel to prevent them drying out. Put a lettuce roll on each wrapper about 3 cm from the side nearest you. Fold the side nearest you over the roll, fold in the sides and roll up firmly. Put the rolls on a plate and cover again with a damp tea towel. Repeat until all the wrappers and ingredients have been used and serve with nuoc cham (see recipe).

Makes 12.

NUOC CHAM (CHILLI SAUCE)
Using a mortar and pestle pound 2 chopped garlic cloves, 2 seeded red chillies and 15 ml (1 T) sugar to make a paste. Add the juice of 1 lime or lemon, 50 ml fish sauce (nuoc mam) and 60 ml (¼ c) water and mix well.

Mini lamb kebabs

Perfect for meat-lovers.

500 g leg of lamb, cut into 2 cm cubes
8 kebab skewers
1 small onion, coarsely grated
1 clove garlic, chopped
5 ml (1 t) grated lemon rind
10 ml (2 t) finely chopped fresh rosemary
1 ml (pinch) cayenne pepper
3 ml (generous ½ t) ground coriander
5 ml (1 t) ground cumin
30 ml (2 T) red wine vinegar
60 ml (¼ c) olive oil

Thread the lamb cubes onto the kebab skewers and put them in a flat dish. Blend the remaining ingredients and pour over the kebabs. Cover and chill for at least 3 hours or overnight. Drain the marinade and set it aside. Grill the kebabs in an oiled griddle pan or over the coals until done and brown, brushing frequently with the reserved marinade.

Makes 8.

Variety of kebabs

Sausage skewers with chutney dip

A typical South African snack made with that old favourite: boerewors.

1 kg boerewors, twisted into small
    plump sausages
oil
80 ml (⅓ c) soft brown sugar
45 ml (3 T) tomato sauce
30 ml (2 T) Worcestershire sauce
30 ml (2 T) mild prepared mustard
5 ml (1 t) chilli sauce (or more if desired)

CHUTNEY DIP
250 ml (1 c) hot fruit chutney
60 ml (¼ c) lemon juice
15 ml (1 T) grated lemon rind
180 ml (¾ c) mayonnaise

Preheat the oven to 200 °C.
    Prick each sausage once, pour oil in a pan and fry until just done. Snip the sausages to separate them and transfer them to an ovenproof dish. Mix the remaining ingredients and pour over the sausages, ensuring they are well coated. Bake for about 20 minutes or until the sausages begin to brown on top. Insert a cocktail stick in each sausage and arrange them on a large platter.

Makes about 48, depending on the size of the sausages.

CHUTNEY DIP
Blend all the ingredients, spoon into a bowl and serve with the sausages.

Chicken tikka kebabs

Skewered chicken with a mild curry flavour.

10 kebab skewers, cut in half
¼ onion, chopped
2 cloves garlic, roughly chopped
15 ml (1 T) grated fresh ginger
5 ml (1 t) grated lemon rind
30 ml (2 T) lemon juice
15 ml (1 T) ground coriander
15 ml (1 T) ground cumin
15 ml (1 T) garam masala
80 ml (⅓ c) plain yoghurt
5 ml (1 t) salt
750 g deboned and skinless chicken
    drumstick or breasts, cubed
1 large red pepper, seeded and cut
    into 2 cm cubes
lemon wedges to serve

Soak the kebab skewers in water for at least 30 minutes to stop them burning. Blitz the onion, garlic, ginger, lemon rind and juice, coriander, cumin and masala in a food processor until smooth. Add the yoghurt and salt. Thread the chicken and pepper cubes onto the kebab skewers and put them in a large flat dish. Spoon the spice mixture over the kebabs, turning them to coat them completely with the mixture. Cover and marinate in the fridge for a few hours or overnight. Grill a few kebabs at a time in a griddle pan, over the fire or under the oven grill for 3–4 minutes on each side or until golden brown. Serve immediately with lemon wedges.

Makes 20.

Chinese spareribs

These deep-fried ribs are delicious.

MARINADE
2 ml (½ t) freshly ground black pepper
2 ml (½ t) Chinese five spice
2 ml (½ t) salt
15 ml (1 T) soy sauce
15 ml (1 T) rice wine (mirin) or rice vinegar
10 ml (2 t) sesame oil

RIBS
1 kg spareribs, cut into 4–5 cm lengths
1 egg, whisked
30–40 ml cake flour
a little water
oil for deep-frying
2 spring onions, finely chopped
2 small red chillies, finely chopped

MARINADE
Mix the marinade ingredients in a glass bowl.

RIBS
Separate the ribs and put them in the marinade, mixing well. Cover and marinate for at least 3 hours or overnight. Mix the egg, flour and a little water if necessary to form a smooth batter the consistency of thick cream. Fill a wok or large pan three-quarters of the way with oil. Heat the oil until a cube of bread turns golden brown in 15 seconds. Dip the spareribs in the batter and fry a few at a time in the hot oil for about 5 minutes or until crisp and brown. Stir occasionally to prevent them sticking together. Remove the spareribs from the wok or pan and set aside. Reheat the oil and fry the spareribs for another 1 minute or until golden brown. Drain on paper towels. Remove the wok or pan from the heat. Put the spring onions and chillies in a sieve and put them in the oil for 2 minutes or until brown. Scatter over the spareribs.

Serves 4.

Bocconcini and tomato skewers

Ordinary mozzarella cheese cubes can be used instead of bocconcini (mozzarella balls).

10 small whole bocconcini or 2 large
    bocconcini, quartered
10 ml (2 t) chopped fresh parsley
5 ml (1 t) chopped chives
20 ml (4 t) olive oil
1 ml (pinch) salt
1 ml (pinch) freshly ground black pepper
10 small cherry tomatoes, halved
20 fresh basil leaves

Put the bocconcini in a mixing bowl, add the parsley, chives, oil, salt and pepper and mix gently. Cover and chill for at least 1 hour. Thread a cherry tomato half, basil leaf, bocconcini, another basil leaf and finally the other cherry tomato half onto a cocktail stick. Repeat with the remaining ingredients. Serve in Chinese spoons if preferred.

Makes 10.

Marinated olives

Marinated olives are a must as part of an antipasti platter.

1 packet each black and green olives
4 cloves garlic, peeled
1 small lemon, thinly sliced
5 sprigs fresh oregano
30 ml (2 T) olive oil

Put the olives, garlic, lemon slices and oregano in a sterilised jar. Pour over the olive oil and seal the jar with a sterilised lid. Leave to marinate for 1–2 days.

Makes 500 ml (2 c) olives.

Stuffed mushrooms

Stuff mushrooms with a piquant feta cheese filling and serve them in small Chinese spoons.

10 large button mushrooms
50 ml olive oil
20 ml (4 t) white wine vinegar
1 ml (pinch) salt
freshly ground black pepper to taste
3 ml (generous ½ t) Dijon mustard
25 ml (5 t) ready-made basil pesto
10 black olives, pitted and chopped
100 g feta cheese, crumbled
10 fresh basil leaves to garnish

Carefully remove the mushroom stems and scoop out the meat in the middle with a melon baller or teaspoon. Whisk together the oil, vinegar, salt, pepper and mustard and marinate the mushrooms in the mixture for 3 hours. Drain the mushrooms. Mix the pesto, olives and feta cheese, season with salt and pepper and spoon a little of the feta mixture into each mushroom. Garnish with basil leaves.

Makes 10.

Patatas

The Spanish love potatoes, most often frying them in olive oil.

POTATOES
1 kg potatoes, peeled and diced
30 ml (2 T) olive oil
salt and freshly ground black pepper

SAUCE
15 ml (1 T) olive oil
1 onion, finely chopped
1 clove garlic, crushed
2–5 ml (½–1 t) chilli powder
5 ml (1 t) dried thyme
1 can (420 g) chopped tomatoes
5 ml (1 t) red wine vinegar
5 ml (1 t) caster sugar
salt and freshly ground black pepper
15 ml (1 T) chopped fresh parsley

POTATOES
Preheat the oven to 200 °C. Arrange the potatoes in a large roasting tin and drizzle with the olive oil. Season well with salt and pepper and roast the potatoes for 30 minutes, stirring occasionally so they can brown evenly.

SAUCE
Meanwhile heat the oil for the sauce and stir-fry the onion until soft. Add the garlic, chilli powder and thyme and stir-fry for another 1 minute.
   Add the tomatoes, red wine vinegar and caster sugar and season with salt and pepper. Bring to the boil, reduce the heat and simmer for 10 minutes or until the sauce thickens slightly and is fragrant. Spoon the roasted potatoes into a dish and spoon the sauce on top. Garnish with fresh parsley.

Serves 6–8.

Stuffed mushrooms

Tortilla

The Spanish love eggs but never eat them hard-boiled. They prefer making a tortilla or large omelette made with plenty of onions and potatoes. The tortilla is served cold in wedges as part of a tapas selection.

60 ml (¼ c) olive oil
3 large potatoes, peeled and diced
1 small onion, finely chopped
2 cloves garlic, crushed
30 g fresh basil, roughly torn
1 chorizo sausage, sliced into thin rings
10 extra-large eggs
30 ml (2 T) water
salt and freshly ground black pepper

Heat the oil in a deep 25 cm pan. Add the potatoes and fry them lightly for 10–15 minutes or until nearly soft. Add the onion and garlic and stir-fry for another 2 minutes. Add the basil and chorizo and stir-fry for 1 minute more. Whisk together the eggs and water and pour into the pan. Season well with salt and black pepper. Heat slowly until the egg is set, shaking the pan occasionally. Meanwhile heat the oven grill. Once the tortilla has set grill it rapidly until golden brown on top. Cool slightly and cut into triangles. Serve lukewarm or cold as part of a tapas selection.

Serves 4–6.

Marinated mushrooms

Marinated mushrooms are ideal for an antipasti platter.

750 g button mushrooms
500 ml (2 c) olive oil
60 ml (¼ c) lemon juice
1 clove garlic, chopped
2 ml (½ t) caster sugar
1 red chilli, seeded and finely chopped
1 green chilli, seeded and finely chopped
20 ml (4 t) chopped fresh coriander leaves
20 ml (4 t) chopped fresh Italian parsley

Wipe the mushrooms with damp paper towels and put them in a large saucepan. Add the olive oil, lemon juice, garlic and caster sugar and cook over high heat for 2 minutes. Remove from the heat and add the chillies and herbs. Pour the mixture into a glass bowl, cover with clingfilm and chill overnight. Alternatively spoon the mixture into a 1 litre sterilised jar and seal. Store in the fridge after opening.

Makes 1 litre (4 c).

Thai spinach cones

These spinach cones are regularly served as part of a Thai meal. Each person prepares his own snack by filling a fresh spinach leaf cone with chopped onions, lemon, ginger, peanuts and coconut.

SPINACH CONES
6–7 fresh spinach leaves, washed
small heap chopped onions
small heap finely chopped lemon
small heap finely chopped red chillies
small heap roughly chopped lemon grass
small heap roughly chopped fresh ginger
small heap roughly chopped peanuts
small heap toasted coconut

DRESSING
15 ml (1 T) tamarind sauce
5 ml (1 t) brown sugar

SPINACH CONES
Spoon a little of the ingredients, except the spinach leaves, into separate shallow dishes and put them on a platter.

DRESSING
Mix the dressing ingredients and put the dressing in the centre of the platter. Let guests assemble their own snacks. Fold the spinach leaves into a cone (like an ice-cream cone) and fill with the ingredients as desired. Spoon a little of the dressing on top and pop the entire cone into your mouth for a wonderfully fragrant Thai taste sensation.

Makes 6.

Spinach empanadillas

These vegetarian snacks are simply delicious.

1 roll (400 g) puff pastry, defrosted
180 ml (¾ c) cooked spinach
50 g sultanas
50 g pine nuts, toasted
5–10 ml (1–2 t) sweet chilli sauce
salt and freshly ground black pepper
1 extra-large egg, whisked

Preheat the oven to 200 °C. Grease a baking sheet.
   Roll out the puff pastry and cut into 16 circles each 8 cm in diameter. Squeeze the spinach to remove excess liquid. Finely chop the sultanas and half the pine nuts and mix with the spinach. Add the whole pine nuts and sweet chilli sauce and season well with salt and freshly ground black pepper. Spoon a little of the filling in the middle of each pastry circle and brush the edges with the whisked egg. Fold over to make a crescent shape and crimp down the edges with a fork to seal. Arrange the tartlets on a baking sheet and bake for 15–20 minutes or until puffed and golden.

Makes 16.

Asian wontons

These tasty Chinese bites are filled with an aromatic pork and cabbage mixture.

FILLING
300 g pork mince
40 g cabbage, shredded
1 small onion, thinly sliced
1 egg
7 ml (1½ t) cornflour
3 ml (generous ½ t) soy sauce
3 ml (generous ½ t) sesame oil
3 ml (generous ½ t) finely chopped
   fresh ginger
3 ml (generous ½ t) finely chopped garlic

WONTONS
10–12 wonton wrappers
1 egg, whisked
oil for deep-frying
soy sauce to serve

FILLING
Mix the filling ingredients and spoon a teaspoonful of the mixture in the middle of each wonton wrapper. Brush the edges of the wrappers with the egg and fold in to make a parcel. Heat the oil and deep-fry the parcels until golden. Drain on paper towels and serve with soy sauce.

Makes 10–12.

Tip
Use phyllo pastry instead of wonton wrappers.

WHAT ARE WONTON WRAPPERS?
These paper-thin wrappers are sold at shops and supermarkets specialising in Asian products and are deep-fried.

The wrappers can also be made at home: Sift together 500 ml (2 c) cake flour and 1 ml (pinch) salt. Add 1 whisked egg and 160 ml water and mix to form a stiff dough. Add more water if necessary. On a floured surface roll out the dough until paper thin and cut into 8–10 cm squares. Cover with a damp tea towel. The wrappers can also be frozen – dust each wrapper with cornflour and freeze with a layer of clingfilm between each.

Chinese spring rolls

The filling for these delicious rolls is made with vermicelli rice noodles and vegetables such as cabbage and carrot.

FILLING
20 g vermicelli rice noodles
15 ml (1 T) sunflower oil
1 onion, thinly sliced
10 ml (2 t) chopped fresh ginger
1 small cabbage, shredded
1 carrot, cut into thin strips
100 g bean sprouts
4 spring onions, finely chopped
1 ml (pinch) salt
1 ml (pinch) freshly ground black pepper
5 ml (1 t) fish sauce
5 ml (1 t) sesame oil
5 ml (1 t) soy sauce

WRAPPERS
6 frozen spring roll wrappers
10 ml (2 t) cornflour
oil for deep-frying
soy or chillie sauce for serving

FILLING
Put the rice noodles in a dish and cover with boiling water. Leave for 3 minutes, drain and cut the noodles into small pieces with scissors. Heat the oil in a large heavy-based saucepan and fry the onion and ginger for 1 minute. Add the cabbage, carrot, bean sprouts and spring onions and stir-fry for 2–3 minutes. Add the salt, pepper, fish sauce, sesame oil and soy sauce. Finally add the rice noodles and remove the pan from the heat.

WRAPPERS
Put a wrapper on a work surface with one corner pointing away from you. Blend the cornflour and a little water to make a paste and brush the edges of the wrapper with the paste. Spoon 1 heaped teaspoon of the vegetable mixture in the corner and fold the flap over the vegetables. Fold in the left and right sides of the wrapper and roll up neatly. Brush the outer flap with extra cornflour paste to seal. Heat enough oil and deep-fry the rolls until crisp and golden. Drain on paper towels and serve with soy or chillie sauce.

Makes 6.

FROZEN SPRING ROLL PASTRY
This is a multipurpose pastry made from cake flour, salt and water. The pastry can also be used to make samoosas. Spring rolls are always deep-fried.

Tip
If you can't find spring roll wrappers make your own using the wonton wrapper recipe (see page 21). Cut the wrappers into 20 cm squares. Alternatively use phyllo pastry.

Chinese spring rolls

Breads and spreads

Homemade bread is always a special treat. Some of these bread recipes require no baking, only time. Others are made with ready-made bread dough. There's also a recipe for pot bread.

New York ciabatta

You don't have to knead the dough for this Italian bread yet it still produces the characteristic open texture. This unique recipe from Jim Lahey of Sullivan Street Baker in Manhattan, New York, published in the *New York Times*, immediately caught our eye. The recipe is unusual in that it requires no special ingredients or kneading. All it requires is plenty of time, a whole day in fact, but the result is outstanding. All the work is done for you during the long resting period. The high moisture content gives the bread its characteristic open texture. To obtain the typical thin crust the bread is baked in a hot pot with a lid.

750 ml (3 c) white bread flour (plus
   extra for dusting)
2 ml (½ t) brewer's yeast
   (not instant yeast)
6 ml (1¼ t) salt
375 ml (1½ c) lukewarm water
bran for shaping

Mix the flour, yeast and salt in a large mixing bowl. Add the water and stir with a spoon until well blended. The dough will be very wet and sticky. Cover the bowl with clingfilm and leave the dough to rest at room temperature for 14–18 hours. The dough is ready when the surface is covered with air bubbles. Put the dough on a floured surface. Dust with flour and fold it once or twice. Cover loosely with clingfilm and leave to rest for 15 minutes.

Shape the dough into a ball and use only enough flour to ensure that it doesn't stick to your fingers or the bowl. Sprinkle bran or white bread flour over a tea towel and put the ball of dough on top of the bran or flour. Sprinkle with more bran or flour.

Cover the dough with another tea towel and leave it to rise for 2 hours or until double in size.

Preheat the oven to 200 °C, 30 minutes before the end of the rising time.

Put a greased 5–7 litre cast-iron, enamel, Pyrex or ceramic pot with a tight-fitting lid in the oven while it's heating. Remove carefully once the oven has reached the right temperature. Put your hands under the tea towel with the dough and carefully tip it into the hot pot, shaking it once or twice to evenly distribute the dough. Cover the pot with the lid and bake for 30 minutes. Remove the lid and bake for another 15–30 minutes or until brown. Leave the bread to cool in the pot before turning out onto a wire rack.

Makes 1 large ciabatta.

Pot bread

Make a delicious pot bread next time you have a braai and serve it with snoek and grape jam or for starters.

1,2 kg (10 c) white bread flour
    (or cake flour)
10 ml (2 t) salt
250 ml (1 c) oats
250 ml (1 c) wholewheat flour
10 ml (2 t) sugar
1 packet (10 g) instant yeast
15 ml (1 T) olive oil
about 750 ml (3 c) lukewarm water

Grease a flat-bottomed cast-iron pot and lid with butter or sunflower oil.

Mix the dry ingredients and sprinkle over the sugar and yeast. Add the oil and mix. Add just enough water to make a slightly slack but firm dough. Knead until the dough no longer sticks to your hands, shape it into a ball and put it in the pot. Cover and leave in a warm place to rise for about 10 minutes. (If leaving the pot near the fire turn it frequently.) Remove the dough from the pot, punch it down and return it to the pot. Leave it to rise until double in size. Put the pot on a stand or bricks over a layer of medium-hot coals. Also put a few coals on the lid and bake the bread for about 1 hour or until done. Test if it's done by turning it out and tapping the bottom. If the bread sounds hollow it's done. A testing skewer must also come out clean. Serve with butter and grape jam.

Makes 1 medium-sized pot bread.

Seed bread

You can also make individual loaves by baking the bread in small tins. The dough requires no kneading.

4 x 250 ml (4 c) wholewheat flour
5 ml (1 t) salt
10 g (1 packet) instant yeast
15 ml (1 T) poppy seeds
15 ml (1 T) linseeds
15 ml (1 T) sunflower seeds
15 ml (1 T) sesame seeds
500 ml (2 c) lukewarm water
30 ml (2 T) oil
30 ml (2 T) honey or golden syrup
extra seeds to sprinkle on top

Preheat the oven to 200 °C. Grease a 25 cm loaf tin.

Combine the flour, salt, yeast and seeds. Mix the water, oil and honey or syrup. Make a well in the dry ingredients and add the liquid. Mix to make a soft dough and put it in the prepared tin so it's about halfway full. Sprinkle extra seeds on top, cover with a damp tea towel and leave in a warm place to rise until double in size. (You can also leave the dough to rise in an oven at 70 °C.) Put the bread in the preheated oven and bake until a testing skewer comes out clean – allow about 45 minutes for a 25 cm tin.

Serve with butter.

Makes 1 medium-sized loaf.

Bread wheels

If you're in a hurry buy ready-made bread dough at your supermarket bakery and turn it into these impressive homemade treats.

1 packet (250 g) bacon, chopped
1 onion, chopped
1 kg white bread dough,
   at room temperature
1–2 cloves garlic, chopped
250 ml (1 c) grated Cheddar cheese

Preheat the oven to 200 °C and grease a large baking sheet with oil.
   Heat a pan over medium heat and lightly fry the bacon. Remove with a slotted spoon and fry the onion in the rendered bacon fat until soft. Flatten the bread dough slightly on a floured surface and roll out as thinly as possible. If you don't have a rolling pin use a wine or cooldrink bottle. Scatter the fried bacon and onion, garlic and cheese over the dough. Neatly roll up the dough and cut it into 3 cm thick slices. Arrange the slices on their sides on the greased baking sheet and bake until well risen, brown and done.

Makes 12.

Variation
Add olives, diced red and green pepper, chopped piquanté peppers and a handful of chopped parsley to the bacon mixture and use as indicated in the recipe.

Braai bread rolls

Anthony Grobler of Faunasig sent us this unusual bread recipe.

1 packet (43 g) Bacon and
   Cheese Potato Bake
250 ml (1 c) cream, at room temperature
250 ml (1 c) milk, at room temperature
1 kg bread dough
200 ml grated Cheddar cheese

Preheat the oven to 180 °C and grease an ovenproof dish with butter, margarine or nonstick food spray.
   Whisk together the Potato Bake, cream and milk and pour half the mixture into the greased dish. Roll the dough into balls and pack them tightly in the dish. Pour over the remaining milk mixture and scatter the cheese on top. Leave for 30 minutes to rise, then bake in the preheated oven for 35–40 minutes or until done.

Serves 6–8.

Tip
Instead of the cream use a mixture of half milk and half mayonnaise and mix with the potato bake, increasing the quantity of milk to 375 ml (1½ c).
Ensure the cream and milk are at room temperature; do not use straight from the fridge as this will cool the dough and it will take longer to rise.

Bread wheels

Brinjal spread

This easy-to-make spread is extremely versatile. Serve it in pittas or with bread or use as a dip with meat and couscous.

500 g small brinjals
2 onions, peeled and quartered
15 ml (5 t) olive oil
1 clove garlic, crushed
45 ml (3 T) fresh coriander leaves
30 ml (2 T) thick plain yoghurt
salt and freshly ground black pepper

Preheat the oven to 200 °C and grease an ovenproof dish with oil. Put the brinjals and onion wedges in the dish and drizzle with olive oil. Bake for about 30 minutes or until soft. Leave to cool and remove the brinjal skins. Blitz the flesh and remaining ingredients in a food processor until smooth. Season to taste with salt and pepper and chill until ready to serve.

Makes about 500 ml (2 c).

Chicken liver pâté

It's much easier to make pâté than you may think. This recipe, made with a port reduction, is a winner. Serve with crisp savoury biscuits or on toasted or plain bread.

1 onion, sliced
200 ml port
2 cloves garlic
6 black peppercorns
2 bay leaves
4 sprigs fresh thyme
15 ml (1 T) olive oil
600 g chicken livers
100 g unsalted butter, cut into
    small cubes
salt and freshly ground black pepper

Put the onion, port, garlic, peppercorns, bay leaves and thyme in a pan and bring to the boil over high heat. Reduce the heat slightly and bubble for 5–6 minutes or until reduced by half. Strain through a fine sieve and discard the solids. Leave the port reduction to cool to room temperature. In a clean pan heat half the oil over high heat and fry half the livers until lightly browned and half-done. Remove from the pan and fry the remaining livers in the remaining olive oil. Blitz the livers in a food processor until smooth. Add the port reduction and blitz. Add the butter one cube at a time and blitz until smooth. Season to taste with salt and pepper. Spoon the pâté into bowls, cover with clingfilm and chill for 2 hours.

Makes 700 ml.

Tips
The butter must be brought to room temperature before it is added to the livers.
This ensures it will be evenly blended and form a smooth, creamy pâté.
The pâté can be sealed with a layer of clarified butter.

Smoked mackerel pâté

2 smoked peppered mackerel fillets
    (about 150 g)
60 g smooth cottage cheese
75 ml (5 T) sour cream
freshly grated nutmeg
salt
capers to garnish

Remove the skin from the mackerel fillets. In a food processor blitz the fish with the remaining ingredients, except the capers. Spoon the mixture into 3 –4 ramekins and garnish with capers. Serve with toasted ciabatta slices.

Makes 250 ml (1 c).

Coarse tuna and pepper spread

This spread improves with time. Serve it with fresh bread or toasted rolls.

30 ml (2 T) olive oil
1 large onion, roughly chopped
3 green peppers, seeded and diced
2 cloves garlic, finely chopped
175 g mixed green and black olives,
    pitted and chopped
50 g drained capers
1 can (410 g) peeled tomatoes
30 ml (2 T) tomato paste
1 jar or can (400 g) pimentos,
    drained and chopped
15 ml (1 T) sherry or wine vinegar
1 can (187 g) tuna, drained
    and flaked
salt and freshly ground black pepper

Heat the oil over medium heat and sauté the onion, green peppers and garlic for about 15 minutes or until soft. Add the olives, capers, tomatoes and tomato paste and simmer for 5 minutes. Add the pimentos and simmer for another 5 minutes. Stir in the vinegar and tuna and season with salt and pepper. Simmer for another few minutes and cool. Chill overnight or until cold.

Makes 750 ml (3 c).

Pimentos are a type of Spanish sweet red pepper and sweeter than other red peppers. They are delicious raw or preserved and are commonly used to stuff green olives.

Pickles and chutneys
Grape pickle

Delicious with an antipasti or cheese platter or with fish.

1 kg red grapes
300 ml caster sugar
300 ml red wine vinegar
170 ml water
6 whole cloves
4 whole star anise
10 whole black peppercorns
1 piece stick cinnamon
5 ml (1 t) English mustard powder

Wash the grapes and prick each once with a cake fork. Heat the sugar and vinegar over low heat, stirring until the sugar has dissolved. Add the grapes and remaining ingredients and bring to the boil. Simmer for 5 minutes over medium heat. Spoon the grapes into sterilised jars and pour over the hot syrup to completely cover the grapes. Seal the jars immediately. The flavour of the preserve will improve with time.

Makes about 750 ml (3 c).

Fresh fig chutney

Delicious with mature cheese and rocket on bruschetta.

1 onion, finely chopped
60 ml (¼ c) brown sugar
10 ml (2 t) grated fresh ginger
5 ml (1 t) mustard seeds
1 piece stick cinnamon
1 whole star anise
60 ml (¼ c) red wine vinegar
4 fresh figs, washed and
    cut into wedges

Heat the onion, sugar, ginger, spices and vinegar over medium heat, stirring until the sugar has melted. Bring to the boil, reduce the heat and simmer for 5 minutes or until the onion is completely soft. Add the fig wedges and simmer for another 5–10 minutes or until the figs just begin to disintegrate. Store the chutney in the fridge, where it will keep for 7 days.

Makes 300 ml.

SOUP FOR EVERY OCCASION

Soup is a great standby, whether served as a starter for a smart dinner party, hearty satisfying meal on a cold winter's day or quick suppertime meal. It's the perfect all-in-one deliciously wholesome meal and can be made from beans, vegetables, meat, fish or chicken.

André Brink's thick pea and vegetable soup

This was originally a pea soup recipe, says André Brink, deputy editor of YOU's sister magazine Huisgenoot. But the first time he made it he didn't have enough peas so he added a cup of red lentils. His wife, Rina, suggested he grate in a potato and carrot. This is a wonderfully rich soup that's a meal on its own. Serve on a cold winter's evening in front of a fire.

500 ml (2 c) split peas (see tip)
250 ml (1 c) dried red lentils
15 ml (1 T) oil
1 large onion, chopped
1 large leek, finely chopped
1 small bunch of soup celery, chopped
  leaves and all (do not overdo the
  celery as it is very potent and can
  dominate the flavour of the soup)
150 g smoked bacon, chopped,
  or smoked pork shank
handful of soup bones
1,5 litres (6 c) chicken stock
1 large potato, grated
1 large carrot, scraped and grated
salt and freshly ground black pepper

Soak the peas and lentils (see tip). Heat the oil in a large saucepan (an old pressure cooker works well) and stir-fry the onion, leek and celery over medium heat for about 5–10 minutes or until soft. Add the bacon and soup bones and stir-fry until the bacon is done. Add the stock (the quantity will depend on the desired consistency: for a thick soup don't add more than 1,5 litres but add more for a thinner soup). Cover and simmer over medium heat for about 20 minutes.

Add the potato, carrot and soaked peas and lentils. Cover and cook over low heat for about 1 hour or until done. Stir occasionally. Season with salt and pepper and serve with freshly baked bread.

Serves 5–6.

Tips
The peas and lentils must be soft or they will spoil the taste and texture of the soup. André puts the peas and lentils in a glass or plastic dish, pours over enough boiling water to cover them and leaves them to soak. Once the peas and lentils have absorbed the water he then microwaves them for 15 minutes.
Only add salt after the lentils or beans are cooked or they will be tough.

André Brink's thick pea and vegetable soup

Minestrone with gremolata

In 2004 we visited Cape foodie Errieda du Toit at her weekend home in Riebeek-Kasteel. She treated us to this excellent Italian soup, which is made in a different way in each region in Italy.

MINESTRONE
30 ml (2 T) olive oil
50 g pancetta or bacon
125 ml (½ c) raw rice
1 large onion, chopped
250 g vegetables in season, such as
    baby marrows, cabbage or peas
4 baby carrots, scraped
4 baby potatoes, scraped and sliced
vegetable stock
125 ml (½ c) vermicelli, broken into
    short pieces
1 can (410 g) butter beans
1 can (420 g) chopped tomatoes
5–10 ml (1–2 t) tomato purée
salt and freshly ground black pepper
pinch sugar

GREMOLATA
250 ml (1 c) chopped fresh parsley
2 cloves garlic, finely chopped
10 ml (2 t) finely grated lemon rind
salt and freshly ground black pepper
Parmesan cheese to serve

MINESTRONE
Slowly heat the oil in a large heavy-bottomed saucepan. Add the bacon, rice and onion and stir-fry until the onion is slightly soft. Add the vegetables, carrots and potatoes and stir until well coated with the oil. Add enough vegetable stock to cover the vegetables and bring the mixture to the boil. Cover and simmer for 10 minutes. Add the pasta, butter beans with their liquid, tomatoes and tomato purée and simmer for about 30 minutes or until fragrant. Season to taste with salt, pepper and a pinch of sugar if necessary.

GREMOLATA
Mix together the gremolata ingredients. Ladle the soup into bowls and spoon a little of the gremolata in the middle of the soup. Serve hot with Parmesan cheese if desired.

Serves 6.

Hearty black-eyed bean soup

Stellenbosch cookery school owner and lecturer Susina Jooste is also a wine expert. She recommends a fruity unwooded white, rosé or red wine such as a chenin blanc or pinotage with this soup. This soup is so thick it's more like a stew. To make a thinner soup add more stock.

25 ml (5 t) olive oil
1–2 small onions, chopped
2 cloves garlic, crushed
2 small chillies, such as jalapeño,
    seeded and chopped
5 ml (1 t) cumin seeds
2 ml (½ t) coriander seeds
1 bay leaf
1 chorizo sausage, sliced
500 g black-eyed beans, soaked in
    water overnight
500 ml–1 litre (2–4 c) chicken stock
1 can (420 g) chopped tomatoes
salt and pepper to taste

Heat the oil and sauté the onions and garlic until soft. Add the chillies and spices and stir-fry until fragrant. Add the sausage. Drain the beans, rinse under cold running water and add to the onion mixture. Cover with the chicken stock and simmer until the beans are soft. Add the tomatoes and simmer for about
10 minutes to allow the flavours to develop. Season with salt, pepper and more chillies if desired.
    Serve with chopped avocado and plain yoghurt to cool the heat of the chilli.

Serves 3–4.

Tuscan bean soup

This deliciously satisfying soup is ready in moments. Italians like using dried beans such as borlotti and cannellini beans in their soups and stews. Canned beans work just as well and save loads of time.

45 ml (3 T) olive oil
2 stalks celery, finely chopped
1 onion, finely chopped
2,25 litres (9 c) hot vegetable stock
250 g potatoes, peeled and diced
500 ml (2 c) raw pasta
500 ml (2 c) Chinese cabbage, shredded
2 cans (420 g each) chopped tomatoes
1 can (410 g) butter beans, drained
salt, freshly ground black pepper
    and sugar
fresh basil leaves, torn

Heat the oil in a large heavy-bottomed saucepan and stir-fry the celery and onion over medium heat for 5–6 minutes or until soft but not browned. Add the stock, potatoes and pasta and bring the mixture to the boil. Boil rapidly for 10 minutes or until the pasta is just done. Add the cabbage, tomatoes and beans and bring the soup back to the boil. Simmer for 3 minutes. Season well with salt, black pepper and a pinch of sugar and add the basil leaves. Serve with Parmesan cheese shavings if desired.

Serves 4–6.

Indian red lentil soup

Coconut milk makes this spicy soup wonderfully creamy.

20 ml (4 t) sunflower oil
1 large onion, chopped
4 cloves garlic, crushed
20 ml (4 t) grated fresh ginger
2 small red chillies, seeded and chopped
10 ml (2 t) ground coriander
45 ml (3 T) ground cumin
5 ml (1 t) turmeric
20 ml (4 t) mild masala
1 piece stick cinnamon
6 cardamom seeds, crushed
8 fresh or dried curry leaves
250 g (½ packet) red lentils
7 x 250 ml (7 c) chicken stock
1 large potato, peeled and chopped
1 large apple, peeled, cored and chopped
500 ml (2 c) coconut milk
40 ml lemon juice
40 ml chopped fresh coriander leaves
whole coriander leaves to garnish

Heat the oil in a large saucepan and stir-fry the onion, garlic, ginger, chillies, spices and curry leaves for 5 minutes or until the onion is soft. Add the lentils, stock, potato and apple, cover and simmer for 20 minutes or until the potato and lentils are soft. Remove the whole spices and curry leaves and reserve the leaves. Blitz the mixture in a food processor until smooth and return the soup to the saucepan. Add the coconut milk, lemon juice, coriander leaves and reserved curry leaves and heat through, stirring frequently. Garnish with fresh coriander leaves.

Serves 6.

Chickpea soup

Canned foods are great time savers.

20 ml (4 t) olive oil
1 large onion, chopped
3 cloves garlic, crushed
20 ml (4 t) grated fresh ginger
7 ml (1½ t) ground cumin
7 ml (1½ t) ground coriander
5 ml (1 t) turmeric
3 ml (generous ½ t) paprika
1 ml (pinch) ground cinnamon
1,5 litres (6 c) chicken stock
2 cans (410 g each) chickpeas, drained
    and well rinsed
2 cans (420 g each) chopped tomatoes
salt and freshly ground black pepper
5 ml (1 t) grated lemon rind
20 ml (4 t) chopped fresh
    coriander leaves
plain yoghurt to serve

Heat the oil in a large saucepan and sauté the onion, garlic and ginger until the onion is soft. Add the spices and stir-fry until the flavours are well developed. Add the stock, chickpeas and tomatoes and bring the mixture to the boil. Reduce the heat and simmer uncovered for 15 minutes or until the soup thickens slightly. Season with salt and pepper to taste. Add the lemon rind and coriander leaves just before serving. Serve the soup with a scoop of plain yoghurt.

Serves 4.

Budget-beating tip
Use 250 g brown lentils instead of the chickpeas and cook them in vegetable stock until soft. Add the tomatoes and proceed as described.

Cream of broccoli and Stilton soup

Broccoli and blue cheese are a winning combination.

40 ml olive oil
2 onions, finely chopped
1 kg broccoli (hard stems removed),
    broken into florets
1 litre (4 c) vegetable stock
2 ml (½ t) freshly grated nutmeg
225 g Stilton cheese, crumbled
salt and freshly ground black pepper
80 ml (⅓ c) Greek yoghurt
80 ml (⅓ c) cream
toasted almond flakes to garnish

Heat the oil in a large saucepan and sauté the onions over medium heat until translucent. Add the broccoli, stock and nutmeg. Bring the mixture to the boil, reduce the heat, cover and simmer for 15–20 minutes or until the broccoli is soft. Leave the soup to cool slightly, then blitz in a food processor until very smooth. If preferred, press through a sieve. Add the Stilton cheese, season with salt and pepper and heat through, stirring continuously. Add the yoghurt and cream and serve in soup bowls. Garnish with almond flakes.

Serves 4.

Cream of broccoli and Stilton soup

Coriander and potato soup

Potato and fresh coriander combine well. This soup makes a wonderful starter.

500 g potatoes, peeled and diced
200 g leeks, cleaned and thinly sliced
30 ml (2 T) butter
50 g fresh coriander leaves, chopped
1 litre (4 c) chicken stock
125 ml (½ c) cream
salt and freshly ground black pepper
100 ml toasted pumpkin seeds
extra fresh coriander leaves

Sauté the potatoes and leeks in the butter for about
5 minutes. Add the coriander and stir-fry for 1 minute longer.
Add the stock, bring to the boil and simmer for 12 minutes or
until the potatoes are soft. Blitz the soup in a food processor
until smooth and add the cream. Season well with salt and
freshly ground black pepper, return the soup to the saucepan
and heat until warm. Serve with the toasted pumpkin seeds
and extra fresh coriander leaves.

Serves 3–4.

Mushroom soup

A thin but rich and creamy mushroom soup.

30 ml (2 T) olive oil
250 g (1 punnet) portebellini
   mushrooms, thinly sliced
2–3 cloves garlic, crushed
2 large potatoes, peeled and
   coarsely grated
1 stalk celery, chopped (optional)
2 onions, finely chopped
1 litre (4 c) chicken stock
250 ml (1 c) milk
250 ml (1 c) cream
15 ml (1 T) sherry (optional)
salt and freshly ground black pepper
fresh parsley to garnish

Heat the oil in a large saucepan and sauté the mushrooms
and garlic until soft and fragrant. Remove a quarter of the
mixture from the saucepan and set aside. Add the potatoes,
celery and onions to the saucepan and sauté over medium
heat for 5 minutes, stirring continuously. Add the stock and
bring the mixture to the boil. Simmer for 10 minutes or until
the potatoes are soft. Add the milk and blitz the mixture in a
food processor until smooth.

Return the soup to the saucepan, add the cream and sherry,
season with salt and black pepper and heat through. Serve in
soup bowls and garnish with the reserved sautéd mushrooms
and parsley.

Serves 4–6.

> **Budget-beating tip**
> Portebellini mushrooms have a robust flavour but
> are fairly expensive. Use more affordable button
> mushrooms instead but then thicken the soup
> slightly with about 30 ml (2 T) cream of mushroom
> soup powder to give it a more intense flavour.

Roasted tomato soup

Bring out the flavour of the tomatoes and other vegetables by grilling and roasting them.
This soup has a lovely creamy consistency but contains no cream.

1,8 kg ripe tomatoes
200 ml olive oil
6 cloves garlic, crushed
4 bay leaves
4 sprigs fresh thyme
4 sprigs fresh rosemary
4 onions, finely sliced
4 stalks celery, finely chopped
1 fennel bulb, finely sliced (optional)
1 red chilli, seeded
10 ml (2 t) tomato paste
10 ml (2 t) sugar
juice of 1 lemon
salt
basil leaves to garnish

Switch on the oven grill.

Halve the tomatoes and put them cut side facing up on a baking sheet. Grill until soft and the edges begin to brown. Remove from the oven and preheat the oven to 190 °C. Heat the olive oil in a large pan and add the garlic, herbs and vegetables. Stir-fry until the vegetables just begin to soften. Transfer the vegetable mixture to a roasting tin and bake uncovered for 30 minutes. Stir occasionally.

Remove the tin from the oven and blitz the vegetable mixture, grilled tomatoes, tomato paste, sugar and lemon juice in a food processor until smooth. Press the mixture through a sieve if desired and pour it into a saucepan. Season with salt and add water if the soup is too thick. Heat through and ladle into soup bowls. Garnish with basil leaves and serve with crusty bread if desired.

Serves 6.

> **Tip**
> Use flavourful tomatoes such as plum or Roma tomatoes to make this soup.

Creamy onion soup

A simple yet elegant soup that's also affordable. The recipe comes from Rita Houghton of George.

2 onions, finely chopped
1 potato, peeled and diced
45 ml (3 T) butter or margarine
500 ml (2 c) milk OR 250 ml (1 c) milk
    and 250 ml (1 c) cream
250 ml (1 c) vegetable stock
1 bay leaf
salt and white pepper

Sauté the onions and potato in the butter over low heat until the onions are soft and translucent. Add the remaining ingredients, except the salt and pepper, and bring the mixture to the boil. Cover and simmer gently for about 20 minutes. Remove the bay leaf, leave the soup to cool slightly and season to taste. Blitz in a food processor until smooth and serve with bread rolls or breadsticks if desired. Alternatively serve the soup with caramelised onions (see tip) and a sprinkling of paprika.

Serves 4.

> **Tip**
> To make caramelised onions stir-fry onion rings in oil until translucent. Sprinkle generously with brown sugar and stir-fry until the onions are caramelised. Add a little balsamic vinegar if desired.

Vegetable soup with French bread

A light, flavoursome soup. Put a slice of bread in the bottom of the soup bowl and ladle
the soup on top.

45 ml (3 T) olive oil
2 small onions, finely chopped
2 stalks celery, finely chopped
4 small carrots, scraped and finely chopped
2 large potatoes, peeled and diced
2 leeks, finely sliced
2 cloves garlic, crushed
2,5 litres (10 c) vegetable stock
100 g green beans, cut into
    short pieces (optional)
100 g frozen peas
150 g cabbage, shredded
80 g Parmesan cheese, grated
salt and white pepper
6 slices French bread

Heat the olive oil in a saucepan and add the onions, celery,
carrots, potatoes, leeks and garlic. Sauté over low heat for
5–6 minutes or until the vegetables are soft but not browned.
Add 375 ml (1½ c) of the vegetable stock and bring the
mixture to the boil. Cover, reduce the heat and simmer for
30 minutes. Add the green beans, peas and remaining stock
and simmer for another 30 minutes. Add the cabbage and
simmer for 10 minutes longer. Stir in the Parmesan cheese and
season the soup with salt and white pepper. Put a slice of bread
in the bottom of each soup bowl and ladle the soup on top.

Serves 6.

Ginger and sweet potato soup

Sweet potatoes make a wonderfully creamy soup.

30 ml (2 T) sunflower oil
finely grated rind of 1 large orange
5 ml (1 t) mild curry powder or
    ground cumin
small handful fresh coriander leaves
5 ml (1 t) sugar
30 ml (2 T) grated fresh ginger
1 kg sweet potatoes, peeled and
    cut into chunks
3–4 leeks, thinly sliced
60 ml (¼ c) water
sea salt and freshly ground black pepper
1 litre (4 c) chicken stock
500 ml (2 c) milk, coconut milk or buttermilk
30 ml (2 T) plain yoghurt
fresh coriander leaves to garnish

Heat the oil in a large heavy-bottomed saucepan. Add the
orange rind, curry powder, coriander, sugar, ginger, sweet
potatoes and leeks and stir well. Add the water, cover and
simmer for 20 minutes, stirring occasionally. Season the soup
with salt and pepper and gradually add the chicken stock and
milk. Cover and simmer until the vegetables are soft.
    Remove the saucepan from the heat and leave the soup
to cool slightly. Blitz in a food processor until smooth and
pour into a clean saucepan. Heat slowly. Stir in the yoghurt
just before serving. Ladle the soup into warmed soup bowls
and garnish with coriander leaves. Serve with Melba toast or
fresh bread.

Serves 4.

Tips
Choose sweet potatoes with a deep yellow colour as they are sweeter than those with creamy
flesh. Sweet potatoes are rich in vitamins A and C. Select medium-sized sweet potatoes with
smooth skins and store in a cool, dry place, not in the fridge.
Leeks have a more subtle flavour than onions. The younger the leeks, the more tender they are. To
clean leeks halve them lengthways and soak and rinse them under running water to remove sand.
Fresh ginger must be plump with smooth skin. Peel with a potato peeler before grating it.
Commercially processed ginger is a convenient, flavoursome alternative to fresh ginger.
Add extra stock or milk to dilute soup to the desired consistency.

Vegetable soup with French bread

Butternut and carrot soup

Butternut soup has become very popular over the years. This variation is made with carrots and is subtly flavoured with orange.

30 ml (2 T) olive oil
1 large leek, thinly sliced
15 ml (1 T) curry powder
5 ml (1 t) ground cumin
10 ml (2 t) ground coriander
5 ml (1 t) turmeric
1 piece stick cinnamon
6–8 large carrots, scraped and cut
    into chunks
1 butternut, peeled, seeded and diced
1,25 litres (5 c) chicken stock
juice and finely grated rind
    of 1 large orange
7 ml (1½ t) brown sugar
salt and freshly ground black pepper
250 ml (1 c) milk
toasted sunflower or pumpkin seeds

Preheat the oven to 190 °C and pour the olive oil into a roasting tin. Put the tin in the oven to heat the oil. Put the leek and spices in the hot oil and stir. Add the carrots and butternut, stirring to coat the vegetables with the spices. Roast for 30 minutes.

Remove the vegetables from the oven and transfer them to a large saucepan. Add the stock and orange juice and rind and bring the mixture to the boil. Cook until the vegetables are soft. Season with sugar, salt and pepper to taste. Blitz the soup in a food processor until smooth and return it to the saucepan. Add the milk and heat through. Ladle the soup into bowls and scatter seeds on top. Serve with sesame rolls.

Serves 6–8.

Chicken soup with glass noodles

Glass or cellophane noodles, made from mung beans, are excellent in soup.
This deliciously spicy soup is flavoured with cinnamon and star anise.

1,5 litres (6 c) chicken stock
500 ml (2 c) water
10 cm fresh ginger, peeled and thinly sliced
2 whole star anise
1 piece stick cinnamon
350 g chicken breast fillets
salt and freshly ground black pepper
250 g dried glass noodles
60 ml (¼ c) lime or lemon juice
15 ml (1 T) fish sauce
4 spring onions, roughly chopped
2 red chillies, seeded and cut into
    thin strips
30 ml (2 T) roughly chopped fresh
    coriander leaves
large handful fresh bean sprouts
lime slices to serve

Bring the stock, water, ginger, star anise and cinnamon to the boil in a large saucepan. Add the chicken, season with salt and pepper to taste and bring to the boil once more. Reduce the heat, cover and simmer for about 15 minutes or until the chicken is done. Remove the chicken and leave it to cool for 10 minutes before shredding it into small pieces.

Bring the stock to the boil again and add the noodles, lime juice and fish sauce. Reduce the heat and simmer until the noodles are just soft. Stir frequently. Add the chicken and remaining ingredients and heat through. Serve immediately with lime slices.

Serves 6–8.

Tip
Serve the soup immediately or the noodles will absorb the liquid, turning it into a stew rather than a soup.

Thai coconut milk and chicken soup

The coconut milk imparts a wonderful flavour to this soup.

500 ml (2 c) chicken stock or water
2 cm piece fresh ginger, grated
1 stem lemon grass, cut into short pieces
500 ml (2 c) coconut milk
6 button mushrooms, thinly sliced
½ onion, sliced into rings
1 tomato, seeded and diced
2 lemon leaves, torn
45 ml (3 T) fresh lemon or lime juice
45 ml (3 T) fish sauce
5–10 ml (1–2 t) sugar
salt and freshly ground black pepper
200 g chicken breast fillets, sliced
    into strips
fresh coriander leaves to garnish

Put the stock, ginger, lemon grass and coconut milk in a saucepan and slowly bring the mixture to the boil. Add the mushrooms, onion, tomato, lemon leaves and juice, fish sauce and sugar. Season to taste with salt and pepper. Add the chicken strips and simmer for about 15–20 minutes or until the chicken is done. Serve the soup in individual bowls and garnish with fresh coriander leaves.

Serves 4.

Goulash soup

The cayenne pepper gives this robust soup bite but if desired you can reduce the amount to make it less hot.

15 ml (1 T) oil
1 onion, finely chopped
1 clove garlic, crushed
4 potatoes, peeled and diced
½ can (210 g) chopped tomatoes
80 ml (⅓ c) tomato purée
1 litre (4 c) beef stock
150 g stewing steak cubes (goulash)
160 ml (⅔ c) red wine
2 carrots, scraped and chopped
2 each red and green peppers, seeded
    and chopped
10 ml (2 t) paprika
5 ml (1 t) cayenne pepper
salt and freshly ground black pepper
25 ml (5 t) finely chopped fresh oregano
fresh bread for serving

Heat the oil in a saucepan, add the onion and garlic, cover and braise gently for about 5 minutes. Add the remaining ingredients and bring the mixture to the boil. Reduce the heat, cover and simmer for about 2 hours or until the meat and vegetables are soft and fragrant. Season to taste and serve the soup with fresh bread.

Serves 4–6.

Chowder

Hettie Bester of Bluff, Durban, makes a robust chowder with smoked haddock, potatoes and a can of sweet corn.

4 chives, chopped
500 g potatoes, peeled and diced
250 ml (1 c) fish or vegetable stock
250 ml (1 c) milk
1 bay leaf
500 g smoked haddock fillets,
    skinned and diced
1 can (410 g) creamy-style sweet corn
salt and freshly ground black pepper

Put the chives, potatoes, stock, milk and bay leaf in a saucepan and bring the mixture to the boil. Reduce the heat and simmer gently until the potatoes are nearly soft. Add the fish and sweet corn and season to taste with salt and black pepper. Simmer gently until the fish is done. Remove the bay leaf and serve the chowder with fresh bread.

Serves 4.

Bouillabaisse

This recipe for the classic seafood soup comes from the chairman of the South African Chefs Association, Martin Kobald, so it's the real thing.

500 g large prawns, shelled and
    deveined (reserve the heads and
    shells for stock)
crab shells (optional)
500 g skinned and deboned white fish
    (reserve the bones for stock), cubed
250 ml (1 c) fish stock
250 ml (1 c) white wine
500 ml (2 c) water
2½ red onions, finely chopped
25 ml (5 t) finely chopped garlic
3 bay or curry leaves
60 ml (¼ c) olive oil
1 small leek, finely sliced
1 can (420 g) chopped tomatoes
45 ml (3 T) tomato paste
1 ml (pinch) saffron powder or turmeric
15 ml (1 T) chopped fresh basil
5 ml (1 t) fennel seeds
4 cm strip orange rind
salt and freshly ground black pepper
12 fresh mussels, scrubbed and
    beards removed
125 ml (½ c) finely chopped fresh parsley

Prepare a stock by bringing the prawn heads and shells, crab shells, fish bones, stock, wine, water, ½ an onion, 10 ml (2 t) of the garlic and 1 bay leaf to the boil in a large saucepan. Reduce the heat and simmer for 20 minutes. Strain the mixture through a sieve and reserve the stock.

Heat the oil in a large saucepan and add the remaining onions and garlic and the leek. Cover and sauté for 10 minutes over low heat or until the onions are soft but not browned. Stir occasionally. Stir in the tomatoes, tomato paste, saffron, remaining bay leaves, basil, fennel seeds, orange rind, salt and pepper. Stir in the reserved stock and cook uncovered for 10 minutes, stirring frequently. Reduce the heat, add the fish and mussels, cover and simmer for 4–5 minutes. Add the prawns, cover and simmer for another 3–4 minutes. Do not overcook the prawns. Remove the orange rind and bay or curry leaves, spoon into soup bowls, garnish with parsley and serve hot.

Serves 4–6.

Bouillabaisse

FISH AND SEAFOOD

Enjoy the fresh taste of the sea with mussels, prawns and calamari and pan-fried or baked fish. Equally delicious whether served with Mediterranean or Asian herbs and spices.

Seafood with Provençale sauce

This seafood dish was created by award-winning chef Nic van Wyk of Stellenbosch. Serve hot or cold.

PROVENÇALE SAUCE
5 ml (1 t) toasted coriander seeds,
    slightly crushed
30 ml (2 T) finely chopped onions
100 ml fresh lemon juice
125 ml (½ c) olive oil
1–2 tomatoes, peeled and finely chopped
10 basil leaves, chopped
salt and freshly ground black pepper

SEAFOOD
2–3 cleaned prawns per person
2 cleaned calamari tubes per person
2 calamari heads per person
salt and pepper
oil

PROVENÇALE SAUCE
Heat the coriander seeds, onions and lemon juice. Strain and reserve the liquid. Discard the solids. Add the olive oil and leave to cool. Add the tomato and basil and season to taste with salt and pepper.

SEAFOOD
Season the seafood with salt and pepper. Separately fry the prawns and calamari in a little well heated oil until just done. Turn the calamari tubes once only. Spoon a little of the sauce on top and serve with bread.

Serves 6.

Variation
Substitute calamari steaks for the seafood and cook as follows: Cut a diamond pattern on both sides of the steaks and fry in heated butter and oil until they turn white. Season with salt and pepper and spoon the sauce on top.
Add a few black olives to the sauce and spoon over the steaks. Top with grated mozzarella cheese and heat under the oven grill until just melted.

Tips
Calamari is done as soon as it turns white.
Prawns are done when they turn pink. Do not overcook seafood or it will become tough.
Soak calamari in milk before cooking it.

Seafood with Provençale sauce

Seafood hotpot

A delicious dish we enjoyed at the Italian restaurant, Zucca, in the heart of Cape Town.

SEAFOOD
1 large onion, roughly chopped
2 bay leaves
500 g fish (selection of kingklip,
    yellowtail or hake), cubed
250 g shelled prawns
3 ml (generous ½ t) fish spice
100 ml water
100 ml white wine

WHITE SAUCE
50 g butter
50 ml cake flour
300 ml milk
2 ml (½ t) mustard powder
60 ml (¼ c) grated Parmesan cheese
60 ml (¼ c) grated mozzarella cheese
2 ml (½ t) paprika

Preheat the oven to 180 °C. Grease a medium-sized ovenproof casserole.

SEAFOOD
Scatter the onion and bay leaves on the bottom of an ovenproof dish and arrange the fish and prawns on top. Season with the fish spice. Add enough water and wine to cover the fish. Cover and bake for 20 minutes or until the fish is done.

WHITE SAUCE
Melt the butter in a saucepan and stir in the flour. Cook for 1 minute. Add the milk, stirring continuously. Bring the sauce to the boil and simmer until it thickens. Stir in the mustard powder and Parmesan cheese. Transfer the cooked fish and prawns to an ovenproof casserole (discard the liquid) and pour over the white sauce. Sprinkle the mozzarella cheese and paprika on top and heat for about 5 minutes or until the cheese has melted. Serve with roasted vegetables.

Serves 3–4.

Fried rice with seafood

Delicious as a quick, light meal.

RICE
250 ml (1 c) white rice
250 ml (1 c) brown rice

SEAFOOD MIX
oil
5 ml (1 t) sesame oil
1 onion, chopped
2 cloves garlic, crushed
1 red pepper, seeded and diced
5 ml (1 t) grated ginger
3 ml (generous ½ t) ground coriander
15 ml (1 T) brown sugar
300 g fish fillets, cubed
250 g prawns
4 chives, chopped
125 ml (½ c) frozen peas
15–30 ml (1–2 T) soy sauce
5 ml (1 t) sweet soy sauce
30 ml (2 T) chopped fresh coriander

RICE
Cook both kinds of rice according to the packet instructions. Drain and leave to cool.

SEAFOOD MIX
Heat a little oil with the sesame oil in a wok or large pan and stir-fry the onion, garlic, red pepper and ginger until soft. Add the coriander and sugar and mix. Add the fish cubes and stir-fry until just done. Add the prawns, cover and braise until the prawns are just done. Add the chives, cooked rice, peas and soy sauces and heat through. Serve in bowls and scatter over the coriander.

Serves 4.

Seafood gumbo

A spicy seafood and rice dish.

1 packet (500 g) frozen seafood (marinara)
15 ml (1 T) Cajun spice
oil
275 g rice
2 cloves garlic, crushed
2 chillies, seeded and chopped
2 green or red peppers, seeded and cut
    into pieces
200 g mushrooms, sliced
600 ml chicken stock
150 ml coconut milk
salt and freshly ground black pepper
coriander leaves to scatter on top

Season the seafood mix with the Cajun spice and stir-fry a little at a time in a little heated oil for at most 2 minutes or until just done – the calamari will turn white and no longer be glassy. Remove from the pan.

Heat more oil and stir-fry the rice, garlic, chillies, peppers and mushroom until lightly browned. Add the chicken stock, coconut milk, salt and pepper and cook until the rice is soft. Return the seafood to the pan and heat through. Scatter over the coriander leaves and serve.

Serves 4.

> **Tip**
> How to defrost seafood in a jiffy: Pour hot water over the seafood and drain rapidly. Pat dry with paper towels before cooking or it will steam instead of frying.

Pakistani prawns

Serve these prawns with naan bread.

PASTE
1 onion, quartered
15 ml (1 T) coriander seeds
2 cloves garlic, peeled
2,5 cm piece fresh ginger
80 ml (1/3 c) fresh coriander leaves
juice and rind of 2 lemons

PRAWNS
30 ml (2 T) oil
600 g large frozen prawns, defrosted
salt and freshly ground black pepper
garam masala

PASTE
Blitz the onion, coriander seeds, garlic, ginger, coriander leaves and lemon juice and rind in a food processor until smooth.

PRAWNS
Heat the oil in a wok or large pan and stir-fry the paste for about 3 minutes or until hot. Add the prawns and stir-fry for about 5 minutes or until just done. Season to taste with salt and pepper and sprinkle over the garam masala.

Serves 6.

Mussels in white wine

Gremolata, a mixture of lemon rind, garlic and parsley, imparts a deliciously pungent flavour to the mussels.

GREMOLATA
30 ml (2 T) chopped flat-leaf parsley
30 ml (2 T) chopped fresh basil
2 cloves garlic, crushed
15 ml (1 T) grated lemon rind

MUSSELS
125 ml (½ c) dry white wine
125 ml (½ c) chicken stock
2 fresh red chillies, seeded and chopped
4 onions, chopped
1 fennel bulb, sliced (optional)
2 kg black mussels, scrubbed
    and beards removed
salt and freshly ground black pepper
Italian bread to serve

GREMOLATA
Mix the ingredients for the gremolata and set aside.

MUSSELS
Mix the wine, stock, chillies, onions and fennel in a large stock pot and cook over high heat until reduced by half. Add the mussels, cover and cook over medium heat for about 10 minutes or until the mussels open. Discard any mussels that don't open. Spoon the mussels into deep pasta plates, season the liquid with salt and pepper to taste and pour over the mussels. Scatter the gremolata on top and serve immediately with chunks of bread.

Serves 6.

> **Variation**
> You can also use frozen mussels in shell halves.

> **Tip**
> Fresh mussels must be cooked while still alive. Discard any mussels that are open and don't close when lightly tapped with a knife.
> Also discard mussels that don't open after they've been cooked. Remember, mussels must be closed before you cook them and open after they've been cooked.

Thai mussels

These mussels are steamed in a fragrant red curry and coconut cream sauce.

½ onion, finely chopped
5 ml (1 t) butter
1–2 chillies, seeded and chopped
15 ml (1 T) red curry paste
4 curry leaves
2,5 cm piece fresh ginger, grated
1 stem lemon grass (hard outer part
    removed), chopped
juice and rind of 1 lemon
1 can (400 g) coconut cream
salt and freshly ground black pepper
500 g frozen mussels in shell
    halves, defrosted
2 handfuls fresh coriander
    leaves, chopped

Sauté the onion in the butter until soft. Add the chillies, curry paste, curry leaves, ginger and lemon grass and sauté for 1 minute over low heat. Stir in the lemon juice and rind and coconut cream and season to taste with salt and pepper.
    Add the mussels, cover and heat for about 3 minutes or until heated through. Scatter over the coriander leaves and serve on rice.

Serves 4.

Thai mussels

Crumbed fish

Shehaam Barnes of Garlandale spoons tartar sauce over fish fillets before topping them with a mixture of cheese and breadcrumbs. Delicious!

TARTAR SAUCE
250 ml (1 c) mayonnaise
10 ml (2 t) fresh lemon juice
15 ml (1 T) chopped capers
4 small gherkins, finely chopped
5 ml (1 t) mustard powder

FISH AND CRUMB TOPPING
2 fresh white fish fillets,
    about 200 g each
salt and freshly ground black pepper
100 ml fresh breadcrumbs
45 ml (3 T) grated Parmesan cheese
15 ml (1 T) chopped fresh coriander leaves
1 ml (pinch) cayenne pepper or
    seafood masala
finely grated rind of 1 lemon

Preheat the oven to 200 °C. Grease a baking sheet.

TARTAR SAUCE
Mix the sauce ingredients.

FISH AND CRUMB TOPPING
Lightly season the fish pieces with salt and pepper and put them on the baking sheet. Spread a little of the tartar sauce on each piece of fish. Mix the remaining ingredients and scatter the mixture over the fish. Bake for 10–15 minutes depending on the thickness of the fish and until the crumb crust is golden brown and the fish flakes easily with a fork. Serve with baby potatoes and a green salad and the rest of the tartar sauce.

Serves 2–3.

> **Budget-beating tip**
> Substitute 80 ml (⅓ c) grated mature Cheddar or mozzarella cheese for the Parmesan cheese.

Fish with couscous topping ✓

The fish is topped with couscous instead of the usual breadcrumbs.

TOPPING
60 ml (¼ c) chopped fresh parsley
10 green olives, pitted and roughly
    chopped (optional)
45 ml (3 T) chopped capers
60 ml (¼ c) pine nuts, toasted and
    roughly chopped
60 ml (¼ c) olive oil
juice and rind of 1 lemon
375 ml (1½ c) couscous
salt and freshly ground black pepper

FISH
4 hake fillets, skinned
salt and freshly ground black pepper
extra olive oil for drizzling on top
500 ml (2 c) water

Preheat the oven to 180 °C. Grease a baking sheet.

TOPPING
Mix the topping ingredients and set aside.

FISH
Arrange the fish fillets in a single layer on the greased baking sheet, ensuring they don't touch. Season with salt and pepper to taste. Drizzle the fillets with a little olive oil and cover with the topping mixture. Pour over the water and drizzle with a little more olive oil. Bake for 20–25 minutes or until done. Serve with tzatziki made with grated cucumber and plain yoghurt.

Serves 4.

> **Tip**
> Substitute toasted sesame seeds and chopped hazelnuts for the pine nuts.

TYPES OF WHITE FISH
White fish includes butter fish, Cape salmon (geelbek), yellowtail, kabeljou, kingklip, steenbras and hake.

TYPES OF OILY FISH
Salmon, trout, mackerel, pilchards, snoek, sardines, kippers, fresh tuna, anchovies and panga are examples of oily fish.

With South Africa's fish resources under threat the South African Sustainability Seafood Initiative has colour-coded different kinds of fish according their availability. Fish types that are most under threat are coded red and may not be caught, fish types that are under pressure are coded orange and may be caught in limited quantities, while code green fish types are still in plentiful supply.

WHICH FISH TYPES ARE ON THE DANGER LIST?
The following well-known kinds of fish have been coded red: galjoen, Cape and Natal stumpnose, white steenbras and white musselcracker.
SMS the fish type to 079-499-8795 to find out if the fish you've ordered is on the danger list.

Fish with tomato sauce

A perfect summer dish that can be made the day before and served at room temperature.

FISH
1,5 kg fresh fish, cut into pieces
  and rinsed well
50 ml olive oil
80 ml (⅓ c) lemon juice
15 ml (1 T) chopped chives
sea salt and freshly ground black pepper
200 g feta cheese, crumbled

TOMATO SAUCE
oil
2 leeks, sliced into rings
3 cloves garlic, crushed
1 red pepper, seeded and diced
1 can (400 g) whole tomatoes, chopped
5 ml (1 t) mustard powder
15 ml (1 T) each chopped fresh basil
  and/or parsley
10 ml (2 t) chopped capers
grated rind of 1 lemon

FISH
Arrange the fish pieces in a non-metallic bowl. Mix the olive oil, lemon juice and chives and pour the mixture over the fish. Leave for 30 minutes. Preheat the oven to 180 °C.

TOMATO SAUCE
Heat a little oil in a pan and sauté the leeks, garlic and red pepper until soft. Add the tomatoes and remaining ingredients and bring the mixture to the boil. Simmer for about 5 minutes or until fragrant. Season the fish with salt and pepper and spoon over the tomato sauce. Bake for about 15–20 minutes or until the fish is just done and flakes easily with a fork. Sprinkle over the feta cheese and heat till melted. Serve with a fresh potato salad (see recipe).

Serves 6.

FRESH POTATO SALAD
Cook baby potatoes in their jackets until done and press gently to break them open. Season generously with sea salt, grated lemon rind and black pepper and drizzle with plenty of olive oil.

Baked snoek with vegetable topping

Mari Olivier of Parow covers snoek with a layer of vegetables and bakes it in the oven.

FISH
1 kg butterflied fresh snoek (backbone
   removed)
30 ml (2 T) melted butter
salt and freshly ground black pepper

SAUCE
60 ml (¼ c) olive oil
60 ml (¼ c) lemon juice
60 ml (¼ c) tomato purée

TOPPING
1 medium-sized onion, thinly sliced
250 g button mushrooms, sliced
1 large tomato, sliced
½ red pepper, sliced into strips
salt and freshly ground black pepper
pinch sugar
5 ml (1 t) chopped fresh rosemary

Switch on the oven grill and grease a baking sheet.

FISH
Put the snoek skin side down on the baking sheet. Pour the butter over and season to taste with salt and pepper. Grill for about 3 minutes on the top oven shelf. Remove, pour off the liquid and remove most of the large bones. Set the oven temperature to 180 °C.

SAUCE
Mix the sauce ingredients and brush the snoek with the mixture.

TOPPING
Cover the fish with the topping ingredients and bake for 5–10 minutes or until the fish is just done and no longer glassy. Serve with freshly baked bread.

Serves 4.

Tip
Scatter mozzarella cheese on top of the vegetable layer and bake until melted.

ASIAN MARINADE FOR SNOEK
Use this marinade when baking snoek in the oven or over a fire.
Blend 60 ml (¼ c) soy sauce, finely grated rind of 2 oranges and 2 lemons, 30 ml (2 T) chutney, 30 ml (2 T) oil, 5 ml (1 t) sesame oil, 2 crushed cloves garlic and 15 ml (1 T) grated fresh ginger. Brush the fish with the mixture while baking.

Fish in coconut milk

I came across this recipe years ago in the Seychelles. It's easy and the results are delicious.

4 hake fillets, cubed
salt and freshly ground black pepper
3 ml (generous ½ t) turmeric
4 cm piece fresh ginger, grated
2 cloves garlic, finely chopped
20 ml (4 t) oil
30 ml (2 T) oil for frying
160 ml (⅔ c) coconut milk
1 piece stick cinnamon
4 curry leaves

Season the fish with salt and pepper. Combine the turmeric, ginger, garlic and oil. Spoon the mixture over the fish cubes and mix well. Brown the fish cubes in a little heated oil. Reduce the heat and add the coconut milk, cinnamon stick and curry leaves. Simmer until most of the liquid has reduced. Serve with rice.

Serves 2–3.

Baked snoek with vegetable topping

Fish and chips

Once you've tasted this deliciously light batter you'll never buy fish and chips from your local corner shop again.

BEER BATTER
180 ml (¾ c) cake flour
80 ml (⅓ c) self-raising flour
250 ml (1 c) cold beer

FISH
oil for deep-frying
4 hake fillets
salt
extra cake flour for dusting
1 lemon, cut into wedges

BEER BATTER
Combine the cake flour and self-raising flour in a large mixing bowl and beat in three-quarters of the beer. Gradually add more beer until the batter has the consistency of thick cream. Chill until needed.

FISH
Heat enough oil for deep-frying. Season the fish fillets with salt and lightly dust them with flour. Dip the fish in the batter, allowing the excess batter to run off. Put two fillets in the oil at a time and fry for about 2 minutes. Turn and fry for another 2 minutes. Remove the fish from the oil and keep warm while frying the remaining fillets. Serve with lemon wedges and chips (see recipe).

Serves 4.

DOUBLE-FRIED CHIPS
Peel 1 kg potatoes and cut them into thick fingers. Wash twice and pat dry with paper towels. Heat the oil for deep-frying until medium hot – a bread cube dropped in the oil will turn pale brown in 70 seconds. Fry the chips for 5–8 minutes until soft but not brown. Remove from the oil and drain. Reheat the oil just before serving and fry the chips until golden brown. Remove from the oil, drain on paper towels and season with salt.

Fish in lemon butter sauce

A classic way to serve fried fish.

750 g white fish fillets, skinned
   and cut in half
seasoned flour
80 g butter
juice and rind of 1 lemon
30 ml (2 T) chopped fresh parsley

Roll the fish fillets in the seasoned flour. Heat half the butter and as soon as it starts foaming add the fish fillets. Fry for about 2 minutes on each side or until golden brown. (Cover the pan and braise the fish until done.) Add the remaining butter, lemon juice and rind and parsley and shake the pan until the butter has melted and the fish is coated in the mixture.

Serves 3–4.

Vietnamese fried fish

In Vietnam fish, which is in plentiful supply, is often dried to preserve it as not everyone has a fridge. Dried fish is an important ingredient in fish sauce or nuoc mam. Fish rolled in cornflour seasoned with turmeric and fried is a typical dish from the north of the country. Serve it with a green mango salsa.

GREEN MANGO SALSA
1 green mango or atjar mango, peeled
    and cut into strips
1 cucumber, peeled, seeded and
    cut into strips
juice of 1 lime
1 red chilli, seeded and cut into long strips
30 ml (2 T) chilli sauce (nuoc cham)
    (see recipe)

FRIED FISH
150 ml cornflour
5 ml (1 t) turmeric
300 g white fish fillets (kabeljou
    or hake), skinned and cubed
vegetable oil for frying
1 handful fresh dill
lime wedges

GREEN MANGO SALSA
Mix all the ingredients except the chilli sauce. Add the chilli sauce just before serving and mix.

FRIED FISH
Combine the cornflour and turmeric and roll the fish in the mixture until completely coated. Heat a little oil in a wok or pan and fry a few fish cubes at a time until golden brown and done. Scatter the dill on a plate and put the fish on top. Serve with mango salsa, extra chilli sauce and lime wedges.

Serves 4.

CHILLI SAUCE
Using a mortar and pestle pound together 4 chopped cloves garlic, 2 seeded red chillies and 15 ml (1 T) sugar. Add the juice of 1 lime, 50 ml fish sauce (nuoc mam) and 60 ml (¼ c) water and mix well.

Fish stroganoff

Mercia Pieterse of Tzaneen makes fish stroganoff with a creamy tomato sauce.

60 ml (¼ c) butter or margarine
1 onion, finely chopped
1 punnet (250 g) button
    mushrooms, sliced
60 ml (¼ c) cake flour
375 ml (1½ c) hot water
salt and freshly ground black pepper
10 ml (2 t) lemon juice
1 can (65 g) tomato paste
25 ml (5 t) dry white wine
250 ml (1 c) sour cream
2 packets (300 g each) frozen hake

Preheat the oven to 180 °C. Grease a large ovenproof dish.
    Heat the butter and sauté the onion until soft. Add the mushrooms and stir-fry until done. Add the cake flour and stir until smooth and the mixture starts to bubble. Gradually add the water and, stirring continuously, bring the mixture to the boil. Remove from the heat and season with salt and pepper. Add the lemon juice, tomato paste, wine and sour cream. Stirring continuously, bring the mixture to the boil once more. Season the fish fillets with salt and pepper and arrange them in the prepared dish. Pour over the sauce and bake for 20–30 minutes or until the fish is just done and no longer glassy.
    Serve with flat noodles.

Serves 4.

Tip
If you prefer a thicker sauce, remove the fish and reduce the sauce until thick and fragrant.

Fish in spicy yoghurt sauce

Serve this fish with a cucumber salad, suggests Dorothy Fiala of Pretoria.

MARINADE
1 onion, chopped
5 ml (1 t) grated fresh ginger
10 ml (2 t) turmeric
1 ml (pinch) ground cumin
1–2 green chillies, seeded and
   finely chopped
500 ml (2 c) plain yoghurt

FISH
675 g white fish, skinned, bones
   removed and cut into big pieces
30 ml (2 T) each butter and oil
1 onion, sliced into rings
juice and rind of 1 lemon
chopped fresh coriander leaves

MARINADE
Mix the ingredients for the marinade.

FISH
Put the fish in a large bowl and pour over the marinade.
Leave for at least 30 minutes. Heat the butter and oil in a pan
and stir-fry the onion rings until fragrant. Add the fish and
marinade, cover and simmer over low heat for 10–15 minutes
or until just done. Sprinkle over the lemon juice and rind and
coriander leaves and serve with rice.

Serves 4–5.

Asian stir-fried fish

45 ml (3 T) vegetable oil
750 g fish fillets, skinned and
   cut into pieces
1 clove garlic, finely chopped
5 ml (1 t) grated fresh ginger
½ red chilli, finely chopped
100 g shitake or oyster mushrooms
1 small carrot, cut into thin strips
3 spring onions, chopped
20 ml (4 t) soy sauce
5 ml (1 t) sesame oil
fresh coriander leaves to garnish

Heat a wok over high heat and add half the oil. Stir-fry the
fish, garlic, ginger and chilli for about 2–3 minutes or until the
fish is just done. Remove from the wok. Heat the remaining oil
in the wok and stir-fry the vegetables until done but still crisp.
Return the fish mixture to the wok and add the soy sauce and
sesame oil. Mix and serve with steamed rice and a scattering
of coriander leaves.

Serves 4.

Budget-beating tip
Use button mushrooms instead of the shitake or
oyster mushrooms.

Fish balls

This is a recipe from Priscilla Petersen, the assistant in *YOU*'s test kitchen.
She says she often makes these fish balls over weekends.

2 slices day-old white bread
water
500 g hake, finely chopped or minced
1 onion, finely chopped
1 extra-large egg
salt and freshly ground black pepper
finely chopped fresh parsley
oil for frying

Soak the bread in water until swollen. Mix the bread with all
the remaining ingredients except the oil. Shape the mixture
into balls and flatten them slightly. Chill for 15 minutes. Fry in
heated oil until done. Serve with tomato sauce.

Serves 6.

Fish in spicy yoghurt sauce

MEAT FOR ALL

Beef, lamb, pork, game; fancy oven and pot roasts, fragrant stews and potjies or budget-beating bobotie and meatballs – you can serve meat in so many interesting ways you never need to serve the same dish twice.

Beef

Beef wing rib with mustard crust

Any meat cut roasted to perfection in the oven is always a treat. Brush the meat with mustard butter to bring out its flavour.

3–3,5 kg beef wing rib on the bone
100 g butter, softened
30–45 ml (2–3 T) Dijon mustard
    or wholegrain mustard
salt and freshly ground black pepper
1 medium-sized onion, thickly sliced
6–8 fairly small onions, unpeeled
15 ml (1 T) chopped fresh thyme leaves
30 ml (2 T) olive oil
250 ml (1 c) red wine
15–25 ml (3–5 t) cake flour

Preheat the oven to 160 °C. Grease a roasting tin. Wipe the meat with a damp cloth. Blend the butter and mustard and season to taste with salt and pepper. Spread the mixture over the rib. Arrange the onion rings down the centre of the roasting tin. Put the meat on top of the onion rings and roast uncovered for 1 hour and 20 minutes. Cut a deep cross in each of the remaining onions and arrange them around the meat. Scatter the thyme sprigs on top and drizzle with olive oil. Roast for another 20–30 minutes, basting frequently with the pan juices and onions.

Heat the red wine and add it to the meat and onions in the tin. Roast for another 40 minutes or until the meat is rare or medium-rare. Transfer the rib to a warm serving platter and surround with the onions. Cover the meat with aluminium foil and rest for about 10 minutes in the warming drawer before carving. Meanwhile heat 30–45 ml (2–3 T) of the fat from the roasting tin in a small saucepan and stir in the cake flour. Stirring continuously, heat for 2 minutes. Stir in the pan juices and heat until the sauce comes to the boil and thickens. Serve the meat with the sauce.

Serves 6–8.

Beef wing rib with mustard crust

COOKING TIMES FOR OVEN ROASTS

Meat roasted in the oven must be cooked at the correct temperature and for the correct time.

HOW TO OVEN-ROAST MEAT

Put the meat on the rack of a roasting tin, fatty side facing up. Do not cover it. Roast at 160 °C (the low temperature prevents moisture loss) according to the times in the table.

Beef and veal is cooked until rare while beef, veal, pork and lamb can be cooked to medium-done.

To test if the meat is done insert a testing skewer in the thickest part of the meat. If the meat juices run clear the meat is well done.

WHICH CUTS ARE SUITABLE FOR OVEN-ROASTING?

Tender whole cuts of meat that have been well ripened are suitable for oven-roasting.

Smaller cuts such as chops are roasted at a high temperature for a short period or grilled.

Tougher meat cuts such as a leg of mutton are covered in aluminium foil to trap the steam inside before being cooked for a fairly long period.

A roast must weigh 1,5 kg or more as smaller cuts will shrink, leaving them dry and tasteless.

	Beef	Pork	Lamb
Rare	15–20 minutes per 500 g plus an extra 15 minutes		
Medium-rare	20–25 minutes per 500 g plus an extra 20 minutes	20–25 minutes per 500 g plus an extra 20 minutes	20–25 minutes per 500 g plus an extra 20 minutes
Well-done	25–30 minutes per 500 g plus an extra 25 minutes	25–30 minutes per 500 g plus an extra 25 minutes	25–30 minutes per 500 g plus an extra 25 minutes

NOTE: Roast meat should always be left to rest in the warming drawer for 10 minutes before being carved. During this time the meat juices are reabsorbed, making the meat juicier and easier to carve.

German pot roast
(Sauerbraten)

Sauerbraten is a well-known German meat dish. The sauce is thickened with ginger cookies, giving it a subtle spicy flavour.

1,5 kg beef (topside or silverside)
275 ml wine vinegar
450 ml water
40 ml brown sugar
1 onion, roughly chopped
1 carrot, roughly chopped
2 stalks celery, chopped
1 bay leaf
3 black peppercorns
3 allspice berries
6 juniper berries
1 whole clove
60 g spek, cut into long strips
salt and freshly ground black pepper
60 g butter
30 ml (2 T) sultanas
2–3 ginger cookies, crumbled
150 ml cream
20 ml (4 t) apple jelly

Put the meat in a deep plastic or glass bowl. Bring the vinegar, water, sugar, vegetables and spices to the boil in a saucepan. Pour the hot mixture over the meat, cover and leave to marinate in the liquid for 2 days in the fridge. Turn the meat a few times. Remove the meat from the marinade and reserve the marinade. Roll the strips of spek in a mixture of salt and pepper and lard the meat by making incisions in the meat and inserting the lard. Season with meat with salt and pepper. Heat the butter in a large heavy-bottomed saucepan and brown the meat all over. Measure the marinade and dilute it with an equal quantity of water. Add the liquid to the meat and bring it to the boil. Cover, reduce the heat and simmer slowly for 2 hours or until the meat is very tender. Remove the meat from the saucepan and keep warm while preparing the sauce. Strain the cooking liquid and reserve 300–350 ml. Add the sultanas, ginger cookies and cream. Add the apple jelly and salt to taste and simmer for 10 minutes. Cut the meat into thick slices, spoon over the sauce and serve.

Serves 6.

Robust pot roast

When I think of pot roast I think of beef, especially tougher cuts such as topside which benefit from long, slow cooking. Topside is also much more affordable than for instance a tender cut such as steak. You can also pot roast a leg of mutton which is tougher but more flavoursome than leg of lamb. Cook a leg of lamb over the fire or in the oven.

about 2 kg topside or silverside
7 ml (1½ t) salt
5 ml (1 t) freshly ground black pepper
cake flour
45 ml (3 T) vegetable oil
2 onions, chopped
1 clove garlic, crushed
2 green chillies, seeded and
    chopped (optional)
2 ml (½ t) cumin seeds
30 ml (2 T) mixed pickling spices
30 ml (2 T) cardamom pods, crushed
300 ml apricot juice or wine, water
    or meat stock
cornflour to thicken the sauce

Season the meat with the salt and pepper and roll it in flour. Heat the oil in a deep heavy-bottomed saucepan and brown the meat over medium heat, turning it continuously to ensure it browns evenly. Remove the meat from the saucepan and set aside. Put the vegetables and spices in the saucepan and stir-fry for 3 minutes or until lightly browned. Return the meat to the saucepan, add the juice, wine, water or stock and bring to the boil. Cover, reduce the heat and simmer slowly over very low heat for 2 hours. Add extra boiling water if the meat becomes too dry. Remove the meat to a carving board. Cover it with aluminium foil and leave to rest for 10 minutes before carving it against the grain. Strain the pan juices to remove the whole spices. Heat the liquid over medium heat and thicken it with a little cornflour blended with water. Serve the pot roast with the gravy, rice and vegetables.

Serves 6–8.

Lamb
Shoulder of lamb with olive stuffing

Mrs SC Labuschagne of Polokwane even serves this roast cold with anchovy mayonnaise (see recipe).

STUFFING
1 packet (200 g) black olives, pitted and
    finely chopped
125 ml (½ c) sun-dried tomatoes,
    drained and chopped
4 anchovies, finely chopped
2 slices white bread, crumbled
60 ml (¼ c) capers, drained
30 ml (2 T) olive oil
1 piece preserved lemon, finely chopped
    (optional)
30 ml (2 T) lemon juice
3 ml (generous ½ t) dried thyme
10 ml (2 t) chopped fresh rosemary

MEAT
1,5 kg deboned shoulder of lamb
salt and freshly ground black pepper
spinach leaves
2 rounds feta cheese, crumbled
fresh rosemary sprigs

Preheat the oven to 160 °C.

STUFFING
Mix the stuffing ingredients.

MEAT
Put the meat on a work surface, fatty side facing down, and season with salt and pepper. Arrange a layer of spinach leaves on the meat and spread the stuffing mixture on top. Sprinkle over the feta cheese and roll up the meat. Season the outside of the roll with salt and pepper. Secure a few rosemary sprigs on top of the roll with string. Put the roll on the rack of a roasting tin and oven-roast until medium-done. Remove the string and carve the meat into slices. Make a sauce from the pan juices and garnish with rosemary.

Serves 6–8.

ANCHOVY MAYONNAISE: Blend 1 finely chopped anchovy with lots of mayonnaise.

Sicilian rack of lamb

The roast racks of lamb are served with a sauce made with lemon, garlic, herbs and olive oil. Use dried oregano which has a more intense, sweet flavour than the fresh equivalent.

MEAT
2 racks of lamb, each with
    about 6–7 ribs
salt and freshly ground black pepper
olive oil for brushing

SICILIAN SAUCE
180 ml (¾ c) olive oil
juice of 1 large or 2 small ripe lemons
10 ml (2 t) dried oregano
2 cloves garlic, crushed
30 ml (2 T) chopped fresh parsley

MEAT
Remove all but a thin layer of fat from the racks of lamb – the fat will help to keep the meat moist while roasting. Rub the meat with salt and black pepper to taste. Brush with a little olive oil.

SAUCE
Blend the ingredients for the sauce until the mixture thickens slightly. Season to taste with salt and pepper. Preheat the oven grill until hot. Arrange the racks fatty sides up on the rack of a roasting tin and grill about 20 cm below the grill for 15–20 minutes. Check occasionally that the fat is not burning. Test doneness with a testing skewer and grill to the required degree of doneness. Transfer the cooked racks of lamb to a hot serving platter and spoon over the sauce. Cover and leave to rest in the warming drawer for at least 10 minutes.

Serves 4–6.

Sicilian rack of lamb

Italian leg of mutton in a tomato and wine sauce

This recipe is ideal for leg of mutton which is tougher but more flavoursome than leg of lamb, especially when cooked in a fragrant tomato and wine sauce.

2,5 kg leg of mutton or leg of lamb
8 cloves garlic, peeled and cut into
    long strips
few sprigs fresh rosemary
30 ml (2 T) olive oil
5 onions, thinly sliced
375 ml (½ bottle) red wine
1 can (420 g) chopped tomatoes
2 red chillies, seeded and
    chopped (optional)
juice of 1 lemon
salt and freshly ground black pepper

Preheat the oven to 160 °C.
Make small incisions all over the leg and insert the garlic strips and small sprigs of rosemary. Heat the olive oil in a large heavy-bottomed saucepan until very hot and brown the leg evenly. Remove from the pan and set aside. Sauté the onions for about 5 minutes until soft and fragrant. Add the remaining ingredients except the lemon juice, salt and pepper and bring to the boil. Put the leg in a deep ovenproof dish and pour over the sauce. Cover and bake for about 3 hours or until the meat is tender. Skim any fat that floats to the surface. Add the lemon juice to the sauce and season to taste with salt and freshly ground black pepper. Serve with pasta or fresh Italian bread.

Serves 6–8.

Pork

Pork is one of the most underrated meats in South Africa despite it being a wonderfully versatile, tender white meat. It combines beautifully with many flavours and is extremely affordable, especially if you buy a whole carcass.

Asian loin of pork

Loin of pork is deliciously succulent provided it's not overcooked. Asian flavours give this dish a new twist.

1,8 kg deboned loin of pork, rolled and
    secured

SAUCE
30 ml (2 T) brown sugar
125 ml (½ c) low-salt soy sauce
10 ml (2 t) dried chilli flakes
3 cloves garlic, crushed
30 ml (2 T) grated fresh ginger
10 ml (2 t) Chinese five spice
juice of 2 limes or 1 lemon
grated rind of 1 orange
salt and freshly ground black pepper

Preheat the oven to 160 °C. Put the pork loin in a nonmetallic dish.

SAUCE
Mix the ingredients for the sauce and pour the mixture over the meat. Marinate for at least 1 hour. Put the meat in a roasting tin and roast until medium-done (see table p. 60). Baste the meat frequently while roasting. Remove it from the oven, cover with aluminium foil and leave to rest for 10 minutes before carving.

Serves 6–8.

> **Variation with orange and apricot glaze**
> Mix 250 ml (1 c) orange juice, 30 ml (2 T) apricot jam, 30 ml (2 T) sherry and 25 ml (5 t) butter together. Brush the loin of pork with the mixture while roasting.

Vietnamese spareribs with hoisin sauce

Pork dishes such as spareribs and chops are popular in Vietnam. Pork mince is also sold everywhere. Sweet caramelised sauces, such as hoisin sauce, are typically served with pork.

45 ml (3 T) hoisin sauce
45 ml (3 T) fish sauce (nuoc mam)
10 ml (2 t) Chinese five spice
45 ml (3 T) sunflower or sesame oil
1 kg spareribs
3 cloves garlic, crushed
20 ml (4 t) grated fresh ginger
1 handful fresh basil leaves, torn

Blend the hoisin and fish sauces, Chinese five spice and 15 ml (1 T) of the oil and set aside. Bring water to the boil in a saucepan and put the ribs in the boiling water. Bring to the boil again and cook the ribs for about 10 minutes or until done. Remove the ribs with a slotted spoon, drain well and set aside. Heat the remaining oil in a clean wok or large heavy-bottomed saucepan and stir-fry the garlic and ginger until fragrant. Add the ribs and stir-fry for 5 minutes or until golden. Add the hoisin sauce mixture and stir-fry for another 10–15 minutes or until most of the liquid has evaporated and the ribs are caramelised and slightly blackened. Add the basil leaves and serve immediately with a salad and sticky rice.

Serves 4.

Eisbein

In Germany pickled or smoked pork shank is served with sauerkraut, which brings out the flavour of the meat. The shanks are served with the rind intact.

Eisbein means 'iced bone' and is derived from the practice of using pork shank bones to make ice skates.

EISBEIN
4 smoked pork shanks, rind scored
6 bay leaves
20 ml (4 t) hot prepared mustard
7 ml (1½ t) black peppercorns
100 ml soft brown sugar
1 large onion, peeled and quartered
6 whole cloves
about 700 ml beer

GLAZE
60 ml (¼ c) honey
60 g butter, melted

EISBEIN
Put the shanks in a large saucepan, add all the ingredients and enough beer to cover the meat. Bring the shanks to the boil, reduce the heat and simmer for 60–90 minutes or until the meat is very tender.

GLAZE
Preheat the oven to 220 °C.
Remove the shanks to a roasting tin and brush with the honey and butter. Roast in the oven until the rind is crisp and brown. Serve with sauerkraut, mashed potatoes and lemon slices.

Serves 4.

Pork belly with sweet mustard sauce

This roast can be served hot or cold. Chef Nic van Wyk from Kleine Zalze near Stellenbosh likes roasting it in a pizza oven.

1,5 kg pork belly, deboned and rind
    and most of the fat removed
5 ml (1 t) crushed whole cumin
    or coriander seeds
salt and freshly ground black pepper
oil
white wine

Cut a diamond pattern on the fatty layer of the meat. Rub the spices, salt and pepper into the meat, cover and leave in the fridge for 1 hour.

Preheat the oven to 220 °C. Rub the meat with oil and roast uncovered for 30 minutes. Add a little wine to the meat, reduce the heat to 160 °C and roast for another 90 minutes. Add more wine to the roasting tin as needed. Cover with aluminium foil and leave to rest for 15 minutes. Serve with sweet mustard sauce and pickled cucumber (see recipes) and the pan juices.

Serves 6–8.

> **Tip**
> The pork belly can be cooked three-quarters of the way in the oven and then grilled over a fire until golden brown.

Sweet mustard sauce

125 ml (½ c) white wine vinegar or cider
125 ml (½ c) lemon juice
150 ml sugar
3 eggs, whisked
15 ml (1 T) mustard powder or
    wholegrain mustard
pinch of salt
plain yoghurt

Mix the white wine vinegar or cider and lemon juice and add the sugar. Stir over medium heat until the sugar has dissolved and add the whisked eggs, mustard and salt. Stir continuously over medium heat until the sauce thickens. Add a spoonful of plain yoghurt if desired.

Pickled cucumber

1 English cucumber, very thinly sliced
10 ml (2 t) sea salt flakes
15 ml (1 T) rice vinegar
20 ml (4 t) caster sugar
15 ml (1 T) chopped fresh dill

Put the cucumber slices in a colander and sprinkle with the salt. Weight down the cucumber with a plate to extract the liquid and leave for about 3 hours. Add the remaining ingredients to the cucumber and cover until needed.

> **Tip**
> Do not overcook pork or it will be dry. It doesn't have to be well-done; it's best cooked medium-done.

Pork belly with sweet mustard sauce

Pork chops with cheese and roasted butternut

Sage goes well with both pork and butternut. The walnuts and mustard add extra flavour to the dish.

MUSTARD BASTING SAUCE
80 ml (⅓ c) sunflower oil
45 ml (3 T) lemon juice or wine vinegar
2–3 cloves garlic, crushed
5–15 ml (1–3 t) honey or sugar
5–15 ml (1–3 t) wholegrain mustard

ROASTED BUTTERNUT
3 kg butternut, peeled and cubed
fresh sage leaves
45 ml (3 T) oil (use 15 ml (1 T) sesame
   oil if desired)
salt

PORK CHOPS AND STUFFING
30 ml (2 T) fresh breadcrumbs
30 ml (2 T) chopped walnuts
30 ml (2 T) chopped fresh sage
15 ml (1 T) chopped fresh thyme
   (optional)
60 ml (¼ c) grated mature
   Cheddar cheese
4–6 pork chops, at least 3 cm thick

TO SERVE
Rocket or baby leaf spinach
1 can (410 g) chickpeas (optional)

MUSTARD BASTING SAUCE
Blend the basting sauce ingredients and set aside.

ROASTED BUTTERNUT
Preheat the oven to 180 °C. Put the butternut in a greased roasting tin and scatter over the sage. Drizzle with the oil and season with salt. Roast for about 20 minutes or until done. Pour over half the mustard basting sauce while the butternut is still warm and set aside.

PORK CHOPS
Mix the stuffing ingredients. Make a horizontal slit in each pork chop to form a pocket, taking care not to cut all the way through. Spoon the stuffing into the pockets and secure with cocktail sticks. Fry in a heated pan for about 10 minutes or until just done but not dry. Baste with the basting sauce while cooking.

TO SERVE
Put a few baby leaf spinach or rocket leaves on a serving platter, mix the butternut with the chickpeas and spoon over the spinach. Arrange the pork chops on top.

Serves 4–6.

Tip
Pork chops, braaied over the coals, can also be served this way.

Pork chops with cheese and roasted butternut

Easter ham with berry and orange glaze

Corli Els prepared this delicious Easter ham for us when she was still chef at Hazendal wine estate near Cape Town. She cooks the gammon in ginger beer.

3–5 kg gammon
2 onions, roughly chopped
6 whole cloves
10 black peppercorns
3 bay leaves
2 litres (8 c) ginger beer

GLAZE
180 ml (¾ c) berry jelly or jam
60 ml (¼ c) fresh orange juice
30 ml (2 T) orange liqueur
15 ml (1 T) Dijon mustard
125 ml (½ c) brown sugar

Bring the gammon, onions, spices and ginger beer to the boil in a large saucepan. Cover and simmer slowly, allowing 30 minutes per 500 g meat. Leave the gammon to cool in the liquid. Remove the rind and cut a diamond pattern in the fatty layer.

Preheat the oven to 160 °C. Transfer the gammon to a roasting tin.

GLAZE
Put the ingredients for the glaze in a saucepan and heat until melted. Spoon the glaze mixture over the gammon and bake for 30–40 minutes. Carve the ham into slices and serve at room temperature or hot with a mustard sauce (see recipe p. 66).

Serves 10.

> **Variation**
> Use smoked loin, neck or leg of pork instead of gammon.

Venison
Oven-roast chine

The venison, currants and marulas are a uniquely South African combination.

RUB
90 ml (6 T) olive oil
25 ml (5 t) lemon juice
2 leeks, finely chopped
15 ml (1 T) freshly ground black pepper
1 bay leaf, crumbled
5 ml (1 t) chopped fresh oregano
5 ml (1 t) chopped fresh thyme
2 ml (½ t) chopped fresh rosemary
1 clove garlic, finely chopped
15 ml (1 T) chopped fresh parsley

MEAT
1 venison chine with fillets
1 piece of caul

MARULA SAUCE
about 500 ml (2 c) beef stock
80 ml (⅓ c) currants
75 ml (5 T) marula liqueur
30 ml (2 T) brandy
salt and freshly ground black pepper
15 ml (1 T) cornflour

RUB
Mix together all the ingredients and rub the mixture into the meat. Cover and marinate in the fridge for 1–2 days. Preheat the oven to 160 °C. Remove the meat from the fridge, wrap it in the piece of caul and secure with cocktail sticks. Put the meat on the rack of a roasting tin and roast for about 50 minutes, allowing 15–20 minutes per 500 g meat plus 15 minutes extra. Do not overcook the meat.

MARULA SAUCE
Measure the pan juices and add enough stock to make up 500 ml (2 c). Add the currants, liqueur and brandy and rapidly boil the mixture for 1 minute. Season to taste. Thicken the sauce with the cornflour and serve with the chine.

Serves 10–12.

Potjies

Martin Moore, the cellar master at Durbanville Hills wine estate near Cape Town not only makes fine wines, he's also a dab hand in the kitchen, especially when it comes to making potjiekos.

Venison potjie

If you don't have venison in the freezer use a leg of lamb instead. This potjie is delicious with shiraz, Martin says.

1 leg of venison such as springbok, deboned and cubed
500 ml (2 c) buttermilk or Bulgarian yoghurt
30 ml (2 T) toasted coriander seeds
10 ml (2 t) black peppercorns
6 whole cloves
7 ml (1½ t) nutmeg
about 6 juniper berries, cracked
10 ml (2 t) salt
30 ml (2 T) brown sugar
375 ml (1½ c) white wine vinegar
60 ml (¼ c) olive oil
1 fairly large onion, finely chopped
150 g bacon
2 bay leaves
500 ml (2 c) white wine
350 ml muscadel
250 ml (1 c) cream

Put the meat cubes in a nonmetallic dish and pour over the buttermilk. Cover and leave to marinate overnight. Using a mortar and pestle, crush the coriander seeds and peppercorns. Add the spices, salt, sugar and vinegar. Remove the meat from the buttermilk and pat dry with paper towels. Cover the meat with the spice mixture, put the meat in a clean nonmetallic bowl and marinate for another 6 hours. Using paper towels pat dry the meat cubes and remove the whole spices. Heat a heavy-bottomed saucepan or black cast-iron pot and brush with oil. Brown the meat cubes and remove them from the saucepan. Stir-fry the onion, bacon and bay leaves until the onion and bacon are golden. Return the meat to the saucepan and add just enough wine to cover the meat. Simmer slowly for about 1½ hours, ensuring the meat remains covered with liquid by adding boiling water when necessary. Add the muscadel and cream and simmer for another 1½ hours or until the meat is tender. Martin likes to cook the meat until it nearly falls apart.

Serves 8.

Tips
Put leftover meat in a pie dish, cover with puff pastry and bake until the pastry is done.
The potjie can also be made with red wine.

HOW TO MARINATE VENISON
Always leave meat to marinate in the fridge in either a glass, earthenware, plastic or enamel dish that will not react with the acid in the marinade. Alternatively put the marinade and meat in a strong plastic bag and fasten it tightly. This also makes it easier to turn the meat. Do not marinate the meat for longer than 3 days or the meat will become 'floury'.

WHAT GOES WITH VENISON?
Side dishes should accentuate the taste of venison by providing contrasting colour, taste and texture. Potatoes in various guises are traditionally served with venison. Samp, crumbly maize meal porridge or fresh bread is also delicious with stews and outdoor meals. Sweet side dishes such as pumpkin, sweet potatoes or a dried-fruit dish go well with venison roasts.

Moroccan lamb neck potjie

Lamb neck is ideal for making potjiekos. Martin seasons this potjie with a Moroccan spice mix, ras el hanout, which literally means 'head of the shop' (see recipe). It can be made from 20 or more spices. Moroccan traders are famous for their spice mixes. Serve this potjie with merlot.

few strands saffron
5 ml (1 t) freshly ground black pepper
5 ml (1 t) salt
5 ml (1 t) ground cinnamon
ras el hanout (see recipe)
2 kg lamb neck, cut into pieces
250 ml (1 c) blanched almonds
60 ml (¼ c) honey
60 g butter
3 onions, finely chopped
80 ml (⅓ c) hot water
250 ml (1 c) raisins
juice and rind of 1 lemon

Mix the saffron, pepper, salt and cinnamon with 10 ml (2 t) ras el hanout and rub the meat with the mixture. Mix the remaining ras el hanout with the almonds and honey. Heat the butter in a large pan or cast-iron pot and brown the meat in batches. Remove from the pan and fry the onions in more butter until soft. Return the meat to the pan, add the water and simmer until the meat is tender. Add the raisins, almond mixture, lemon rind and juice and cook for another 30 minutes or until fragrant and heated through. Serve with rice.

Serves 6–8.

> **RAS EL HANOUT**
> Using a mortar and pestle, pound together the following: 6 allspice berries, 4 whole cloves, 7 ml (1½ t) black peppercorns, 6 ml (1 large t) toasted coriander seeds, 5 ml (1 t) cumin seeds. Add 1 ml (pinch) cayenne pepper, 7 ml (1½ t) ground cinnamon and 5 ml (1 t) ground ginger and mix.

Curried flat rib and dried fruit potjie

This is a different version of foodies Peter Veldsman and the late Sannie Smit's original recipe, Martin says. It goes down well with a bottle of chardonnay or merlot.

30 ml (2 T) grape seed or sunflower oil
1,5 kg beef flat rib, cut into individual ribs
15 ml (1 T) salt
2 large onions, coarsely chopped
4 cloves garlic, crushed
30 ml (2 T) grated fresh ginger
20 ml (4 t) mild curry powder
10 ml (2 t) turmeric
7 ml (1½ t) paprika
1 piece stick cinnamon
60 ml (¼ c) wine vinegar
125 ml (½ c) desiccated coconut
125 ml (½ c) sultanas
125 ml (½ c) pitted prunes
125 ml (½ c) halved Turkish apricots
750 ml (3 c) hot meat stock
750 ml (3 c) dry white wine
    (sauvignon blanc)
30 ml (2 T) chutney

Heat the oil in a flat-bottomed saucepan and brown the meat in batches. Season with salt and remove from the saucepan. Heat a little more oil in the same saucepan and fry the onions and garlic. Stir in the ginger, curry powder, turmeric and paprika and mix well with the onions and garlic. Return the meat to the saucepan and add the cinnamon. Pour the vinegar over the meat and add the coconut and dried fruit. Cover with the hot stock and wine and simmer for about 2 hours or until the meat is tender. Stir in the chutney and serve with pearl wheat or pot bread.

Serves 6–8.

Moroccan lamb neck potjie

Waterblommetjie potjie

Martin adds a generous dash of wine to this traditional potjie.

60 g butter
1 kg whole mutton shanks or 500 g
    breast of lamb and 500 g lamb shanks
3 medium-sized onions,
    roughly chopped
3 cloves garlic, crushed
5 ml (1 t) freshly ground black pepper
5 ml (1 t) salt
5 ml (1 t) ground ginger
5 ml (1 t) ground cloves
5 allspice berries
5 ml (1 t) grated whole nutmeg
4 bay leaves
125 ml (½ c) wine vinegar
250 ml (1 c) dry white wine
3 large potatoes, peeled and diced
1 kg fresh waterblommetjies,
    cleaned and well rinsed
1 large cooking apple (such as Granny
    Smith), peeled and cut into strips
juice and rind of 2 lemons

Heat a flat-bottomed saucepan and melt the butter. Brown the meat in batches. Remove the meat from the saucepan and heat more butter. Stir-fry the onions and garlic until soft and fragrant. Return the shanks to the saucepan and season with the spices. Add the vinegar and wine and simmer the meat for 1 hour. Layer the potatoes, half the waterblommetjies and apple on top of the meat. Cover and simmer for about 30 minutes. Add the remaining waterblommetjies and simmer until they are tender but still slightly crisp. Season with lemon juice and grated rind and mix. Serve with rice.

Serves 8–10.

> **Tip**
> Break off the hard outer leaves of the waterblommetjies and remove the stems. You can also remove the backs of the flowers which will reduce the cooking time but then they will disintegrate.

Stews
Mutton and butter bean stew

André Brink, assistant editor at *YOU*'s sister magazine, *Huisgenoot*, found this recipe on an American website and simplified it. It's the perfect dish for cold winter evenings.

cake flour to coat meat
salt and freshly ground black pepper
1 kg mutton shanks or other stewing
    lamb or mutton
olive oil for shallow-frying
a little butter for shallow-frying
1 large onion, grated
1 large carrot, grated
1 leek, finely sliced (optional)
2–3 cloves garlic, crushed
1 large glass red wine
2 tomatoes, peeled and chopped
40 ml finely chopped fresh parsley
5 sprigs fresh mint, finely chopped or
    15 ml (1 T) dried mint
3 pieces lemon rind, finely chopped
1 can (420 g) butter beans

Season the flour with salt and pepper. Roll the shanks in the seasoned flour and brown in olive oil and butter over high heat. Remove from the saucepan and set aside. Reduce the heat and sauté the onion, carrot and leek in the same pan for about 5–10 minutes or until the vegetables are soft. Scrape loose the bits of meat stuck to the bottom of the saucepan and add more oil if necessary. Add the garlic and heat for another 5 minutes. Add the red wine, tomatoes, parsley, mint and lemon rind. Return the meat to the saucepan and add the butter bean liquid (reserve the butter beans for later use). There must be enough liquid in the saucepan to cover the contents (add water if necessary). Cover and simmer over low heat for about 30 minutes. Add the butter beans and simmer until the meat is tender and nearly falls off the bone. Serve with fresh bread or rice.

Serves 6.

Greek stifado

André is a past master of simple cooking. 'We spent a family holiday on the small Greek island of Paxos and the first night there I had stifado. Afterwards I searched long and hard to find a recipe that produced the same result as that of the Greek taverna. This one comes closest.'

30–45 ml (2–3 T) olive oil
15–20 pickling onions, halved
1,5 kg lean stewing steak, cubed
15 ml (1 T) vinegar (use balsamic vinegar
  if desired)
2 cans (420 g each) chopped tomatoes
3–4 cloves garlic, crushed
5 ml (1 t) ground cinnamon
1–2 sprigs fresh rosemary, leaves
  stripped off and finely chopped
10 ml (2 t) dried oregano
  (or fresh if available)
250–300 ml chicken stock or dry red wine

Preheat the oven to 180 °C. Heat the oil in a large ovenproof casserole. Add the onions and sauté over medium heat for about 5 minutes. Add the meat and brown. Add the remaining ingredients and simmer for about 10 minutes. Cover the casserole and bake the dish for about 1 hour.
Check if there is enough liquid in the casserole after 30 minutes. Add stock or red wine (or a mixture of the two) if the casserole becomes too dry but take care that you don't end up with soup instead of a stew.
  The stifado is done when the meat is tender. Serve with bread or garlicky mashed potatoes (see recipe).

Serves 4.

Variations
Add a few rashers of bacon and mushrooms if desired.

Sprinkle over gremolata just before serving if desired: Mix the finely grated rind of 1 lemon with 125 ml (½ c) chopped fresh parsley and 2 crushed cloves garlic.

To make a Portuguese trinchado add 2–3 chillies and 100 g black olives. Stir in a few spoonfuls plain yoghurt for an extra-creamy texture.

Garlicky mashed potatoes

60 ml (¼ c) unpeeled cloves garlic
1,2 kg potatoes, peeled
60 g butter
180 ml (¾ c) hot milk
60 ml (¼ c) grated Parmesan cheese

Wrap the garlic cloves in aluminium foil and bake at 180 °C for 40 minutes or until very soft. Open the parcel and leave to cool. Meanwhile cook the potatoes until soft and drain.
  Put the potatoes in a mixing bowl, add the butter, milk and Parmesan cheese and mash. Snip off the tips of the garlic cloves and squeeze out the purée. Mix well and season to taste.

Serves 4.

Tip for mutton and butter bean stew
Save time and effort by putting the flour, salt and pepper in a sturdy plastic bag.
Add the shanks a few at a time and shake until well coated with the seasoned flour.
Ensure you use a strong plastic bag and don't overload it or it will tear.

Hearty beef stew with beans

André discovered this recipe in British supermarket Sainsbury's magazine while working in London. It's easy, colourful and packed with flavour. If you prefer your food less hot, adjust the quantity of chilli powder. André suggests you add it a little at a time, tasting as you go along. Remember, the longer the stew cooks the less hot it becomes.

olive oil for shallow-frying
1,5 kg stewing steak, cubed
salt and freshly ground black pepper
2 large onions, chopped
2–3 cloves garlic, crushed
1 red pepper, seeded and diced
1 yellow pepper, seeded and diced
10 ml (2 t) ground cumin
5 ml (1 t) dried marjoram
2 bay leaves
60 ml (¼ c) tomato purée
500 ml (2 c) beef stock
5 ml (1 t) chilli powder (peri peri)
1 can (420 g) red kidney beans (use
    other beans if desired but the red
    kidney beans add colour to the dish)
180 ml (¾ c) plain yoghurt

Heat a little olive oil in a heavy-bottomed saucepan. Season the meat cubes with salt and pepper and brown. Remove from the saucepan and set aside. Sauté the onions and garlic in the same saucepan until soft and add the peppers. Stir-fry for 1–2 minutes, then add the cumin, marjoram and bay leaves. Stir-fry for 1 minute more. Return the meat to the saucepan and add the tomato purée and stock. Add the chilli powder a little at a time, tasting as you go along. Reduce the heat and simmer until the meat is tender. Stir occasionally. Add the beans and simmer until heated through. Gradually stir in the yoghurt and simmer for another 5 minutes. Serve with rice.

Serves 6.

Delicious lamb tagine

This traditional Moroccan dish is usually served on couscous but is also delicious with coconut rice.

30 ml (2 T) oil
1 kg lamb cubes
salt and freshly ground black pepper
1 large onion, chopped
4 cloves garlic, finely chopped
15 ml (1 T) ground cumin
15 ml (1 T) ground coriander
15 ml (1 T) paprika
1 large piece cassia, broken into pieces
1 piece stick cinnamon
1 can (420 g) chopped tomatoes
600 ml vegetable stock
175 g dried apricots or pears
15 ml (1 T) brown sugar
3 thick strips fresh orange rind
50 g toasted pine nuts

Heat half the oil in a large saucepan and fry the meat in batches until golden. Season with salt and pepper. Remove the meat from the saucepan and set aside.
    Heat the remaining oil and fry the onion and garlic until soft. Add the spices and stir-fry for 1 minute. Add the remaining ingredients, except the pine nuts. Return the meat to the saucepan and bring to the boil. Reduce the heat and simmer uncovered for about 2 hours or until tender and juicy. Scatter over the pine nuts and serve with coconut rice (see recipe p. 176).

Serves 6.

Variation
Make pumpkin stew by adding 1 kg cubed pumpkin to the meat 1¼ hours into the cooking time.

Oven casserole

Hester Heuer of Durban serves this stew, made with lentils and beer, with herbed dumplings.

STEW
butter, margarine or nonstick food spray
500 g beef, cubed
5 ml (1 t) soy sauce
45 ml (3 T) olive oil
2 large onions, chopped
5 carrots, cut into chunks
5 potatoes, peeled and cut into chunks
2 bay leaves
15 ml (1 T) cake flour
250 ml (1 c) red lentils
1 can (340 ml) beer
375 ml (1½ c) beef stock
30 ml (2 T) chutney and/or tomato paste
salt and freshly ground black pepper

DUMPLINGS
625 ml (2½ c) self-raising flour
1 clove garlic, crushed
3 ml (generous ½ t) prepared mustard
10 ml (2 t) finely chopped fresh parsley
60 ml (¼ c) oil
3 ml (generous ½ t) salt
5 ml (1 t) mixed herbs
150 ml cold water

STEW
Preheat the oven to 160 °C and grease a 30 cm x 20 cm ovenproof dish.
　Sprinkle the beef cubes with the soy sauce, heat 30 ml (2 T) of the oil and fry the beef cubes until done. Spoon into the ovenproof dish. Heat the remaining 15 ml (1 T) oil and stir-fry the onions until done. Add the carrots, potatoes and bay leaves and stir-fry for 2 minutes. Sprinkle over the flour and stir well. Add the lentils, beer, stock and chutney. Season with salt and pepper and bring to the boil. Spoon the mixture into the ovenproof dish, cover and bake for about 1½–2 hours or until the meat is tender.

DUMPLINGS
Increase the oven temperature to 180 °C. Mix all the ingredients to make a soft dough. Shape into 12 balls and arrange them on top of the meat. Bake uncovered for another 20–25 minutes or until the dumplings have risen and are done. Serve with caramelised pickle onions (see recipe) if desired.

Serves 6–8.

Caramelised pickle onions

20 pickling onions
2 bay leaves
2 cloves garlic
200 g seeded raisins
100 g brown sugar
100 g butter
50 ml wine vinegar

Put all the ingredients in a small saucepan and simmer slowly for about 1 hour or until most of the liquid has evaporated and the onions are caramelised.

Enough for 3 people.

SUITABLE CUTS FOR STEW
One of the big attractions of making a stew is that you can use more affordable cuts to make dishes packed with flavour. Mutton, especially mutton rib, cut into cubes makes the best stew but you can also make wonderful stews with stewing beef, pork and chicken.
Beef: thick rib, brisket, neck, bolo, shin, thin flank, flat rib, topside, thick flank and silverside.
Lamb and mutton: neck, thick rib, shank, brisket and flank.
Pork: brisket, shank and trotters, flank and ribs.
Spices for stews: The trinity is allspice berries, peppercorns and whole cloves. Cardamom, ginger and cassia go well with sweetish stews such as pumpkin, quince and tomato stew.

TIPS FOR STEWS

- Fry the meat with the onions and spices before adding the vegetables.
- I prefer using whole spices in stews – fry them with the onions so they can release their flavours.
- Do not add too much water or stock when making a stew or else it becomes more like a soup than a stew. Add the liquid a little at a time. Remember, vegetables also release moisture into the gravy.
- Heat the liquid before adding it to the stew or the meat will be dry.
- Vegetables are mostly added raw except in the case of cabbage stew where the cabbage is first blanched in boiling water.
- Heat the saucepan in which you're making the stew before adding oil; this way you will use considerably less.
- Reduce the heat after frying the meat and onions and cover the saucepan.
- Try to keep the heat constant while cooking the stew. Medium heat allows the stew to simmer slowly for about 1 hour and the flavours to develop and marry.
- Lemon, especially lemon rind, imparts a delicious flavour to any stew. Mix it with chopped parsley to make a gremolata (see p. 75) and sprinkle over the stew just before serving.
- A spoonful of plain yoghurt stirred into the stew just before serving makes the gravy deliciously creamy.

Fragrant lamb shanks

This dish is infused with flavours of the Mediterranean.

4 whole lamb shanks
salt and freshly ground black pepper
5 ml (1 t) fresh coriander
10 ml (2 t) seeded and finely chopped
  fresh red chilli,
5 ml (1 t) finely chopped fresh rosemary
5 ml (1 t) chopped fresh oregano
15 ml (1 T) cake flour
15 ml (1 T) olive oil
1 clove garlic, crushed
1 large carrot, scraped and diced
2 large onions, finely chopped
6 stalks celery, finely chopped
30 ml (2 T) balsamic vinegar
180 ml (¾ c) red wine
6 anchovies, chopped
2 cans (420 g each) whole peeled tomatoes
1 handful fresh basil leaves, torn

Season the lamb shanks with salt and freshly ground black pepper. Mix the coriander, chilli, rosemary and oregano. Roll the lamb shanks in the spice mixture and press it firmly onto the meat. Dust the shanks with flour. Heat the oil in a large saucepan and brown the shanks evenly over medium heat. Remove from the saucepan and set aside. Add the garlic, carrot, onions, celery and a pinch of salt. Cover the saucepan and braise the vegetables until soft. Add the balsamic vinegar and bring to the boil. Add the wine and simmer for about 2 minutes. Add the anchovies and whole tomatoes. Stir and return the shanks to the saucepan. Heat until the sauce starts bubbling, cover and simmer slowly for about 1½ hours. Remove the lid and simmer for another 30 minutes or until the sauce is fragrant. Skim any surface fat and season with salt and freshly ground black pepper if necessary.

Add the basil leaves and serve on couscous.

Serves 4.

Fragrant lamb shanks

Moroccan shanks

These shanks are cooked in an aromatic African spice mix consisting of cumin, coriander and cassia. Add more vegetables if desired.

olive oil
4 whole lamb shanks
2 large onions, chopped
10 ml (2 t) finely chopped fresh ginger
3 cloves garlic, crushed
2 fresh red chillies, seeded and
    finely chopped
10 ml (2 t) ground cumin
10 ml (2 t) ground coriander
5 ml (1 t) freshly ground black pepper
5 ml (1 t) paprika
2 large tomatoes, finely chopped
425 ml hot water
1 large piece cassia
450 g carrots, scraped and cut into
    chunks (optional)
450 g butternut, cut into chunks (optional)
140 g dried peaches or apricots (optional)
5 ml (1 t) honey
1 can (410 g) chickpeas, drained (optional)

Preheat the oven to 160 °C. Heat oil in a large pan and brown the shanks. Put the shanks in a large casserole. Stir-fry the onions in the same pan until just soft. Mix the ginger, garlic, chillies, cumin, coriander, black pepper and paprika and add half the mixture to the onions. Add the tomatoes and stir-fry for 2–3 minutes until fragrant. Add the mixture to the shanks. Add the water, cover and bake for 1 hour or until the shanks are nearly soft. Remove from the oven, add the remaining spice mix, cassia, vegetables, dried fruit and honey. Cover and return the casserole to the oven. Bake for another 45 minutes to 1 hour or until the meat is tender and the vegetables are done. Add the chickpeas if desired and heat through. Serve with couscous mixed with chopped almonds and fresh coriander leaves.

Serves 4.

Variation
Add mashed preserved lemon peel and garnish with chopped coriander leaves.

Cabbage stew

South African stews are based on the Malay culinary tradition. Their ability to combine spices turns an ordinary stew into a heavenly meal. This recipe for cabbage stew comes from Cape Town food writer Cass Abrahams. It's an excellent example of how you can prepare delicious food using basic ingredients.

1 cabbage, shredded
oil
2 large onions, sliced
10 ml (2 t) cumin seeds
4 whole cloves
2 allspice berries
1 kg mutton, cubed
meat stock or water
8 small potatoes, peeled
2 leeks, washed and sliced
1 stalk celery, chopped
1 green chilli, seeded and
    chopped (optional)
salt and freshly ground black pepper
5 ml (1 t) sugar

Blanch the cabbage in boiling water for 5 minutes. Drain, rinse under cold water and set aside.
    Heat oil in a heavy-bottomed saucepan and sauté the onions and cumin seeds until glassy. Add the whole spices and meat and fry until brown. Add a little meat stock or water, cover and reduce the heat. Simmer until the meat is nearly tender. Add the potatoes, cabbage, leeks, celery and chilli and simmer until the potatoes are soft. Add more water or meat stock if necessary. Season to taste with salt and pepper and sprinkle over the sugar. Serve with rice and chutney.

Serves 6.

Oxtail stew

1,8 kg oxtail, cut into pieces at the joints
125 ml (½ c) cake flour
5 ml (1 t) salt
freshly ground black pepper
25 ml (5 t) oil
50 g butter
250 g (1 punnet) mushrooms, quartered
4 large onions, chopped
6 stalks celery, chopped
2 large carrots, scraped and grated
4 large cloves garlic, crushed
250 ml (1 c) dry white wine
6 large tomatoes, peeled and diced
375 ml (1½ c) beef stock
1 bay leaf
coarse salt
45 ml (3 T) cream or plain yoghurt

Preheat the oven to 180 °C. Remove all visible fat from the meat and set aside. Combine the flour, salt and pepper and coat the meat pieces with the flour mixture. Heat the oil and butter in a heavy-bottomed saucepan and brown the meat. Remove from the saucepan and set aside. Sauté the mushrooms in the remaining oil and set aside. Sauté the onions, celery, carrots and garlic in the same saucepan for 3 minutes. Add the wine, bring the mixture to the boil and simmer for 3 minutes. Add the oxtail, mushrooms, tomatoes, stock, bay leaf and salt to taste. Bring to the boil, remove from the heat and stir in the cream or yoghurt. Spoon everything into an ovenproof dish, cover and bake for 4–5 hours or until tender. Serve with rice or samp.

Serves 6.

Spicy oxtail stew

It couldn't be easier – the oxtail and spices are cooked in water on top of the stove until fragrant and tender.

2 kg oxtail, cut into 3 cm pieces
2 whole star anise
1 piece stick cinnamon
salt and freshly ground black pepper
1–2 ml (¼–½ t) dried chilli flakes
   or chilli powder
50 ml brown sugar
50 ml soy sauce

Put the oxtail in a deep saucepan and cover with water. Bring the water to the boil and simmer the oxtail for 10 minutes, skimming the foam continually. Drain the oxtail and rinse. Return the oxtail to the saucepan and add 1,5 litres (4–6 c) hot water. Add the star anise and cinnamon. Season with salt and black pepper. Cover, bring the water to the boil, reduce the heat and simmer for 1 hour over low heat. Add the chillies, brown sugar and soy sauce and simmer for another 2 hours.
If the liquid evaporates add a little more water until the meat is tender and falls off the bone. Serve with mashed potatoes.

Serves 6.

Mince
Cape moussaka

Elna de Klerk of Kuruman adds herbs and spices to impart a delicious Cape flavour to this traditional Greek dish.

VEGETABLES
2 large potatoes, peeled
1 large brinjal, thinly sliced and
    sprinkled with salt
olive oil

MINCE MIXTURE
1 large onion, finely chopped
5 cloves garlic, crushed
1 kg mince
1 can (420 g) chopped tomatoes
1 can (65 g) tomato paste
30 ml (2 T) finely chopped fresh parsley
15 ml (1 T) finely chopped fresh thyme
15 ml (1 T) finely chopped fresh
    coriander leaves
5 ml (1 t) ground coriander
1 ml (pinch) nutmeg
1 ml (pinch) ground cumin
3 ml (generous ½ t) cayenne pepper
60 ml (¼ c) dry red wine

WHITE SAUCE
1 litre (4 c) milk
1 bay leaf
4 cardamom pods
1 ml (pinch) nutmeg
125 g butter
125 ml (½ c) cake flour
salt and freshly ground black pepper
1 extra-large egg, whisked
150 ml grated Cheddar cheese
100 ml grated Parmesan cheese

Preheat the oven to 180 °C and grease a large ovenproof dish with butter, margarine or nonstick food spray.

VEGETABLES
Cook the potatoes until just done and set aside. Meanwhile rinse the brinjal slices under cold water and pat dry. Fry in the olive oil until done. Slice the potatoes and arrange in the bottom of the dish.

MINCE MIXTURE
Sauté the onion and garlic in the same pan until done. Add the mince and fry until done. Add the rest of the ingredients and simmer for at least 15 minutes or until done and fragrant. Spoon the mince mixture on top of the potato slices and arrange the brinjal slices on top.

WHITE SAUCE
Bring the milk, bay leaf, cardamom pods and nutmeg to the boil while the mince mixture is cooking. Remove from the heat and leave to stand for 10 minutes. Remove the bay leaf and cardamom pods. In a separate saucepan, melt the butter and stir in the cake flour. Heat until the mixture begins to bubble. Stirring continuously, add the hot milk a little at a time. Bring to the boil and, stirring continuously, simmer until the sauce thickens and is done. Remove from the heat, season with salt and pepper and stir in the whisked egg. Spoon the sauce over the brinjal layer and sprinkle over the cheeses. Bake for 30 minutes or until the topping is golden. Serve with a tomato and onion salad.

Serves 8–10.

Cape moussaka

Carrot bobotie

Mandy Brown of Brentwoodpark adds carrots and apple to this spicy bobotie which give it a loose texture and also make the dish go further.

1 slice white bread
375 ml (1½ c) milk
30 ml (2 T) butter, melted
25 ml (5 t) curry powder
10 ml (2 t) garam masala
5 ml (1 t) ground cumin
5 ml (1 t) ground coriander
5 ml (1 t) turmeric
30 ml (2 T) lemon juice
5 ml (1 t) sugar
7 ml (1½ t) salt
1 can (410 g) tomato and onion mix
1 kg lean mince
3 carrots, finely grated
1 Granny Smith apple, grated
4 eggs
5 bay leaves

Preheat the oven 180 °C. Grease a 2,5 litre ovenproof dish.
Soak the bread in the milk. Mix the butter, spices, lemon juice, sugar and salt. Add the tomato and onion mix, mince, carrots, apple and 1 of the eggs. Squeeze the bread to extract the milk. Reserve the milk. Crumble the bread and add it to the mixture. Mix well and spoon into the prepared dish. Whisk the remaining 3 eggs and reserved milk and pour over the meat mixture. Insert the bay leaves into the meat mixture and bake the bobotie for 90 minutes or until golden brown on top. Serve hot with fragrant yellow rice (see p. 176) and tomato sambal (see recipe).

Serves 6–8.

> **Variation**
> Add 125 ml (½ c) sultanas and/or 50 ml almond flakes.

Tomato sambal

3 ripe tomatoes
1 onion, finely chopped
30 ml (2 T) chopped fresh
   coriander leaves
15 ml (1 T) caster sugar
10 ml (2 t) white wine vinegar
5 ml (1 t) lemon juice
1 ml (pinch) salt
2 ml (½ t) white pepper

Halve the tomatoes horizontally and scoop out the seeds. Dice the tomatoes with a sharp knife and mix with the remaining ingredients.

Tomato and meatball bake

Meatballs seasoned with cumin, oregano and rosemary and baked in a tomato sauce with a cheese topping. Delicious!

BASIC TOMATO SAUCE
1 large clove garlic, finely chopped
30 ml (2 T) olive oil
1 small dried red chilli, crushed
10 ml (2 t) dried oregano
3 cans (420 g each) whole tomatoes
15 ml (1 T) red wine vinegar
1 handful fresh basil leaves, chopped
1 handful fresh marjoram, roughly chopped
salt and freshly ground black pepper

MEATBALLS
1 kg lean mince
2 slices white bread, crumbled
30 ml (2 T) dried oregano
3 ml (generous ½ t) cumin seeds, crushed
1 fresh red chilli, finely chopped
15 ml (1 T) finely chopped fresh rosemary
2 egg yolks
salt and freshly ground black pepper
1 onion, finely chopped
1 clove garlic, crushed
75 ml (5 T) olive oil
15 ml (1 T) Dijon mustard
375 ml (1½ c) torn fresh basil leaves
60 g mozzarella cheese, grated
60 g Parmesan cheese, grated

BASIC TOMATO SAUCE
Stir-fry the garlic in the olive oil until fragrant. Add the chilli, oregano and tomatoes. Bring to the boil and simmer for about 40 minutes or until fragrant. Add the vinegar and season with the fresh basil, marjoram, salt and pepper. Set aside.
    Preheat the oven to 200 °C. Grease an ovenproof dish.

MEATBALLS
Put the meat in a large mixing bowl and add the breadcrumbs, oregano, cumin, chilli, rosemary, egg yolks, salt and pepper. Sauté the onion and garlic in 15 ml (1 T) olive oil until soft and add the mustard. Cool slightly and add to the mince mixture. Wet your hands and shape the mince mixture into balls. Heat the remaining olive oil in a large pan and fry the meatballs until brown, taking care not to break them. Transfer the meatballs to the ovenproof dish and pour over the tomato sauce. Add the basil and sprinkle over the mozzarella and Parmesan cheese. Bake for 20–25 minutes or until the cheese is golden. Serve with rice.

Serves 6.

> **Budget-beating tip**
> Fry the meatballs in a large pan until done, pour over the tomato sauce and heat through. Serve with rice.

Asian meatballs in a curry and coconut sauce

Thai curry with a twist: meatballs cooked in a coconut milk sauce.

MEATBALLS
500 g pork and beef mince
3 cloves garlic, finely chopped
2 stems lemon grass,
    finely chopped (optional)
3 cm piece fresh ginger, grated
salt

CURRY SAUCE
20 ml (4 t) oil
20–40 ml (4–8 t) green curry paste
375 ml (1½ c) coconut milk
250 ml (1 c) water
35 ml fish sauce
10 ml (2 t) soft brown sugar
fresh coriander leaves

MEATBALLS
Mix together the ingredients for the meatballs and shape into small balls.

CURRY SAUCE
Heat the oil in a wok or deep pan and stir-fry the curry paste over low heat for 1 minute. Add the coconut milk and water. Stir until the mixture comes to the boil, reduce the heat and simmer uncovered for 5 minutes. Add the meatballs and simmer for another 5 minutes or until the meat is done. Add the fish sauce and sugar. Scatter over coriander leaves and serve with Asian egg noodles.

Serves 6.

VERSATILE CHICKEN

Pot-roasted, oven-roasted, whole or in pieces, flavoured with Mediterranean herbs or fiery Asian spices, chicken is always a winner. It's versatile, nourishing and, best of all, affordable.

Whole chicken with feta and olive stuffing

The feta cheese, olive and caper stuffing is inserted between the skin and flesh of the bird, which is then roasted on a bed of potatoes.

1 whole chicken, cleaned and patted dry

STUFFING
3 rounds feta cheese, roughly crumbled
15 ml (1 T) capers, rinsed
60 ml (¼ c) calamata olives, pitted
    and quartered
15 ml (1 T) chopped fresh rosemary
salt and freshly ground black pepper
olive oil

POTATOES
1 kg baby potatoes, washed and halved
coarse salt
1 handful rosemary sprigs

Preheat the oven to 220 °C and brush a deep roasting tin with olive oil.
   Lightly mix the stuffing ingredients. Season the chicken generously with salt and pepper. Loosen the skin over the breast from the neck to the wings and bottom of the breastbone, taking care not to tear the skin. Spoon the stuffing under the skin, spreading it over the breast. Pull the skin back in place and secure with cocktail sticks. Stuff the cavity with any remaining stuffing and secure with cocktail sticks. Brush the bird with olive oil and season with salt and ground black pepper.
   Arrange the baby potatoes in the roasting tin and season with coarse salt and rosemary. Sprinkle over 30 ml (2 T) boiling water. Put the chicken breast down on the potatoes and roast for 30 minutes. Reduce the temperature to 200 °C. Turn the chicken breast up and roast for another 45–60 minutes or until tender and done.
   Transfer the chicken and potatoes to a large platter and garnish with a scattering of fresh rosemary sprigs.

Serves 4.

The secret to roasting a whole chicken is to initially put it in the oven at a very high temperature to crisp the skin. Roast it at 220 °C until golden all over. Reduce the temperature to 200 °C to prevent the oven being spattered with fat.

Variations
Vary the stuffing as desired by adding for instance bacon, onion and parsley mixed with breadcrumbs.
OR
Mix 500 ml (2 c) cooked rice with 1 chopped onion and 2 crushed and sautéed cloves garlic, 1 small chopped apple, 60 ml (¼ c) dried apricots, 60 ml (¼ c) sultanas, 60 ml (¼ c) chopped nuts, 2 ml (½ t) ground cumin, 5 ml (1 t) turmeric and 5 ml (1 t) paprika.

Whole chicken with feta and olive stuffing

Milky chicken

The lemon makes the sauce slightly thick and sticky. Delicious!

1 whole chicken
salt and freshly ground black pepper
1 medium-sized onion, peeled
1 generous handful fresh thyme sprigs
10 ml (2 t) cumin seeds
15 ml (1 T) mustard seeds
rind and juice of 2 lemons
10 whole cloves garlic, peeled
500 ml (2 c) milk
8 small carrots, scraped
4 small cabbages, halved (optional)

Preheat the oven to 220 °C. Grease an ovenproof dish with butter, margarine or nonstick food spray.

Clean the chicken, remove any excess fat, rinse and pat dry. Season the chicken inside and out with salt and freshly ground black pepper. Put the whole onion and a few sprigs of thyme in the cavity. Put the chicken in the ovenproof dish. Scatter over the cumin and mustard seeds, remaining thyme, lemon rind and garlic. Mix the milk and lemon juice and pour the mixture over the chicken. Bake for 30 minutes. Lower the temperature to 200 °C and bake for another 45 minutes till done.

Meanwhile steam the carrots and cabbages until just tender. Transfer the vegetables to the ovenproof dish and mix them with the pan juices. Roast with the chicken until the vegetables are lightly browned and the chicken is golden brown and succulent. Serve with mashed potatoes.

Serves 4.

> **Tip**
> I sometimes use whole breyani spices instead of cumin and mustard seeds to sprinkle over the chicken, and use maas (sour milk) instead of fresh milk.

Pot-roasted chicken

An old-fashioned method of cooking chicken until it's golden brown and succulent.

1 whole chicken
cake flour
butter and oil
salt and white pepper
250 ml (1 c) white wine or water

Rub the chicken with flour. Heat a little butter and oil in a large pot and brown the chicken all over, turning it frequently. Season with salt and white pepper and add the white wine or water. Cover with a lid, lower the heat and pot-roast until done. Add more wine or water if necessary.

Serves 4.

How to flatten a chicken

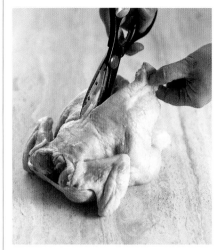

Using kitchen scissors, cut open the chicken on both sides of the backbone and remove the bone

Put the chicken on an even surface, skin side facing up, and flatten it by pressing down on the breast with the palm of your hand. Insert two skewers crossways into the chicken to ensure it retains its shape while cooking.

Stuffing and trussing a chicken

Fold the neck skin over and secure with a meat skewer. Spoon the stuffing into the cavity, taking care not to overstuff it as the stuffing expands during the cooking process.Secure the drumsticks to the tail: Tie a piece of string around the ends of the drumsticks so they lie against each other. Tie the piece of string around the tail, pulling the string tight so the tail lifts and covers the cavity. Tie the string around the drumsticks.
Lift the wings and twist them at the joints so they lie flat across the back of the chicken. Tie a piece of string around the carcass and wings to hold them in place.

Fragrant braised chicken

Full of flavour and with a crisp skin.

250 ml (1 c) buttermilk
4 cloves garlic, crushed
1 onion, finely chopped
1 ml (pinch) chilli flakes (optional)
4–6 large chicken pieces
90 ml (6 T) cake flour
2 ml (½ t) salt
2 ml (½ t) cayenne pepper
2 ml (½ t) paprika
oil for roasting

Mix the buttermilk, garlic, onion and chilli flakes. Put the chicken pieces in a nonmetallic dish and pour over the buttermilk marinade. Cover and marinate for at least 1 hour but preferably overnight. Combine the cake flour and spices. Remove the chicken pieces from the marinade and drain well. Roll them in the flour mixture until well coated.

Heat the oil in a pan and brown the chicken pieces all over. Cover the pan and braise the chicken pieces until done.

Serve with a salad.

Serves 4–6.

Tip
Make incisions all over the meaty parts of the chicken pieces to allow the flavours of the marinade to infuse the meat.

Chicken in blue cheese sauce

Chicken pieces cooked in a heavenly blue cheese sauce. The dish is not too rich as the sauce is made with yoghurt instead of cream.

4 chicken breast fillets
30 ml (2 T) olive oil
salt and freshly ground black pepper
1 clove garlic, crushed
150 ml white wine
150 ml chicken stock
2 sprigs fresh rosemary
180 ml (¾ c) full-cream Greek yoghurt
15 ml (1 T) cornflour
80 g blue cheese, crumbled

Cut the chicken breasts into pieces. Heat the oil in a pan and lightly brown the chicken pieces. Season with salt and pepper and remove from the pan. Stir-fry the garlic clove and add the wine and stock to the pan. Add the rosemary and bring the mixture to the boil. Reduce the sauce by two-thirds. Remove the rosemary sprigs. Blend about 30 ml (2 T) yoghurt with the cornflour to make a paste and mix with the remaining yoghurt. Set aside.

Return the chicken pieces to the pan and add the yoghurt mixture and blue cheese. Season to taste with salt and pepper. Heat slowly until the sauce just comes to the boil, the chicken is done and the cheese has melted. Serve with boiled baby potatoes and a salad.

Serves 3–4.

Tip
Never overcook chicken breasts. Cook them until the meat just turns white and is no longer pink. The fillets must still be succulent – if overcooked they will be dry and tasteless.

Chicken in blue cheese sauce

Chicken stroganoff

Mrs E Mundell of Bellville says she used chicken to make stroganoff and it was delicious.
Serve it with pasta and vegetables or a green salad.

50 g butter
1 onion, sliced
1 clove garlic, crushed
500 g chicken breasts
½ green pepper, finely chopped
250 g (1 punnet) button mushrooms,
    sliced
100 ml white wine
80 ml (⅓ c) chicken stock
150 ml sour cream or plain yoghurt
30 ml (2 T) tomato purée
5 ml (1 t) Worcestershire sauce
10 ml (2 t) prepared mustard
10 ml (2 t) lemon juice
30 ml (2 T) chopped fresh parsley
15 ml (1 T) cornflour (maizena)
salt and freshly ground black pepper

Heat the butter and sauté the onion and garlic until soft.
Debone the chicken breasts if desired and cut them into
strips. Stir-fry until lightly browned. Add the green pepper
and mushrooms and stir-fry until just done. Add the wine
and stock, reduce the heat and simmer until the meat is
tender and done. Stir in the sour cream, tomato purée,
Worcestershire sauce, mustard, lemon juice and parsley and
mix. Blend the cornflour with a little water to form a paste
and stir into the mixture.
  Bring the stroganoff to the boil, season with salt and
pepper and serve with pasta such as tagliatelle, or with rice.

Serves 4–6.

Coronation chicken

This old favourite, specially created for the crowning of Queen Elizabeth II in 1953,
is given a healthy twist by using less mayonnaise. Celery is substituted for the grapes
and instead of frying the chicken it is poached in stock.

CHICKEN
4 chicken breast fillets, skin removed
250 ml (1 c) water
5 ml (1 t) chicken stock powder
1 clove garlic, crushed
50 ml white wine vinegar
1 bay leaf

SAUCE
10 ml (2 t) olive oil
1 medium-sized onion, chopped
10 ml (2 t) curry powder
60 ml (¼ c) dry white wine
150 ml stock used to cook the chicken
10 ml (2 t) grape vinegar
10 ml (2 t) smooth apricot jam
    or mango chutney
1 ml (pinch) cayenne pepper
60 ml (¼ c) low-fat mayonnaise
100 ml plain yoghurt

EXTRAS
200 g celery stalks, chopped
60 ml (¼ c) walnuts, halved
fresh watercress to garnish

CHICKEN
Put the chicken breasts in a shallow saucepan. Blend the
water, stock powder, garlic, white wine vinegar and bay leaf
and pour the mixture over the chicken. Bring to the boil and
simmer for 15–20 minutes or until the chicken breasts are just
done. Strain the liquid and set aside for the sauce.

SAUCE
Heat the olive oil in a pan and sauté the onions and curry
powder until the onion is soft. Add the strained liquid and the
remaining ingredients except the mayonnaise and yoghurt and
simmer for 5 minutes. Spoon the mixture into a food processor
and blitz until smooth. Allow the sauce to cool to room
temperature. Add the mayonnaise and yoghurt and mix well.
  Cut the chicken breasts into thin slices and pour over the
sauce. Mix gently, cover and chill until needed. Add the celery
and nuts just before serving and garnish with watercress.
Serve with rye bread.

Serves 4.

Poached chicken parcels

If you're trying to lose weight or simply watching your kilojoule intake chicken breast fillets are always a good option as they contain hardly any fat. For this recipe the chicken is poached in stock and no fat or oil is used. Serve the parcels with an orange sauce. Deliciously light and ideal for hot summer days.

CHICKEN
6 chicken breast fillets
30 ml (2 T) good-quality
   wholegrain mustard
salt and freshly ground black pepper

SAUCE
375 ml (1½ c) orange juice
180 ml (¾ c) hot chicken stock
60 ml (¼ c) white wine
2 oranges, cut into segments
20 ml (4 t) chopped fresh thyme
salt and freshly ground black pepper
15 ml (1 T) cornflour

CHICKEN
Put a chicken breast fillet between 2 sheets of clingfilm and pound gently with a meat mallet to an even thickness. Turn over the fillet and remove one sheet of clingflim. Spread 5 ml (1 t) mustard over the fillet and season it with salt and pepper. Fold the fillet in half by lifting the ends of the clingfilm and holding them together. Secure with a piece of string so the fillet forms a neat parcel. Repeat with the remaining fillets.

Fill a saucepan three-quarters of the way with water and bring to just below boiling point. Carefully put the chicken parcels in the water, cover and poach in barely simmering water for 10–12 minutes or until just done. (Do not let the water boil too rapidly or the chicken will be tough.) Remove the parcels to a plate and remove the clingfilm. Cover the parcels and keep warm.

SAUCE
Prepare the sauce while the chicken is poaching. Bring the juice, stock and wine to the boil in a saucepan and simmer for 10–15 minutes. Add the orange segments to the sauce and season with thyme, salt and pepper. Blend the cornflour with a little water to make a paste and stir into the sauce. Simmer until the sauce thickens. Thinly slice each chicken parcel and serve with the orange sauce, rice and vegetables.

Serves 6.

Delicious chicken rolls

Gently flatten 5 chicken breast fillets with a meat mallet. Put a large steamed spinach leaf on each fillet. Mix together 1 round crumbled feta cheese, 2 finely chopped garlic cloves, 6 chopped piquanté peppers, a few chopped pine nuts, chopped fresh herbs such as thyme or parsley and freshly ground black pepper to taste. Divide the mixture among the chicken breast fillets, roll them up and secure with cocktail sticks. Dip the chicken breasts in whisked egg and then in fine dry breadcrumbs. Chill for 20 minutes or until firm. Steam fry in heated oil until golden brown and just done. Leave to cool slightly, remove the cocktail sticks and cut each roll into 5 thin slices. Serve lukewarm or cold.

Serves 4–6.

HOW TO STEAM FRY MEAT
Rapidly brown the meat in hot oil. Cover and cook until the meat is just done. Do not add any water.

Chicken breyani

Breyani is one of the best-known Cape Malay dishes. The dish, made with layers of chicken, rice and lentils, is a perfect one-dish meal.

oil
5 medium-sized onions, finely chopped
1 green pepper, seeded and chopped
3 ripe tomatoes, peeled and chopped
15 ml (1 T) ginger paste
10 ml (2 t) garlic paste
30 ml (2 T) breyani masala
5 ml (1 t) ground cinnamon
5 ml (1 t) ground coriander
2 ml (½ t) ground cumin
150 ml chopped fresh coriander leaves
250 ml (1 c) water
5 potatoes, peeled and cut into chunks
1,5 kg chicken pieces
salt and freshly ground balck pepper
500 ml (2 c) raw rice
3 ml (generous ½ t) turmeric
1 piece stick cinnamon
3 cardamom pods, crushed
250 ml (1 c) cooked lentils
butter

Preheat the oven to 120 °C.

Heat a little oil in a saucepan and stir-fry the onions and green pepper until soft. Add the tomatoes and ginger and garlic pastes and stir-fry until well blended. Add the spices, coriander leaves and water and simmer for 10 minutes. Add the potatoes and chicken pieces, cover and simmer until the chicken and potatoes are done. Season with salt and pepper.

Cook the rice with the turmeric, spices and a pinch of salt in enough water until done. Mix the lentils with the rice.

Arrange layers of chicken and rice in an oven dish, dotting each layer with butter. Cover and put in the oven for 15–20 minutes or until heated through. Serve with cucumber raita and a tomato and onion sambal (see p. 122).

Serves 8.

Chicken peri peri

Froza Chenia of Qualbert in KwaZulu-Natal makes chicken peri peri with fresh, ripe tomatoes. The chicken is not browned beforehand.

1 whole chicken, cut into pieces
salt
30 ml (2 T) oil
1 small onion, finely chopped
2 cloves garlic, finely chopped
7 large ripe tomatoes, grated
4 green chillies, seeded
5–10 ml (1–2 t) peri peri powder
2 ml (½ t) ground saffron
2 ml (½ t) ground cardamom
60 ml (¼ c) sour milk, maas or yoghurt
25 ml (5 t) chutney

Season the chicken pieces with salt. Heat the oil in a pan large enough to hold all the chicken pieces and stir-fry the onion and garlic until fragrant. Remove from the heat, add the tomatoes, chillies, spices, sour milk and chutney and mix well. Add the chicken to the pan and mix well to coat with the sauce. Cover the pan and simmer slowly over low heat for 30–45 minutes or until the chicken is done. Serve with potato chips and a salad.

Serves 4.

Chicken breyani

Cinnamon chicken

Chicken flavoured with orange and cinnamon. The yoghurt gives the sauce a creamy consistency.

45 ml (3 T) oil
1 large onion, cut into thin wedges
2 cloves garlic, crushed
7 ml (1½ t) ground cinnamon
1 ml (pinch) cayenne pepper (optional)
500 g chicken breast fillets,
    cut into strips
10 ml (2 t) finely grated orange rind
60 ml (¼ c) orange juice
30 ml (2 T) sultanas
30 ml (2 T) brown sugar
60 ml (¼ c) plain yoghurt
80 ml (⅓ c) almond splinters, toasted

Heat a large pan and add 30 ml (2 T) of the oil, the onion, garlic and spices. Stir-fry for 3 minutes or until the onion is soft. Remove the mixture from the pan and set aside.

Heat the pan once more, add the remaining oil and stir-fry the chicken until golden brown and just done. Return the onion mixture to the pan and add the orange rind and juice, sultanas and sugar. Stir-fry until most of the liquid has evaporated. Remove from the heat, stir in the yoghurt and scatter over the almond splinters. Serve with rice.

Serves 3–4.

> **Tip**
> Heat a pan well before adding the oil. This will ensure you use less oil.

Moroccan chicken strips

Elna Mattheus of Faerie Glen in Pretoria has over the years sent us many wonderful recipes. Her handwriting is easy to recognise and I always put her letters aside without reading them first because I know they'll contain yet another of her culinary gems. This is one of her interesting creations. Delicious!

CHICKEN
250 ml (1 c) apricot jam
60 ml (¼ c) smooth peanut butter
90 ml (6 T) orange juice
90 ml (6 T) dry sherry
30 ml (2 T) balsamic vinegar
30 ml (2 T) lemon juice
2 cloves garlic, crushed
5 ml (1 t) salt
10 ml (2 t) curry powder
3 ml (generous ½ t) ground cinnamon
3 ml (generous ½ t) cardamom seeds
3 ml (generous ½ t) ground cumin
500 g chicken breast fillets, cut into strips

COUSCOUS
250 ml (1 c) seedless raisins
boiling water
500 ml (2 c) chicken stock
10 ml (2 t) sugar
1 ml (pinch) ground cinnamon
1 ml (pinch) cardamom seeds
3 ml (generous ½ t) turmeric

30 ml (2 T) finely grated orange rind
500 ml (2 c) couscous
125 ml (½ c) toasted, salted peanuts, finely chopped

Preheat the oven to 180 °C. Grease an ovenproof dish with butter, margarine or nonstick food spray.

CHICKEN
Mix all the ingredients except the chicken. Add the chicken to the sauce and mix to coat well. Cover and chill for at least 1 hour. Spoon the chicken and sauce into the ovenproof dish and bake for 30–40 minutes or until just done.

COUSCOUS
Soak the raisins in just enough boiling water until soft and plump. Heat the stock, sugar, spices and orange rind and bring to the boil. Add the couscous. Remove from the heat, cover the saucepan and leave for 5–10 minutes. Fluff the couscous with a fork. Drain the raisins and add to the couscous along with the peanuts. Serve with the chicken.

Serves 4–6.

Vietnamese stir-fried chicken

This dish is quick and easy to make. The stir-fried chicken is given an interesting twist with a sweet syrup.

15 ml (1 T) sugar
5 ml (1 t) water
30 ml (2 T) sesame or peanut oil
2 cloves garlic, crushed
2 green or red Thai chillies, seeded and
    finely chopped
2 stems lemon grass, finely chopped
1 onion, finely sliced
350 g chicken breast fillets, cut into
    strips
30 ml (2 T) soy sauce
15 ml (1 T) fish sauce
salt and freshly ground black pepper
1 handful chopped fresh coriander leaves

Heat the sugar and water over medium heat until lightly caramelised and golden brown. Immediately remove from the heat and set aside. Heat a wok or large pan and add the oil. Stir-fry the garlic, chillies, lemon grass and onion until golden brown and fragrant. Add the chicken and stir-fry until just done.

Add the caramelised syrup and soy and fish sauces and heat through. Season to taste with salt and pepper. Scatter over the coriander leaves and serve with rice.

Serves 4.

Chicken satay

We published the first Thai food article in *YOU* in 2000 after eating at the Cape Thai restaurant in Cape Town.

MARINADE
5 ml (1 t) turmeric
5 ml (1 t) sugar
5 ml (1 t) salt
100 g chicken breasts, cut into strips

MARINADE
Blend the turmeric, sugar and salt and marinate the chicken in the mixture for 30 minutes or until fragrant. Thread the chickens strips onto skewers and grill in the oven or over coals until just done.

PEANUT SAUCE
45 ml (3 T) oil
7 ml (1½ t) Massaman curry paste
100 ml coconut milk
100 ml water
30 ml (2 T) finely chopped peanuts
15 ml (1 T) sugar
5 ml (1 t) palm sugar, dissolved in a
    little water in the microwave oven
    OR brown sugar
5 ml (1 t) salt
5 ml (1 t) turmeric

PEANUT SAUCE
Heat the oil in a large wok or pan, add the curry paste and stir-fry until fragrant. Add the coconut milk and water and bring to the boil, stirring continuously. Add the remaining ingredients and mix. The sauce must be fairly sweet.

Serve with the chicken skewers and Thai atjar.

Serves 2–3.

THAI ATJAR
60 ml (¼ c) sugar
50 ml white wine vinegar
2 ml (½ t) salt
1 onion, diced
¼ English cucumber, diced
2 red chillies, seeded and finely chopped

Blend all the ingredients and serve with the chicken satay.

Italian chicken

This chicken dish with its fragrant tomato, olive and anchovy sauce is the ideal dinner party dish.

40 ml olive oil
12 chicken pieces
1 large onion, halved and sliced
2 cloves garlic, chopped
125 ml (½ c) dry white wine
30 ml (2 T) vinegar
125 ml (½ c) chicken stock
1 can (410 g) whole tomatoes
20 ml (4 t) tomato paste
5 ml (1 t) chopped fresh thyme
5 ml (1 t) sugar
3 anchovies, finely chopped
125 ml (½ c) black olives,
   pitted and halved
40 ml roughly chopped Italian parsley

Preheat the oven to 180 °C.

Heat the oil in a large pan and brown the chicken pieces. Put the fried chicken in an ovenproof dish. Pour off the pan juices, leaving about 20 ml (4 t) in the pan. Reserve the pan juices. Fry the onion and garlic until soft.

Add the wine and vinegar to the onion mixture, bring the liquid to the boil and reduce by half. Add the chicken stock and heat over high heat for 2 minutes. Press the tomatoes through a sieve and add them to the pan, along with their juice, the tomato paste, thyme and sugar. Cook for another 1 minute. Pour the tomato mixture over the chicken pieces, cover and bake for 1 hour.

Bring the reserved pan juices to the boil in a small saucepan and bubble for 1 minute. Add the anchovies, olives and half the parsley and heat for another 1 minute. Pour the mixture over the chicken and sprinkle over the remaining parsley. Serve with mashed potatoes and green beans.

Serves 6.

> **Tip**
> Soak the anchovies in a little milk to remove the excess salt.

Chicken parmigiana

Gaynor Tapson of Dubai in the United Arab Emirates sent us the recipe for this delicious chicken dish. The chicken is rolled in Parmesan cheese, fried and then topped with a slice of mozzarella cheese before being baked in the oven in a fragrant tomato sauce.

100 ml cake flour
salt and freshly ground black pepper
50 g freshly grated Parmesan cheese
4 chicken breast fillets
1 egg, whisked
10 ml (2 t) butter
100 g mozzarella cheese,
   cut into 4 slices
15 ml (1 T) olive oil
1 onion, chopped
2 cloves garlic, crushed
4 baby marrows, sliced
1 can (420 g) peeled, chopped tomatoes
15 ml (1 T) tomato paste
5 ml (1 t) chopped fresh oregano
5 ml (1 t) chopped fresh basil leaves
salt and freshly ground black pepper

Preheat the oven to 180 °C and grease a medium-sized ovenproof dish that will hold the chicken breast fillets in a single layer.

Combine the flour, salt, pepper and half the Parmesan cheese. Dip the chicken breasts in the whisked egg and then in the flour mixture, coating them well. Heat the butter in a pan and fry the chicken breasts until golden brown all over. Put them in the prepared dish and top each with a slice of mozzarella cheese.

Wipe the pan with a paper towel and heat the oil. Sauté the onion and garlic over medium heat for 5 minutes. Add the baby marrows and sauté for another 2 minutes. Add the tomatoes, tomato paste, herbs, salt and pepper and simmer uncovered over low heat for 15 minutes. Pour the tomato mixture over the chicken, cover with aluminium foil and bake for another 25–30 minutes. Sprinkle over the remaining Parmesan cheese just before serving.

Serves 4.

Italian chicken

Coq au vin potjie

Winemakers have a good sense of smell and taste so are often excellent cooks as well. Martin Moore of Durbanville Hills wine cellars near Cape Town prepares this classic French dish in a cast-iron pot.

250 g bacon, diced
30 ml (2 T) butter
1 whole chicken, cut into pieces
salt and freshly ground black pepper
5 cloves garlic, crushed
125 ml (½ c) brandy
750 ml (3 c) red wine such as a light
    pinotage or older shiraz (use good-
    quality wine)
250 ml (1 c) chicken stock
5 ml (1 t) tomato purée
few sprigs fresh thyme
2 sprigs fresh rosemary
few sprigs fresh parsley
2 bay leaves
15 ml (1 T) soft brown sugar
20 pickling onions, peeled
30 ml (2 T) olive oil
45 ml (3 T) butter
250 g (1 punnet) button mushrooms
45 ml (3 T) cake flour

Heat a flat-bottomed pot and fry the bacon in a little melted butter. Remove the bacon from the pot. Season the chicken to taste and brown a few pieces at a time. Set aside. Wipe the pot with paper towels and sauté the garlic until soft. Return the chicken and bacon to the pot. Pour over the brandy and ignite it (use extra-long matches for safety). Once the flames have died down return the pot to the heat or fire. Add the wine, chicken stock and tomato purée. Make a bouquet garni with the herbs and add to the pot. Sprinkle over the sugar. Cover and simmer over medium heat for about 45 minutes or until the chicken is done. Put the onions in a small saucepan or pan. Pour over boiling water and cook for about 30 minutes or until soft. Pour off the water and add the oil and 15 ml (1 T) butter to the onions. Season to taste and return the saucepan to the heat and brown the onions, shaking the saucepan occasionally. Remove the onions from the pan and fry the mushrooms in the same pan until brown, adding a little more butter if necessary.

Melt the remaining 30 ml (2 T) butter and mix with the flour to make a paste. Add more butter if necessary.

Remove the chicken from the heat and remove half the chicken and the bouquet garni from the pot. Add small knobs of the butter paste to the pot, stirring continuously. Return the pot to the heat, stirring until the sauce thickens slightly. Return the rest of the chicken to the pot and add the onions and mushrooms. Heat until warmed through. Garnish with fresh rosemary sprigs. Serve the chicken with mashed potatoes.

Serves 4–6.

Curry chicken casserole

This curry is mild and fragrant rather than hot. The dish is made with lentils and butternut and seasoned with both coriander seeds and fresh leaves. The plain yoghurt that's added at the end gives the curry a lovely creamy consistency.

8 chicken pieces, excess fat and
  skin removed
cornflour to coat chicken pieces
sea salt and freshly ground black pepper
30 ml (2 T) sunflower oil
2 ml (½ t) whole coriander seeds
2 ml (½ t) mustard seeds
5 ml (1 t) chilli flakes
10 ml (2 t) turmeric
1 onion, finely chopped
4–6 cloves garlic, crushed
4 leeks, cut into 3 cm pieces
125 ml (½ c) lentils
10 ml (2 t) grated fresh ginger
leaves of 1 small bunch fresh coriander
500 ml (2 c) chicken stock
1 small butternut, peeled and cubed
125 ml (½ c) fat-free plain yoghurt

Preheat the oven to 180 °C and grease an ovenproof dish.

Roll the chicken pieces in the cornflour, coating them well, and season with salt and pepper. Heat the oil in large heavy-bottomed saucepan and brown the chicken pieces. Remove from the pan and arrange them in the ovenproof dish.

Stir-fry the coriander and mustard seeds in the pan for 1–2 minutes. Add the chilli flakes, turmeric, onion, garlic and leeks, cover and fry until soft. Add the lentils, ginger, most of the coriander leaves and stock, cover and simmer for 10 minutes.

Spoon the mixture over the chicken in the ovenproof dish and add the butternut. Cover and bake for 30–40 minutes or until the lentils are soft and the chicken pieces are done. Stir in the yoghurt and heat through. Scatter over the remaining coriander leaves. Serve with basmati rice or noodles and a fresh green salad made with orange segments, radishes and onion rings.

Serves 6–8.

Chicken casserole

Mercia Pieterse of Tzaneen cooks chicken pieces in a sauce made with mango atjar, mayonnaise and onion soup powder. Delicious.

oil
6–8 chicken pieces
salt and freshly ground black pepper
1 packet (60 g) thick white onion
  soup powder
250 ml (1 c) mayonnaise
125 ml (½ c) mango atjar
  OR 100 ml smooth apricot jam
  OR 125 ml (½ c) chutney

Preheat the oven to 180 °C.

Heat a medium-sized heavy-bottomed pan and brush it with a little oil. Season the chicken pieces with salt and pepper and fry skin side down until crisp and golden brown. Turn the chicken pieces and brown the other side. Remove from the pan and arrange them in an ovenproof dish.

Mix the onion soup powder with 500 ml (2 c) water and mix in the mayonnaise, atjar or jam or chutney. Pour the mixture over the chicken pieces and bake for about 40 minutes or until done. Serve hot with rice and vegetables.

Serves 6–8.

> **Variation**
> To give the sauce extra zip add 5 ml (1 t) curry powder and 45 ml (3 T) tomato sauce.

Mexican chicken casserole

The chicken and bean mixture is layered with a cheese sauce and corn chips. Delicious!

CHICKEN AND BEAN MIXTURE
30 ml (2 T) oil
1 onion, chopped
2 cloves garlic, crushed
200g–300 g chicken breast fillets,
    cut into strips
1 green pepper, seeded and chopped
5 ml (1 t) ground cumin
5 ml (1 t) dried oregano
2 ml (½ t) dried chillies
2 ml (½ t) salt
1 can (440 g) red kidney beans, drained
45 ml (3 T) chopped fresh coriander leaves
juice of ½ lemon

CHEESE SAUCE
45 ml (3 T) butter
45 ml (3 T) cake flour
375 ml (1½ c) milk
125 ml (½ c) grated Cheddar cheese
2 ml (½ t) dried oregano

TO ASSEMBLE
150 g corn chips (Doritos)
125 ml (½ c) grated Cheddar cheese
paprika

Preheat the oven to 220 °C. Grease a large ovenproof dish.

CHICKEN AND BEAN MIXTURE
Heat the oil in a large heavy-bottomed saucepan. Add the onion and garlic and sauté until soft. Add the chicken and green pepper. Stir-fry until the onion is soft and the chicken is just done. Remove the pan from the heat and add the spices, kidney beans, coriander and lemon juice. Set aside.

CHEESE SAUCE
Melt the butter in a large saucepan and add the flour. Stir to form a smooth paste. Heat until it starts to bubble. Gradually add the milk, stirring continuously. Bring to the boil and simmer until the sauce is done. Remove from the heat and stir in the cheese and oregano.

TO ASSEMBLE
Arrange half the corn chips in the bottom of the prepared ovenproof dish. Spoon the chicken and bean mixture on top and cover with the remaining corn chips. Pour over the cheese sauce and sprinkle with the cheese and paprika. Bake for 15–20 minutes or until golden brown. Serve with avocado salsa (see recipe).

Serves 6.

Budget-beating tip
Use breadcrumbs instead of cheese for sprinkling on top.

AVOCADO SALSA
Peel and dice 1 avocado, add 3 chopped spring onions and the chopped flesh of 1 Roma tomato. Season with lemon juice, salt and pepper.

Mexican chicken casserole

Citrus and olive chicken

This quick chicken dish is ideal for an everyday meal or dinner party. The chicken skin is removed to cut down on kilojoules but the stuffing keeps the meat moist and flavoursome.

CHICKEN
8 chicken pieces, skin removed
20 calamata olives, pitted
rind of 1 lemon, cut into thin strips

STUFFING
4 fat cloves garlic, crushed
250 ml (1 c) chopped Italian parsley and
    chives (adjust proportion to taste)
sea salt and freshly ground black pepper
30 ml (2 T) olive oil

SAUCE
juice and rind of 1 lemon and 1 orange
125 ml (½ c) chicken stock
125 ml (½ c) white wine
60 ml (¼ c) olive oil
5 ml (1 t) sugar

Preheat the oven to 200 °C.

CHICKEN AND STUFFING
Make shallow incisions in each chicken piece.
    Mix the stuffing ingredients to make a coarse paste and press the stuffing into the incisions. Rub the chicken pieces with the remaining stuffing mixture.

SAUCE
Mix the sauce ingredients, season with salt and pepper and pour the mixture into a roasting tin. Put the chicken pieces in the sauce, cover and bake for 20 minutes. Add the olives and lemon rind and bake for another 10–15 minutes or until done. Serve with couscous or garlic and olive mashed potatoes.

Serves 8.

> **Variation**
> Use pesto and a slice of cheese and/or bacon instead of the stuffing.

Chicken with wine and cream

Verity Lake of Piketberg enjoys experimenting with ingredients.

8 chicken pieces
chicken spice
olive oil for frying
1 large onion, roughly chopped
2–4 cloves garlic, crushed
250 g (1 punnet) button mushrooms,
    sliced
1 red pepper, seeded and diced
5 ml (1 t) chopped fresh oregano
    or tarragon
1 sprig fresh thyme
5 ml (1 t) paprika
250 ml (1 c) dry white wine
250 ml (1 c) chicken stock
15 ml (1 T) cornflour
250 ml (1 c) sour cream
salt and freshly ground black pepper

Season the chicken pieces with the chicken spice. Heat the oil in a large saucepan and fry the chicken until cooked and golden. Remove the chicken pieces from the saucepan and set aside. Sauté the onion, garlic, mushrooms and red pepper in the same saucepan for 10 minutes. Add the herbs, paprika, wine and stock and reduce by two-thirds. Return the chicken pieces to the saucepan.
    Blend the cornflour with 30 ml (2 T) of the sour cream and blend with the remaining sour cream. Add the sour cream mixture to the chicken. Simmer slowly until the chicken is done and the sauce thickens. Season to taste. Serve with rice or pasta or baked potatoes and vegetables.

Serves 6–8.

Chicken and brinjal stew

The chicken and brinjal are cooked in a fragrant tomato sauce.

olive oil for frying
375 g young, thin brinjals, cut into
   3 cm thick slices
8 pickling onions, quartered
1 can (420 g) chopped tomatoes
2 cloves garlic, crushed
10 ml (2 t) ground cumin
cake flour
salt
500 g chicken breast fillets, cut into
   3 cm thick slices
100 ml apple cider vinegar
125 ml (½ c) water
3 sprigs fresh thyme
30 ml (2 T) toasted chopped cashew
   nuts (optional)

Heat 40 ml olive oil in large heavy-bottomed saucepan and fry a few brinjal slices at a time over high heat. Add more oil if necessary. Drain the brinjal slices on paper towels and set aside. Add more oil to the pan if necessary and fry the onions over medium heat for 5 minutes.

Add the tomatoes, garlic and cumin and simmer for 2 minutes. Set aside.

Combine some of the flour and salt in plastic bag, put the chicken in the bag and shake well to coat with the flour mixture. Shake off the excess flour. Heat more oil in a large pan or saucepan and fry the chicken slices over moderate heat until golden brown. Remove from the pan and set aside.

Add the apple cider vinegar to the pan and, stirring, heat for 1–2 minutes. Add the water, thyme and tomato and onion mix and return the chicken to the pan. Layer the fried brinjal slices on top of the chicken, cover partially and simmer for another 20 minutes until the chicken is tender. Add the cashew nuts just before serving and serve with pasta such as penne.

Serves 4–5.

Tip
Brinjal is inclined to absorb oil when fried. To prevent this first heat the pan, preferably a nonstick griddle pan, and then brush with oil. Fry a few brinjal slices at a time, pressing them down with a spatula.

DELICIOUS CURRIES

No two curry recipes are the same. Curries also vary from region to region. There are hot and spicy Indian curries from KwaZulu-Natal, mild and fragrant Malay curries from the Cape and creamy Thai curries, to mention but a few.

Malay curries

Cape Town foodie and renowned chef (Cass Abrahams) introduced me to the secrets of Malay cooking and more specifically Malay curries, which are fragrant and aromatic rather than hot. Since then I've fallen in love with the exotic aromas of cumin, cardamom, coriander and cinnamon.

Malay curried offal with beans

This recipe originates from the time when slaves were given offal by their masters which they cooked on the square in front of the Groote Kerk in Cape Town. Families would get together to swop news and the curry would be shared among everyone. Some of it would be sent back to the farms as *barakat* (a gift) for those who were unable to attend the event. This tradition still exists: Family get-togethers are held on Sundays and food is sent back home with guests as a gift.

1 beef offal and 6 sheep trotters,
   cleaned and cut into pieces
2 large onions, chopped
2 cardamom pods
3 pieces whole cassia
4 whole cloves
80 ml (1/3 c) oil
3 tomatoes, peeled
   and roughly chopped
10 ml (2 t) masala
5 ml (1 t) ground cumin
5 ml (1 t) ground coriander
5 ml (1 t) turmeric
15 ml (1 T) crushed garlic
5 ml (1 t) ginger paste
2 cans (410 g each) butter beans
   (do not drain)
salt and freshly ground black pepper
   fresh coriander leaves, chopped

Bring the offal and trotters to the boil in water and cook until tender. Drain and set aside. Sauté the onions and whole spices in a large saucepan in the heated oil until the onions are soft. Add the offal, trotters and tomatoes and simmer for 10–15 minutes. Stir in the ground spices and add the garlic, ginger and butter beans including the liquid. Simmer for another 5–10 minutes or until heated through and fragrant. Season to taste with salt, pepper and chopped coriander. Serve with rice, or samp and beans (see recipe).

Serves 6–8.

SAMP AND BEANS
Soak 500 g samp-and-bean mixture in cold water overnight. Drain and transfer to a large saucepan. Cover with water. Add 2 chicken stock cubes and boil until the mixture is soft. Season to taste with salt and pepper and stir in a knob of butter. Sauté together 1 chopped onion, 2 cubed potatoes, 5 ml (1 t) masala and garlic in a little oil until the onion and potatoes are soft. Add a little water, heat and add to the samp mixture.

Malay curried offal with beans

Cape Malay chicken curry

This traditional recipe, which has been given a slight twist with the addition of chickpeas, can be used as the basis for any other curry. Use it to make lamb or vegetable curry for instance; the method and basic ingredients are the same.

1 large onion, chopped
2 cardamom seeds
2 whole pieces cassia
5 ml (1 t) cumin seeds
80 ml (⅓ c) oil
500 g chicken (excess fat and skin removed), cut into pieces
1 can (420 g) chopped tomatoes
10 ml (2 t) mild masala
5 ml (1 t) turmeric
10 ml (2 t) ground cumin
5 ml (1 t) ground coriander
10 ml (2 t) crushed garlic
5 ml (1 t) ginger paste,
1 can (410 g) chickpeas, drained
salt
½ bunch fresh coriander leaves, washed and finely chopped

Sauté the onion and whole spices in the heated oil until the onion is soft and the spices fragrant. Add the chicken pieces and stir-fry gently. Add the tomatoes and their juice and mix. Add the ground spices, garlic and ginger paste and stir until the chicken is coated with the tomato mixture. Reduce the heat and simmer until the chicken is nearly tender. Add the chickpeas and simmer until heated through and the chicken is done and fragrant. Season with salt and scatter the coriander leaves on top.

Serve in a roti or with braised rice (see p. 178) and a fresh sambal (see p. 122).

Serves 4–6.

Indian curry contains hardly any or no sweet ingredients while Malay curry is sweeter and is often made with fruit or dried fruit.

Sweet *boere* curry

Real *boere* curry is mild with a slightly sweet flavour. Dried fruit is often added to the dish.

30 ml (2 T) oil
1,2–1,5 kg mutton rib or shoulder or stewing beef, cubed
2 large onions, chopped
25–30 ml (5–6 t) mild curry powder
6 cloves garlic, crushed
1 can (420 g) chopped tomatoes
2 pieces whole cassia
2 bay leaves
hot meat stock
30 ml (2 T) brown sugar or apricot jam to taste
salt and freshly ground black pepper

Heat the oil in a heavy-bottomed saucepan and brown the meat cubes in batches. Remove from the saucepan and set aside. Sauté the onions in the remaining oil until soft. Sprinkle over the curry powder and stir-fry for about 15 seconds. Add the garlic and stir-fry for about 1 minute. Return the meat cubes to the saucepan and add the tomatoes. Bring the mixture to the boil. Add the cassia, bay leaves and a little meat stock, cover and simmer for about 2 hours over low heat until the meat is tender. Season with brown sugar or apricot jam, salt and pepper to taste.

Serve with yellow rice, chutney and banana slices mixed with yoghurt.

Serves 6–8.

Variations
Spinach curry: Add 2 bunches finely shredded spinach about 30 minutes before the end of the cooking time.

Fruit curry: Add 250 g dried fruit such as apricots, apples, prunes, pears or peaches that have been soaked in water or rooibos 40 minutes before the end of the cooking time. Serve with chutney and toasted coconut.

KwaZulu-Natal curries

On the KZN coast curries are made the Indian way – hot and spicy. I was treated to a real Indian curry at Neville and Shamen Reddy's curry eaterie in Tinley Manor Beach on the North Coast. Shamen says the secret is in the unique mixture of masalas, fresh ginger and garlic and fresh curry and coriander leaves. No fruit, cream or yoghurt is added to this curry with its intense deep-red colour.

> The masalas (spice mixtures) for KZN curries are very basic. It's advisable to buy ready-mixed masala at Indian spice shops. Most KZN curries are made with a hot curry mixture (garam masala), chillies, tamarind, garlic paste, curry leaves and fresh coriander.

Prawn curry

This curry takes only a few minutes to make.

1 large onion, finely chopped
1 sprig curry leaves
3–4 whole green chillies
oil
15 ml (1 T) garlic and ginger paste
6 medium-sized tomatoes, puréed
30–45 ml (2–3 T) mixed masala
1 ml (pinch) turmeric
500 g prawns, peeled and deveined
    but tails kept intact
salt
fresh coriander leaves

Stir-fry the onion, curry leaves and chillies in a little heated oil until the onion is golden brown. Add the garlic and ginger paste and mix well. Add the tomatoes, mixed masala and turmeric, stir-fry slightly and simmer until fragrant. Add the prawns, cover and simmer for 5–7 minutes or until just done. Season with salt, remove the chillies and scatter fresh coriander leaves on top.
    Serve with rice or rotis and sambals (see p. 122).

Serves 3–4.

Chicken curry

Everyone knows Cindy's, the charming little shop in Umhlali on the KwaZulu-Natal North Coast where you can buy anything from garden-fresh veggies to fragrant spices. Owner Cindy Valayadam, who gave me a wonderful insight into the art of Indian cuisine, is a dab hand at rustling up a tasty curry for a crowd on the huge gas burners at her home.

1 medium-sized onion, sliced into rings
oil
5 ml (1 t) garlic paste
5 ml (1 t) ginger paste
15 ml (1 T) mixed masala
15 ml (1 T) curry powder
3 ripe plum tomatoes, mashed
1 can (420 g) tomato purée
500 g chicken, skin and bones removed
5–7 curry leaves
5 ml (1 t) fennel powder
5 ml (1 t) garam masala
fresh coriander leaves

Fry the onion in a little heated oil until soft. Add the garlic and ginger pastes. Stir in the mixed masala followed by the curry powder. Add the tomatoes and tomato purée. Simmer for a few minutes until fragrant. Add the chicken pieces and curry leaves and simmer slowly until the chicken is done and fragrant. Add the fennel powder and garam masala towards the end of the cooking time and scatter fresh coriander leaves on top. Serve with rotis or rice.

Serves 3–4.

Dry curry

The sauce for this curry is reduced which accounts for its dry texture.

45 ml (3 T) oil
15 ml (1 T) finely grated fresh ginger
4 cloves garlic, crushed
10–15 dried or fresh curry leaves
500 g deboned shoulder of lamb, cubed
10 ml (2 t) garam masala or
    hot curry powder
5 ml (1 t) ground cumin
1 ml (pinch) turmeric
1 ml (pinch) chilli powder
1 fresh green chilli, seeded and
    finely chopped
salt and freshly ground black pepper
5–10 ml (1–2 t) lemon juice
fresh coriander leaves

Heat the oil in a heavy-bottomed saucepan and stir-fry the ginger, garlic and curry leaves until fragrant. Add the meat cubes in batches and stir-fry until lightly browned. Add the spices and chilli and mix well. Reduce the heat, add about 30 ml (2 T) water, cover and simmer until the meat is tender. Add more water if necessary. Remove the lid towards the end of the cooking time and allow the liquid to evaporate. Braise the meat until brown and fragrant. Season with salt and pepper and add lemon juice to taste. Scatter fresh coriander leaves on top and serve with poppadums, naan bread or rice and sambals as desired.

Serves 4.

Lamb curry

Indian lamb curry is often made with meat on the bone which gives the dish a more robust flavour. Eating the last morsels of meat off the bone by hand is part of the fun. This curry is made with potato for extra body.

1 large onion, sliced into rings
1 sprig fresh curry leaves
oil
15 ml (1 T) garlic and ginger paste
60 ml (¼ c) mixed masala
2 ml (½ t) turmeric
2 medium-sized plum tomatoes
1 kg leg of lamb, or shoulder sliced in
    pieces
salt
4–5 medium-sized potatoes,
    peeled and quartered
fresh coriander leaves, chopped

Fry the onion and curry leaves in a little heated oil until the onion is soft and lightly browned. Add the garlic and ginger paste, masala and turmeric and mix well. Add the tomatoes and braise them for about 5 minutes or until fragrant. Add the meat and season with salt. Cover the saucepan, reduce the heat and simmer until the meat is nearly tender. Add the potatoes and a little water and simmer until the potatoes are soft. Add more water if necessary. Add the coriander leaves at the end of the cooking time.

Serve with rice and sambals such as chopped onion and tomato.

Serves 6.

FRESH CORIANDER
Also known as dhania in Indian cooking. The leaves are often referred to as cilantro, Chinese parsley or Mexican parsley in foreign cookbooks. Choose fresh coriander with uniformly green leaves. To store, remove any wilted or discoloured leaves immediately and place the bunch of coriander in a jug of water as you would a bunch of flowers. Cover the leaves with a plastic bag and place in the fridge. Wash the leaves just before using. Fresh coriander enhances the flavour of Indian, Asian and Mexican dishes. In Thailand the roots are used to add flavour to meat and curry dishes.

Lamb curry

Indian vegetable curry

Cindy Valayadam of Umhlali also loves making this vegetable curry, adding cooked butter beans to provide essential protein.

oil
1 onion, chopped
7 ml (1½ t) garlic paste
7 ml (1½ t) ginger paste
20–30 ml (4–6 t) curry powder
   or masala
5 ml (1 t) garam masala
1 kg ripe tomatoes, peeled
   and finely chopped
1 can (50 g) tomato paste
few curry leaves
few garlic chives
salt, sugar and black pepper
500 g brinjal, cubed
500 g cooked butter beans
fresh coriander leaves

Heat a little oil in a heavy-bottomed saucepan and stir-fry the onion until translucent. Stir in the garlic and ginger pastes, curry powder and garam masala. Add the tomatoes, tomato paste, curry leaves and garlic chives, reduce the heat and simmer slowly for 15–20 minutes or until fragrant. Season well with salt, sugar and black pepper. Fry the brinjal cubes in a little heated oil until lightly browned and add to the curry sauce along with the butter beans. Simmer until fragrant. Adjust the seasoning to taste and stir in the coriander leaves. Serve with rice or poppadums.

Serves 6.

Priscilla's fish and vegetable curry

Priscilla Petersen, who has been the kitchen assistant in the *YOU* test kitchen for many years, learnt to make curry in KwaZulu-Natal. One lunchtime she treated us to this excellent fish curry using leftover ingredients from the kitchen. It's now become one of our standbys.

45 ml (3 T) oil
600 g hake, cubed
2 onions, halved and sliced
2 cloves garlic, crushed
10 ml (2 t) fish masala
5 ml (1 t) garam masala
5 ml (1 t) turmeric
10 ml (2 t) sugar
25 ml (5 t) tomato paste
250 ml (1 c) water
125 ml (½ c) chopped fresh coriander
   leaves
salt and freshly ground black pepper
250 g frozen or fresh mixed vegetables,
   cut into pieces
fresh coriander leaves to garnish

Heat 20 ml (4 t) of the oil in a large pan over high heat and brown the fish all over. Remove from the pan and heat the remaining oil in the same pan. Stir-fry the onions and garlic until the onion is soft. Add the fish masala, garam masala and turmeric and stir-fry for 1 minute so the flavours can develop. Add the sugar, tomato paste, water and 125 ml (½ c) coriander leaves and bring to the boil. Simmer for a few minutes then return the fish to the pan. Season with salt and pepper and simmer until the sauce is thick and fragrant. Add the vegetables and simmer until they are done but still firm. Garnish with fresh coriander leaves on top just before serving.

Serves 4.

Banana curry

Cooling green banana is delicious in a hot curry and also thickens the sauce.
This is also one of *YOU* test kitchen assistant Priscilla Petersen's recipes.

oil
1 kg stewing beef cubes
2 onions, chopped
1 green pepper, seeded and chopped
5 ml (1 t) curry powder
5 ml (1 t) turmeric
10 ml (2 t) roasted masala
1 chilli, seeded and chopped
500 ml (2 c) water
salt to taste
4 green bananas, cut into pieces
fresh coriander leaves

Heat a little oil in a heavy-bottomed saucepan and brown the meat in batches. Remove from the saucepan and set aside. Fry the onions and green pepper in the same saucepan until soft. Add the spices and chilli and fry for about 5 minutes or until fragrant. Return the meat to the saucepan, add 250 ml (1 c) water, cover and bring the mixture to the boil. Simmer for 1½–2 hours or until the meat is tender. If the curry is too dry add more water. Season with salt and add the bananas. Heat through rapidly and remove from the heat.

Leave the curry to stand for a few minutes. Scatter coriander leaves on top and serve with rotis or rice.

Serves 8.

Penang curry

Joey Rasdiem of Johannesburg is not only a comedienne, she's also an excellent cook.
This curry is named after Penang in Malaysia.

4 onions, sliced into rings
30 ml (2 T) oil or ghee (clarified butter)
15 ml (1 T) garlic paste
30 ml (2 T) ginger paste
1–2 chillies, seeded and finely chopped
150 g tamarind, soaked in
   250 ml (1 c) water
1–2 sprigs fresh curry leaves (optional)
5 ml (1 t) ground coriander
5 ml (1 t) ground cumin
15 ml (1 T) turmeric
10 ml (2 t) mixed masala
15 ml (1 T) mild curry powder
1 kg beef fillet, cubed
5 tomatoes, halved
5 ml (1 t) salt
3 ml (generous ½ t) sugar
6 hard-boiled eggs, shelled

Fry the onions in the oil or ghee, add the garlic and ginger pastes and chilli and mix. Add the tamarind water to the onion mixture and stir in the curry leaves and spices. Simmer for 5–7 minutes or until a fragrant sauce forms. Add the meat, mix well with the onion mixture and reduce the heat. Cover and simmer for 15–20 minutes or until the meat is just done. Add the tomatoes and simmer for 5–10 minutes or until fragrant. Season to taste with salt and a little sugar. Add the whole eggs and heat through. Serve with basmati rice, mango atjar, tomato chutney and tomato and onion sambal (see p.122).

Serves 6.

> **Tip**
> Tamarind, the pulpy fruit of the Indian tamarind tree, imparts a tart flavour to stews and curries.
> If unobtainable use the juice of two lemons instead.

Rogan josh

Rogan josh, a delicious dish from the Kashmir region, is made of spices with a strong, intense flavour. This recipe is from Cathy Smith who says her house in Bakoven near Cape Town has been destroyed twice: once by massive waves and the second time when tenants forgot a pot of food on the stove and burnt down the house. Perhaps they were making Rogan josh, she jokes. This dish is outstanding.

15 ml (1 T) oil
15 ml (1 T) butter
2 onions, chopped
5 ml (1 t) chilli powder or 1 chilli,
　finely chopped
15 ml (1 T) ground coriander
10 ml (2 t) ground cumin
5 ml (1 t) ground cardamom
5 ml (1 t) turmeric
3 cloves garlic, crushed
15 ml (1 T) grated fresh ginger
125 ml (½ c) plain yoghurt
5 ml (1 t) salt
1 can (420 g) chopped tomatoes
30 ml (2 T) brown sugar
30 ml (2 T) chutney
1 kg deboned lamb, cubed
15 ml (1 T) garam masala
fresh coriander leaves, chopped

Heat the oil and butter in a large saucepan and sauté the onions until soft. Add all the spices (except the garam masala), garlic and ginger and stir-fry for 1 minute or until fragrant. Add the yoghurt, salt, tomatoes, sugar and chutney and simmer for about 10 minutes. Add the meat and stir to cover it with the sauce. Cover and simmer for 60–90 minutes over low heat or until the meat is tender. Remove the lid and simmer for another 10 minutes so the liquid can evaporate. Stir in the garam masala and scatter over the coriander leaves just before serving. Serve with rice.

Serves 5–6.

Tandoori chicken

Tandoori chicken is the best-known dish made in a tandoor, an ancient clay oven with a funnelled lid. Few people have a tandoor but you can successfully cook the dish in a conventional oven, especially if you have a rotisserie. Smaller pieces of meat threaded onto skewers and cooked in a tandoor are called tikka. The spices used are similar to those used for tandoori chicken.

1 onion, chopped
3 cloves garlic, crushed
15 ml (1 T) grated fresh ginger
35–40 ml (7–8 t) tandoori masala
　(see p. 121)
8 ml (generous 1½ t) salt
10 ml (2 t) sugar
500 ml (2 c) plain yoghurt
30 ml (2 T) chopped fresh mint
2 red chillies, seeded and finely chopped
1,5 kg chicken pieces
30 ml (2 T) butter

Blitz together all the ingredients, except the chicken and butter, in a food processor or pound them using a mortar and pestle. Rub the chicken with the mixture and marinate for at least 6 hours. Preheat the oven to 220 °C. Grease an ovenproof dish with butter. Put the chicken pieces in the dish skin side facing up. Roast uncovered for about 45 minutes or until tender. Serve with rice and sambals (see p. 122).

Serves 6–8.

> **Tip**
> Most tandoori dishes have a typically orange or reddish colour obtained by adding food colouring. We prefer to omit this.

Tandoori chicken

Butter chicken

To make butter chicken butter is used instead of clarified butter or ghee. Zaidah Howell
of Salt River near Cape Town cooks the chicken in an aromatic buttermilk sauce which makes
it less rich than traditional butter chicken.

60 g butter
1 large onion, grated
1 kg chicken breast fillets, cut into strips
2 cloves garlic, crushed
45 ml (3 T) garam masala
2 ml (½ t) ground cumin
2 ml (½ t) ground coriander
500 ml (2 c) buttermilk
1 can (420 g) chopped tomatoes
125 ml (½ c) cream
5 ml (1 t) cornflour
10 ml (2 t) chopped fresh coriander leaves
1 green chilli, chopped

Heat the butter and sauté the onion until soft. Add the
chicken and garlic and stir-fry until the chicken is done.
Add the spices and stir-fry for 2 minutes. Pour over the
buttermilk and add the tomatoes. Bring to the boil and
simmer for 10 minutes. Mix the cream and cornflour and add
to the buttermilk mixture along with the coriander leaves and
chilli. Bring to the boil and, stirring continuously, simmer for
about 3 minutes or until the sauce thickens slightly.
    Serve with rotis or naan bread.

Serves 6.

Korma

In Kashmir a few korma dishes are traditionally served at weddings – a white one with cream
and ground nuts, a green one with herbs, and a hot red one with plenty of chillies.

Lamb korma

This fairly mild lamb korma is deliciously creamy. For a hotter version add 1–2 green chillies
to the spice paste.

60 ml (¼ c) oil
1 kg lamb, cubed
1 packet (100 g) blanched almonds
    or cashew nuts, toasted
45 ml (3 T) sesame seeds
5 cm piece fresh ginger, peeled
4 cloves garlic, peeled
3 onions, quartered
juice of 1 lemon
15 ml (1 T) ground coriander
15 ml (1 T) ground cumin
3 ml (generous ½ t) turmeric
2 ml (½ t) ground cloves (optional)
6 cardamom pods
2 pieces stick cinnamon
200 ml plain yoghurt
10 ml (2 t) cornflour
600 ml water
salt and freshly ground black pepper
200 ml sour cream (optional)
2 large onions, sliced into rings
    and fried until crisp
toasted sesame seeds

Heat 30 ml (2 T) oil in a heavy-bottomed saucepan and brown
the meat. Blitz the nuts, sesame seeds, ginger, garlic, onions
and lemon juice in a food processor to make a paste. Remove
the meat from the saucepan. Heat the remaining oil in the
same saucepan and stir-fry the paste for about 5 minutes or
until golden brown. Stir continuously to prevent it sticking
to the bottom of the saucepan. Add the remaining spices
and stir-fry for 1–2 minutes. Return the meat cubes to the
saucepan and add the yoghurt which has been blended with
the cornflour as well as the water. Season generously with salt
and black pepper. Cover and simmer slowly for 1–1½ hours or
until the meat is tender. Adjust the seasoning if necessary.
    To serve, pour over the sour cream, scatter the onion rings
and sesame seeds on top and serve with rice.

Serves 6.

Fragrant chicken korma

This recipe comes from Mrs R Coetzee of Kyalami.

MARINADE
125 ml (½ c) plain yoghurt
10 ml (2 t) lemon juice
5 ml (1 t) black pepper
2 ml (½ t) ground nutmeg
2 ml (½ t) ground cinnamon

CHICKEN
1 kg chicken pieces, skin removed
   and cut into bite-sized pieces
60 ml (¼ c) oil
5 ml (1 t) mustard seeds
3 onions, finely chopped
5 cm piece fresh ginger, finely grated
4 cloves garlic, crushed
2–3 bay leaves
5 ml (1 t) paprika
5 ml (1 t) ground coriander
2 ml (½ t) ground cumin
60 ml (¼ c) ground almonds
6 sprigs fresh coriander leaves,
   finely choppped
½ red chilli, seeds removed
50 ml (1 sachet) tomato paste
1 can (400 ml) coconut milk
5 ml (1 t) ground cardamom
salt
fresh coriander leaves

Mix together the marinade ingredients. Wash the chicken pieces and pat dry. Put them in a non-metallic dish and pour over the marinade. Marinate in the fridge, preferably overnight.

Heat 30 ml (2 T) oil in a heavy-bottomed saucepan and lightly stir-fry the mustard seeds. Add the onions, ginger, garlic and bay leaves and stir-fry over medium heat until lightly browned. Add the paprika, coriander and cumin and stir-fry until fragrant. Mix the ground almonds with the coriander leaves and chilli and add to the saucepan along with the tomato paste. Stir-fry until a fragrant paste forms. Add the coconut milk and ground cardamom to the paste mixture. Heat slowly, stirring continuously until the mixture forms a thick sauce.

Heat the remaining oil in a separate saucepan and stir-fry the chicken pieces until golden brown and just done. Add the chicken pieces to the sauce, season with salt, cover and simmer for 15–20 minutes or until fragrant. Remove the lid 5 minutes before the end of the cooking time.

Scatter fresh coriander leaves on top. Serve with sticky rice and/or poppadums.

Serves 6.

> **Tip**
> Microwave a poppadum on high for about 40 seconds or until puffed up.

CUMIN
This wonderful spice with its distinctive taste and aroma is used mostly in heavily spiced dishes such as meat stews, curries, roast or grilled meat (especially lamb), chilli con carne, Portuguese sausages, Middle Eastern fish and chicken dishes, couscous and even vegetable dishes. It's also an essential ingredient in curry powder. It comes in these forms:
- **Cumin seeds** should preferably be toasted so the flavour can be released.
- **Ground cumin.** Some recipes call for ground cumin. It's best to make your own by toasting whole cumin and pounding it using a mortar and pestle. This way the flavour is fresher and more intense than if you use bought ground cumin. Store ground cumin in an airtight container to retain its flavour.
- **Black cumin.** In its raw form it has a bitter taste but when used in cooking it imparts an aromatic, nutty flavour. Available from stores specialising in Eastern and Indian ingredients.

Thai curries

Many Thai curries are enriched with coconut milk which gives them their characteristic creamy taste and texture. Yet Thai curries are by no means mild – the chillies in the green or red curry paste add heat and flavour. Unlike other curries Thai curries are flavoured with a generous dash of fish sauce.

Thai coconut milk curry

This is a basic recipe for chicken or pork which you can flavour with green or red curry paste and enrich with coconut milk. I prefer to use green curry paste with chicken and vegetables and red curry paste with beef and pork. Add vegetables to taste.

30 ml (2 T) oil
15 ml (1 T) grated fresh ginger
10 ml (2 t) finely chopped garlic
2 spring onions, chopped
30 ml (2 T) Thai green or red curry paste
   (see recipes p. 120)
650 g deboned, skinless chicken thighs
   or breasts OR pork, cubed
125 g variety of vegetables, such as
   baby corn, mushrooms, green beans,
   baby carrots and eggplant, cubed
1 can (400 ml) coconut milk
30 ml (2 T) Thai fish sauce
5 ml (1 t) brown sugar
1 green chilli, seeded and
   finely chopped
fresh basil leaves

Heat the oil in a wok or heavy-bottomed saucepan. Add the ginger, garlic and spring onions and stir-fry until soft and fragrant. Add the curry paste and stir-fry for another 2 minutes. Add the meat pieces and stir-fry for 3 minutes, ensuring the pieces are coated with the curry mixture. Add the vegetables and stir-fry gently. Stir in the coconut milk and bring the mixture to the boil. Reduce the heat and simmer the curry for 10 minutes or until the meat is done and the sauce has reduced. Stir in the fish sauce, brown sugar and chilli. Simmer for about 3 minutes. Adjust the seasoning to taste and serve with basil leaves and jasmine rice or Asian noodles.

Serves 4.

> **Quick tip**
> Use ready-made curry paste instead of making it from scratch.

> **Tip**
> To make a Thai vegetable curry omit the meat and use vegetables that are quick to stir-fry, such as baby corn, sweet peppers, green beans, brinjal and cabbage.

> **THE SECRET OF MAKING CURRY**
> • Whole spices are added at the beginning and fried with the onions and meat.
> • Ground spices are very potent and are only added once you've added the liquid or tomatoes.
> • Do not fry ground spices as they will dominate the dish and may also impart a bitter taste.
> • Garlic and ginger are added with the ground spices. Always add garlic with the liquid to bring out its sweet flavour and to prevent any unpleasant after effects.

Thai coconut milk curry

Curry mixes

Masala is a mixture of spices used to make curry. You get various kinds of masala: fish or chicken masala, leaf masala, roasted masala, mixed masala and garam masala. Masalas vary in heat, depending on how much chilli has been added. Mother-in-law masala for instance is hot and spicy. Pakco makes a good commercial pure roasted masala. It contains no chillies or thickening agent. The proportion of masala to turmeric should be 2:1. Wet masala contains oil and fresh garlic. It can be used as a rub and forms a crust when pan-frying fish or chicken. Alternatively rub it into the meat when making curry. Dry masala is a mixture of dried spices used to impart flavour to curries.

Wet masalas

Our recipes for green and red masala pastes are based on those for Thai curries while the mild masala can be used to impart flavour to Cape Malay curries.

Red masala paste

15 ml (1 T) coriander seeds
10 ml (2 t) cumin seeds
5 ml (1 t) black peppercorns
10 ml (2 t) fish sauce
5 ml (1 t) ground nutmeg
12 red chillies, roughly chopped
1 onion, chopped
30 ml (2 T) oil
4 stems lemon grass, finely chopped
12 small cloves garlic, chopped
60 ml (¼ c) chopped fresh coriander
    leaves
6 fresh curry leaves, chopped
10 ml (2 t) grated lime rind
10 ml (2 t) salt
10 ml (2 t) turmeric
5 ml (1 t) paprika

Roast the coriander and cumin seeds in a dry pan for 2–3 minutes, shaking the pan constantly. Using a mortar and pestle, pound together the roasted seeds and peppercorns or blitz them in a food processor until fine. Add the fish sauce, nutmeg and chillies and pound or process for 5 seconds. Add the remaining ingredients and pound or process to make a smooth paste. If using a food processor constantly scrape the sides of the bowl with a spatula.

Makes about 250 ml (1 c).

Green masala paste

15 ml (1 T) coriander seeds
10 ml (2 t) cumin seeds
5 ml (1 t) black peppercorns
10 ml (2 t) fish sauce
8 green chillies, seeded and
    roughly chopped
2 medium-sized onions, chopped
5 cm piece fresh ginger, chopped
30 ml (2 T) oil
3 stems lemon grass, finely chopped
12 small cloves garlic, chopped
250 ml (1 c) chopped fresh coriander leaves
6 fresh curry leaves, chopped
10 ml (2 t) grated lime rind
10 ml (2 t) salt

Proceed as for the red masala.

Makes about 250 ml (1 c).

WHAT IS THE DIFFERENCE BETWEEN RED AND GREEN MASALA?
The difference is in the type of chillies used. Red masala is made with red chillies and green masala with green chillies. They are both hot so use judiciously.

Cass Abrahams' mild wet masala

150 g cumin seeds
50 g coriander seeds
10 g pure roasted masala
20 g garlic paste
50 ml oil

Coarsely grind the cumin and coriander seeds in a coffee grinder and add the masala, garlic paste and enough oil to make a paste. Store in the fridge.

Makes about 200 ml.

> **Tip**
> Store wet masalas in the fridge or freeze them.

Dry masalas
Basic garam masala

Garam means hot so garam masala is a mixture of hot spices. This mixture goes well with onion-based sauces for meat or poultry.

25 ml (5 t) cumin seeds
30 ml (2 T) coriander seeds
15 ml (1 T) green or black cardamom
10 ml (2 t) black peppercorns
½ piece stick cinnamon,
   broken into pieces
1 bay leaf, crushed
1 ml (pinch) whole cloves
1 ml (pinch) ground nutmeg
   or mace

Heat a heavy-bottomed frying pan and add the whole spices. Roast them over medium heat until they begin to change colour. Shake the pan constantly to prevent the spices from burning. Leave them to cool. Add the nutmeg or mace and using a mortar and pestle pound the mixture or process in a food processor until fine.

Makes about 80 ml (⅓ c).

Tandoori masala

Use this mixture to make chicken tandoori or tikka.

60 ml (¼ c) cumin seeds
30 ml (2 T) coriander seeds
2 ml (½ t) fenugreek seeds (optional)
seeds of 2 cardamom pods
2 whole cloves
2 ml (½ t) whole black peppercorns
1 ml (pinch) fennel seeds
1 bay leaf
1 cm piece stick cinnamon
1 ml (pinch) ground nutmeg or mace
5 ml (1 t) turmeric

Proceed as for the basic garam masala.

Makes about 100 ml.

> **Tip**
> Store dry masalas in air-tight containers, preferably in the fridge. Do not make too much at a time as masala loses its flavour over time.

Sambals

Sambals are served with nearly all kinds of curries: cool sambals are served with hot curries and hot sambals with more neutral dishes to add spice. Chutney, toasted coconut and banana slices mixed with a little chilli are among the most common sambals.

Tomato and onion sambal: Finely chop tomatoes, onions and chilli.
Add a little vinegar and chopped coriander leaves.

Sweet pepper sambal: Finely slice red and yellow peppers. Add finely chopped tomato and onion and chopped coriander leaves. Sprinkle with a little vinegar and sugar.

Cucumber sambal: Mix chopped cucumber with chopped onion and coriander leaves and moisten with a little vinegar.

Raita: Grate 1 English cucumber and drain the liquid. Add finely chopped garlic, mint and coriander leaves and 250 ml (1 c) plain yoghurt. Season with salt, a pinch of cayenne pepper and a little sugar. You can also add a pinch of ground cumin if desired. Delicious with hot curries.

Carrot sambal: Grate 4 carrots, add plenty of chopped coriander leaves, about 60 ml (¼ c) orange juice, 1 chopped chilli and salt and pepper to taste.

Prepare sambals just before serving so they are crisp and fresh.

ACCOMPANIMENTS FOR CURRY
Curry is mostly served with basmati or jasmine rice.
Flat breads such as naan, chapati or paratha (fried chapati) are served with
Indian curries. Alternatively flat pancakes such as rotis are filled with curry.
Another favourite accompaniment with curry is poppadums.

Chillies

All chillies start off green then change to yellow, orange or red as they ripen. There's hot debate about which chillies are hotter: the green or red ones. Our rating in brackets indicates the degree of heat – the higher the score the hotter.

Cayenne (3–5)
Available everywhere and easy to grow. These red or green chillies can be used in most dishes.

Jalapeño (5)
Green or red with a rounded end. Jalapeños have a distinctive flavour and are ideal used fresh in salads.

Serrano (6–7)
Green or red and shaped like a bullet. Perfect for salsas, sauces and pickles.

Bird's Eye (7–8)
Small green or red chillies that work well in atjar, stir-fries and chutney.

Thai (8–10)
Green or red and long and thin with a sharp point. Hot and excellent in curries and Eastern dishes.

Habañero (10+)
Use these bulbous dark olive-green, orange or red chillies judiciously as they're extremely fiery. Used mostly in Mexican dishes.

Spices

The Yin and Yang principle: certain spices complement each other, cardamom goes with cloves, cassia with peppercorns, cumin with coriander and garlic with ginger. One is sweet and delicate, the other potent and pungent.

Galangal
This ginger variety is available in SA mostly in dried form. Soak it in water for at least 1 hour before use. It has a more lemony and peppery taste than ordinary ginger.

Star anise
The fruit of an Eastern tree and as the name indicates the spice is star-shaped. The fruit is picked before it ripens then left to dry. Star anise is used to flavour sweet and savoury dishes and combines well with beef and duck.

Cardamom
The spice of the moment. The seeds have a distinctive flavour that impart a wonderful taste to curries and desserts. No wonder some call it the spice of life.

Curry leaves
These pointy leaves with their spicy, lemony flavour are available fresh or dried. The fresh leaves obviously have more flavour. They're widely used in Asian cooking, especially in curry dishes. Ask your greengrocer to order fresh curry leaves from KZN.

PIES AND QUICHES

Chicken pie reminds me of Christmas on the farm, venison pie of a trip to the Kalahari and tomato tarte Tatin of seaside suppers. Quiches are great for entertaining or light suppers. We've included fool-proof pastry recipes, including puff pastry.

Pastry to pick and choose

Here are various kinds of pastry in varying degrees of flakiness which you can easily make at home. Even the recipe for puff pastry is easy. The recipes were all sourced and tested by YOU's former assistant food editor, Daleen van der Merwe.

Rich shortcrust pastry

Rich shortcrust pastry is ideal for quiches. It's crisp and more moisture resistant than ordinary shortcrust pastry.

375 ml (1½ c) cake flour
1 ml (pinch) salt
125 g chilled butter, diced
1 egg yolk, lightly whisked
5 ml (1 t) lemon juice
20 ml (4 t) ice-cold water

Put the cake flour and salt in a food processor and add the diced butter. Pulse until the mixture resembles fine breadcrumbs. Add the egg yolk, lemon juice and ice-cold water and process until the ingredients just bind. Turn out the pastry onto a floured work surface and lightly gather it into a ball. Cover with clingfilm and chill for at least 1 hour. Remove from the fridge and leave to rest at room temperature for a while before carefully rolling out. Chill for 20 minutes before baking.

Makes enough for lining a 30 cm quiche tin.

TO MIX BY HAND
Sift together the flour and salt and lightly rub in the butter with your fingertips until the mixture resembles breadcrumbs. Whisk together the egg yolk, lemon juice and ice-cold water and add just enough of the liquid to bind the pastry. Gather into a ball, cover with clingfilm and chill.

Variations
Wholewheat: Substitute wholewheat flour for 150 ml of the cake flour.
Sweet shortcrust pastry: Sift in 30 ml (2 T) caster sugar with the flour.
Substitute **phyllo or puff pastry** for shortcrust pastry when making a quiche or savoury tart. Brush each layer of phyllo pastry with butter before layering them.

HOW TO MAKE PERFECT SHORTCRUST PASTRY
- Use ice-cold butter and water to make the pastry.
- Handle the dough as little as possible.
- Leave the pastry to rest in the fridge before rolling it out and before baking it.
- Roll out the pastry carefully: do not stretch or pull it, also when lining the tin.
- An easy way to line the tin is to roll the pastry onto the rolling pin and to unroll it over the tin. Lightly press the pastry onto the base and along the sides of the tin.

PIE TINS
A flan tin with a loose bottom is the most suitable for baking quiches. For pies with a runny filling preferably use a pie dish. Cheesecakes are mostly baked in a loose-bottomed spring-form tin which is deeper than a flan tin. The pie tin or dish measurement given in a recipe refers to the base. Put a loose-bottomed tin on a baking sheet before putting a quiche or pie in the oven; because the bottom is loose a little of the filling may leak out.

LINING A QUICHE TIN OR PIE DISH
Roll out the pastry about 4 cm bigger than the quiche tin or pie dish. Lift the pastry onto a rolling pin to prevent it breaking and ease it into the tin or dish. Dust your fingers with flour and gently push the pastry into the corners and up the sides of the tin or dish. Roll the rolling pin over the tin or dish to trim the excess pastry. Gently ease the pastry over the rim of the tin or dish. Prick the base with a fork and leave the pastry shell to rest in the fridge for 30 minutes before baking it.

HOW TO BAKE PASTRY BLIND

To bake a pastry crust blind means to bake it without a filling.
There are three ways that work well:

Brushed with egg white: The easiest but not necessarily the most efficient method is to lightly brush the pastry with whisked egg white and to then bake it at 200 °C until the crust is just done but not brown.

With baking paper and beans: Cover the pastry with a sheet of baking paper, ensuring it overlaps the quiche tin. Fill the pastry shell with dried beans or raw rice and bake at 200 °C for 10–15 minutes. Remove the baking paper and beans and bake for another 5–10 minutes until the pastry casing is just done but not browned.

With light-weight aluminium foil: Cover the pastry with light-weight aluminium foil, ensuring it overlaps the sides of the quiche tin. Lightly press the foil onto the pastry, working it into the corners and up the sides of the tin. This will ensure the crust retains its shape during the baking process. Bake for about 15 minutes at 200 °C, remove the aluminium foil and bake for another 5–10 minutes at 180 °C or until the pastry casing is done but not browned as it will be baked again.

Sour-cream pastry

The sour cream gives the pastry a fine, crumbly melt-in-the-mouth texture.

500 ml (2 c) cake flour
2 ml (½ t) salt
100 g ice-cold butter
7 ml (1½ t) vinegar or lemon juice
150 ml sour cream

Sift together the flour and salt. Grate the butter over the flour and rub in roughly. Mix the vinegar and sour cream and stir the mixture into the flour mixture. Mix lightly with a fork until the pastry holds together. Press gently with your hands to mix well. Chill in the fridge for at least 2 hours. Roll out the pastry between 2 sheets of wax paper and use as needed.

Hot-water pastry

Hot-water pastry contains less butter or margarine, making it less flaky. The layers are slightly thicker and the pastry doesn't rise as much as puff pastry. Hot-water pastry is perfect for sausage rolls and tartlets.

500 ml (2 c) cake flour
2 ml (½ t) salt
250 g ice-cold butter, grated
1 egg yolk
5 ml (1 t) ice-cold water
5 ml (1 t) lemon juice
125 ml (½ c) boiling water

Sift together the flour and salt in thin layers, alternating them with layers of the grated butter to distribute the flour and butter evenly. Whisk together the egg yolk and ice-cold water and sprinkle over the flour mixture. Rub in gently with your fingers. Add the lemon juice to the boiling water and rapidly cut into the flour mixture to form a slack pastry. Leave the pastry to rest in the fridge overnight. Roll out to a thickness of 5 mm on a floured surface. Fold into thirds and refrigerate again. Roll out gently and use as needed.

Oil pastry

This is the easiest of all pastries. The pastry is made without butter so doesn't form flaky layers.

500 ml (2 c) cake flour
10 ml (2 t) baking powder
5 ml (1 t) salt
80 ml (⅓ c) oil
170 ml milk or water

Sift together the flour, baking powder and salt. Mix the oil and milk and cut into the dry ingredients with a knife. Divide the pastry in half and chill for at least 2 hours. Roll out between 2 sheets of wax paper and use as needed.

Stirred pastry

The ingredients for this quick pastry are stirred together. It requires no rolling out.

180 ml (¾ c) milk
160 ml (⅓ c) oil
2 eggs
300 ml cake flour
15 ml (1 T) baking powder
1 ml (pinch) salt

Stir together all the ingredients and spoon over the filling.

Quick puff pastry

Puff pastry contains the most fat of all pastries, giving it a delicate, flaky texture. This flop-proof recipe comes from master baker and food writer Carolié de Koster of Gauteng.

500 ml (2 c) cake flour
1 ml (pinch) salt
250 g ice-cold butter
   or margarine, grated
1 egg yolk
15 ml (1 T) white wine vinegar
125 ml (½ c) ice-cold water

Combine the flour and salt. Add the butter or margarine and mix lightly with a fork to separate the butter flakes. Do not break them up too much.

Whisk together the egg yolk, vinegar and water and add to the flour mixture. Mix with a fork until just blended – the pastry will still be slightly crumbly.

Shape the pastry into a ball and put on a floured surface. The pastry will still not be evenly mixed.

Dust the work surface, pastry and rolling pin with flour. Roll the pastry into a 2 cm thick rectangle.

Fold the short sides of the rectangle inwards so they meet in the middle.

Fold the other 2 sides inwards so they also meet in the middle.

Dust the work surface, pastry and rolling pin with more flour if necessary and roll out the pastry again. Repeat the folding process and roll out again.

Repeat the folding and rolling out process four more times. After each rolling process the pastry will look smoother. If the pastry becomes warm or the shortening becomes soft chill it after each rolling and folding process. Put the pastry in a plastic bag and chill for at least 2 hours before using. Roll out the pastry gently without stretching it and avoid rolling over the edges of the pastry onto the work surface.

The secret when making pastry is that it must remain as cold as possible to ensure the butter or margarine flakes stay intact. This gives the pastry its characteristic flaky texture.

Proceed as follows:
Put the butter or margarine in the freezer, grate it and return it to the freezer.
Put the flour in the fridge the day before or if you're short of time in the freezer for 1 hour.
Chill the mixing bowl in the freezer.
Handle the dough as little as possible and if it becomes warm put it in the fridge to cool before proceeding.
Shape the sausage rolls or tartlets and chill in the fridge. This will prevent the pastry shrinking while baking.

Pies
Old-fashioned chicken pie

When I think of pies a chicken pie with puff pastry on the top and bottom always springs to mind. Every Christmas on the farm chicken pie was the favourite on the menu. This recipe is for an old-fashioned chicken pie seasoned with bay leaf, allspice and lemon. Minette van Rensburg of Brits shared her mother-in-law's standby recipe with us.

PASTRY
2 x recipe puff pastry (see p. 128)
1 egg yolk, lightly whisked
   to brush the pastry shell

FILLING
2 kg chicken pieces, excess skin
   and fat removed
2 large onions, roughly chopped
1 clove garlic, crushed
salt and freshly ground black pepper
10 ml (2 t) light brown sugar
300 ml water
1 bay leaf
10 allspice berries
24 black peppercorns
30 ml (2 T) sago, soaked in water
   for a few hours
30 ml (2 T) vermicelli, broken into pieces
30 ml (2 T) butter
2 egg yolks, whisked
juice of 2 lemons
2 hard-boiled eggs, sliced

> **Variations**
> Add a few sprigs chopped fresh thyme for extra flavour.
>
> For a creamier filling add a little cream, sour cream or plain yoghurt or even cream cheese or creamed cottage cheese to the thickened stock.
>
> Add about 100 g chopped smoked ham to make a chicken and ham pie.

PASTRY
Prepare the pastry as described and chill until needed.

FILLING
Put the chicken, onions, garlic, salt, pepper, sugar and water in a saucepan. Tie the bay leaf, allspice berries and black peppercorns in a piece of muslin and add it to the saucepan. Bring to the boil, reduce the heat and simmer slowly until the chicken is done and falls off the bone. Remove the bouquet garni and chicken. Debone the chicken and cut the meat into smaller pieces.

Grease a large ovenproof dish or two smaller pie dishes with butter, margarine or nonstick food spray. Add the sago, vermicelli and butter to the stock in the saucepan and stir over low heat until it begins to thicken. Whisk together the egg yolks and lemon juice and beat in a little of the hot stock. Add the egg yolk mixture to the remaining stock in the saucepan and simmer gently for 1 minute. Return the chicken pieces to the saucepan and heat through. Leave to cool.

On a floured surface roll out the pastry until 3–4 mm thick. Cut out pieces of pastry to line the base and sides of the pie dish. Spoon the cooled chicken filling into the pie dish and arrange the hard-boiled egg slices on top. Brush the pastry edges with the whisked egg yolk. Cut another piece of pastry to cover the filling, press the pastry edges firmly together and brush the top with the whisked egg yolk. Prick holes in the pastry topping with a fork or make a small incision in the middle to allow the steam to escape. Chill for 30 minutes.

Meanwhile preheat the oven to 200 °C. Bake the chilled pie for 15 minutes, reduce the temperature to 180 °C and bake for another 20 minutes or until the pastry is crisp and golden.

Serves 6–8.

Creole chicken pie

The paprika, cumin and Cajun spice in this chicken pie give it extra kick. Make individual pies by spooning the filling into small ramekins and topping them with phyllo pastry.

20 ml (4 t) olive oil
3 rashers bacon, chopped
2 leeks, sliced
4 cloves garlic, crushed
1 medium-sized yellow pepper,
  seeded and chopped
1 stalk celery, chopped
1 carrot, scraped and chopped
10 ml (2 t) paprika
10 ml (2 t) ground cumin
10 ml (2 t) Cajun spice
10 ml (2 t) chopped fresh thyme
1 kg chicken pieces, deboned
40 ml cornflour
20 ml (4 t) water
250 ml (1 c) chicken stock
80 ml (⅓ c) sour cream or plain yoghurt
salt and freshly ground black pepper
6 sheets phyllo pastry
50 g butter, melted

Preheat the oven to 200 °C and grease 6 small 250 ml (1 c) ovenproof ramekins with butter, margarine or nonstick food spray.
    Heat the oil in a pan and stir-fry the bacon, vegetables, spices and thyme until the leeks are soft. Add the chicken and stir-fry until the chicken is done. Blend the cornflour and water and add to the chicken mixture. Add the chicken stock and stir until the mixture comes to the boil and thickens. Remove from the heat, stir in the sour cream and season with salt and black pepper to taste.
    Spoon the chicken mixture into the prepared ramekins. Brush the phyllo pastry sheets with the melted butter. Scrunch the sheets and place them on top of the filling in the ramekins. Bake for about 20 minutes or until the pastry is golden.

Serves 6.

Pinotage chicken pie

During Cape governor Simon van der Stel's time poultry was mostly pot-roasted and turned into ragout or pie. Chicken was the most common kind of poultry and chicken pie topped with puff pastry the favourite poultry dish. This recipe is a two-in-one dish combining the French classic, coq au vin or chicken cooked in red wine, which is then topped with pastry to turn it into pie. This is one of Beyerskloof winemaker Beyers Truter's signature dishes.

CHICKEN
100 g butter
16 chicken pieces
salt and freshly ground black pepper
250 g pickling onions, peeled
1 clove garlic, crushed
175 g lean bacon, finely chopped
250 g (1 punnet) button mushrooms
80 ml (⅓ c) cake flour
300 ml chicken stock
600 ml pinotage

PASTRY
1 x recipe sour-cream pastry
  (see p. 127)
milk and egg yolk to brush on top

Preheat the oven to 190 °C and grease a medium-sized ovenproof dish with butter, margarine or nonstick food spray.

CHICKEN
Melt the butter in a large saucepan. Season the chicken pieces with salt and pepper and brown. Remove from the saucepan and set aside. Stir-fry the onions, garlic, bacon and mushrooms in the same saucepan until slightly browned. Stir in the flour. Add the stock and wine and bring to the boil. Return the chicken pieces to the saucepan. Reduce the heat and simmer slowly until the chicken is tender and the sauce has thickened slightly. Remove the chicken from the saucepan and leave to cool slightly. Remove the bones and spoon the chicken meat and sauce into an ovenproof dish and leave to cool completely. Roll out the pastry and cover the filling. Cut out shapes from the remaining pastry and use to decorate the pastry. Brush the pastry with a little milk and egg yolk and bake for about 30 minutes or until golden.

Serves 6–8.

Oxtail pie

This pie was a hit among *YOU's* editorial staffers.

60 ml (¼ c) cake flour
salt and freshly ground black pepper
2 kg oxtail, cut into pieces at the joints
100 ml oil
2 large cloves garlic, crushed
1 large onion, chopped
2 carrots, sliced
1 stalk celery, chopped
200 g smoked bacon, chopped
250 ml (1 c) dry red wine
4 sprigs fresh thyme
1 sprig fresh rosemary
4 sprigs fresh parsley
2 bay leaves
750 ml (3 c) beef stock
80 ml (⅓ c) tomato paste
1 x recipe sour-cream or hot-water
   pastry (see p. 127)
1 packet (250 g) pitted prunes (optional)
1 egg yolk, whisked

Mix the flour, salt and pepper in a plastic bag. Add the oxtail pieces and shake well to coat them with the flour mixture. Heat 80 ml (⅓ c) of the oil in a large pan and brown the oxtail in batches.

Heat the remaining oil in a large saucepan or pressure cooker and stir-fry the garlic, onion, carrots, celery and bacon until lightly browned. Add the wine and simmer uncovered to reduce the wine by half. Tie the herbs and bay leaves together with a piece of string and add to the vegetable mixture. Add the stock, tomato paste and oxtail, stirring well to mix. Cover and cook for 3 hours (90 minutes if pressure-cooking) or until the meat is soft and falls off the bone. Remove the bouquet garni and leave the meat to cool.

Grease a large ovenproof dish. Roll out the pastry on a floured surface and use to line only the base of the greased dish. Skim the fat from the meat and remove the bones. Add the prunes to the meat mixture and spoon it into the pastry-lined dish. Cut out another piece of pastry to cover the filling, place on top and brush with the egg yolk. Chill for 30 minutes.

Meanwhile preheat the oven to 200 °C. Bake the pie for 15 minutes, reduce the temperature to 180 °C and bake for another 20 minutes or until the crust is crisp and golden.

Serves 8.

Tips
If desired remove all the bones from the meat mixture. I, however, love eating the last morsels of meat off the bone by hand. This pie can also be made with lamb shanks.

Pierce a hole in the pastry with a testing skewer to allow the steam to escape while the pie is baking. This prevents the pastry from becoming soggy instead of deliciously crisp and flaky.

Oxtail pie

Venison pie

After cutting biltong from game killed for the pot the leftover bits of meat were cooked until fine. This meat makes the best venison pie.

FILLING
2 kg shoulder of venison,
   cut into 25 mm cubes
250 ml (1 c) buttermilk
500 g lamb shanks, cut into pieces
25 ml (5 t) oil
1 litre (4 c) water
1 onion spiked with 10 whole cloves
2 bay leaves
5 ml (1 t) ground coriander
15 ml (1 T) salt
beef stock

SAUCE
2 onions, chopped
30 ml (2 T) oil
250 ml (1 c) red wine
125 ml (½ c) wine vinegar
15 ml (1 T) prepared mild mustard
30 ml (2 T) cornflour, blended with
   a little water

PASTRY
1 x recipe stirred pastry (see p.127)
1 onion, sliced in rings (optional)

FILLING
Coat the venison with the buttermilk and marinate for 2 days in the fridge. Pat the meat dry with paper towels. Brown the lamb shanks in heated oil in a large heavy-bottomed saucepan. Remove with a slotted spoon and set aside. Brown the venison in the same saucepan, remove from the pan and set aside.

Pour off any excess oil and put the remaining filling ingredients in the saucepan. Bring to the boil and return the venison and shanks to the saucepan. Cover and simmer slowly for 2–3 hours or until the meat falls off the bones. Leave to cool, remove the bones and cut the meat into smaller pieces. Keep the sauce in the saucepan and fill up with beef stock to make 500 ml (2 c). Keep aside.

Preheat the oven to 200 °C. Grease a 2 litre ovenproof dish.

SAUCE
Sauté the onions in the oil until golden. Add the wine and vinegar and boil rapidly until the liquid has reduced to about 45 ml (3 T). Add the 500 ml (2 c) meat sauce and mustard. Thicken with the cornflour paste. Mix the meat and sauce and spoon into the prepared dish.

PASTRY
Prepare the pastry as described and spoon over the meat mixture in the dish. Put onion rings on top if desired and bake for about 20 minutes or until the crust is done and golden brown.

Serves 8.

Puff pastry tartlets

These tasty open-face tartlets are each attractively decorated with a row of tomato halves.

150 g black olives, pitted
4 anchovies in oil, drained
40 g capers
15 ml (1 T) Dijon mustard
30 ml (2 T) olive oil
400 g puff pastry, bought or homemade (see recipe p. 128)
1 egg yolk, whisked
10 plum tomatoes, halved
fresh thyme leaves
fresh basil leaves
fresh rosemary leaves

Preheat the oven to 200 °C and grease a baking sheet with butter, margarine or nonstick food spray.

Pulse the olives and anchovies in a food processor until the olives are roughly chopped. Add the capers and pulse 5 times. Finally add the mustard and olive oil and pulse until the olives are just finely chopped.

Cut the puff pastry into 6 rectangles of 15 cm x 6 cm each and arrange them on the greased baking sheet. Brush the edges with the egg yolk. Spread the pastry rectangles with a little of the olive mixture (tapenade), leaving a 1 cm uncovered edge all around. Arrange 3 tomato halves on the tapenade and dot with more of the tapenade. Bake for 20–25 minutes. Sprinkle with the herb leaves and serve warm.

Makes 6.

Fish and vegetable pies

Once you've tasted these tartlets you won't want to touch commercial pies again.
Kids also love these tartlets.

125 ml (½ c) water
60 ml (¼ c) lemon juice
60 ml (¼ c) white wine
4 spring onions, chopped
300 g whites fish fillets, cubed
1 small broccoli, broken into small florets
2 egg yolks
45 ml (3 T) sour cream
salt and freshly ground black pepper
250 ml (1 c) grated Cheddar cheese
20 ml (4 t) finely chopped fresh parsley
1 x recipe hot-water, oil or sour-cream
    pastry (see p. 127)
1 egg, whisked

Bring the water, lemon juice, white wine and spring onions to the boil in a pan or saucepan with a lid. Add the fish, cover, reduce the heat and simmer for 5 minutes. Drain the fish and discard the liquid. Blanch the broccoli in rapidly boiling water for 2 minutes and drain well. Mix the egg yolks, sour cream, salt, pepper, cheese and parsley in a mixing bowl. Add the fish and broccoli, mix well and leave to cool.

Grease a patty pan with butter, margarine or nonstick food spray. On a floured surface roll out the pastry to a thickness of 2–3 mm. Cut out 18 circles 10–12 cm in diameter. Line 9 of the patty pan hollows with pastry circles. Spoon the filling into the lined hollows. Brush the pastry edges with the whisked egg and cover the tartlets with the remaining pastry circles. Press the edges together and brush the tops with the whisked egg. Chill for 30 minutes.

Meanwhile preheat the oven to 200 °C. Bake the tartlets for 10 minutes, reduce the temperature to 180 °C and bake for another 15 minutes or until the pastry is pale brown.

Makes 9.

Butternut and cheese pie

The recipe for this delicious pie was developed by *YOU*'s former assistant food editor,
Daleen van der Merwe. She wraps the filling in the pastry which is beautifully plaited on top.

1 butternut, peeled and diced
50 ml fresh sage leaves
45 ml (3 T) olive oil
salt and freshly ground black pepper
1 x recipe sour cream or hot-water
    pastry (see p. 127)
150 ml grated Emmenthaler cheese
150 ml grated mozzarella cheese
100 ml grated Parmesan cheese
1 egg, lightly whisked

Preheat the oven to 200 °C.
Put the diced butternut in a roasting tin and sprinkle over the sage leaves and olive oil. Season with salt and pepper and mix gently. Roast for 15 minutes or until done – the butternut must not be mushy. Leave to cool.

On a floured surface roll out the pastry into a 36 cm x 25 cm rectangle. Spoon the cooked butternut down the middle of the pastry in a 13 cm wide strip. Mix the three cheeses and spoon on top of the butternut.

Cut the pastry diagonally in 2,5 cm strips on both sides of the filling. Fold the two uncut ends of the pastry over the filling. Brush the pastry strips with the whisked egg and fold them over the filling, alternating them from each side of the filling so they cross each other. Brush the top of the pie with more whisked egg and chill for 40 minutes.

Meanwhile preheat the oven to 200 °C. Bake the pie for 30–40 minutes or until the crust is golden brown.

Serves 4–5.

Ricotta and sun-dried tomato rolls

A delicious variation on conventional sausage rolls and much healthier.

300 g ricotta cheese
grated rind of 1 lemon
8 sun-dried tomatoes, quartered
15 ml (1 T) chopped fresh parsley
10 ml (2 t) chopped fresh basil leaves
2 eggs, whisked
salt and freshly ground black pepper
1 x recipe hot-water pastry (see
    p. 127)
1 egg, lightly whisked
30 ml (2 T) sesame seeds

Grease a baking sheet with butter, margarine or nonstick food spray.

Press the ricotta cheese through a sieve or blitz it in a food processor until smooth. Add the lemon rind, sun-dried tomatoes, herbs and 2 eggs. Season with salt and pepper and spoon the filling into a plastic bag or piping bag with a wide nozzle. Chill until needed.

Roll out the pastry into a 3 mm thick rectangle. Trim one of the long edges of the pastry. Snip off a corner of the plastic bag and pipe the filling down the trimmed pastry edge.

Roll the pastry over the filling to cover it. Brush whisked egg down the seam and cut the pastry. Repeat the process until all the filling has been used. Brush the rolls with the whisked egg and sprinkle with sesame seeds. Prick the pastry at regular intervals with a fork and cut the rolls into 5–6 cm lengths. Put them on the prepared baking sheet and chill for 40 minutes.

Meanwhile preheat the oven to 200 °C. Bake the rolls for 10 minutes, reduce the temperature to 180 °C and bake for another 15–20 minutes or until golden.

Makes about 24.

Mushroom and goat's cheese tart

For best results use a semihard goat's cheese such as gotino, which has the same texture as mozzarella cheese. Alternatively use goat's feta cheese.

400 g puff pastry
4 large brown mushrooms
165 g sun-dried tomato pesto
salt and freshly ground black pepper
250 g goat's cheese
1 egg yolk, whisked with 15 ml (1 T) water
100 g piquanté peppers
10 ml (2 t) fresh thyme

Preheat the oven to 200 °C and grease a baking sheet with butter, margarine or nonstick food spray.

Cut the puff pastry into an 18 cm x 35 cm rectangle and put it on the greased baking sheet. Wipe the mushrooms with damp paper towels (do not wash them in water). Remove and discard the mushroom stems. Spoon 15 ml (1 T) pesto into each mushroom hollow. Season with salt and pepper.

Divide half the goat's cheese among the stuffed mushrooms. Spread the puff pastry with the remaining pesto, leaving a 2 cm pastry edge. Brush the pastry edge with the whisked egg yolk mixture. Arrange the mushrooms in a row down the middle of the pastry, packing them tightly together. Stuff the piquanté peppers with the remaining goat's cheese and arrange them on both sides of the mushrooms. Scatter the thyme leaves on top and bake for about 25 minutes or until the pastry is golden and the cheese begins to melt.

Serves 4.

Mushroom and goat's cheese tart

Quiches
Basic egg custard

This egg custard is enough to fill a 30 cm pie crust. Use any of the fillings with the custard.

250 ml (1 c) full-cream milk
125 ml (½ c) cream
3 extra-large eggs
1 ml (pinch) mustard powder
salt and freshly ground black pepper

Whisk together the milk, cream and eggs. Season to taste with mustard, salt and freshly ground black pepper and carefully pour over the filling in a baked pie crust.

Egg custard variations
Use milk instead of the cream and use 1 extra egg yolk.
Add 20 ml (4 t) pesto to the custard for extra flavour.
Add a pinch of cayenne pepper for extra bite.
Add finely grated Parmesan cheese.
For a lighter custard use yoghurt instead of cream.

Chorizo and tomato quiche

1 x recipe rich shortcrust pastry
  (see p. 124)
2 chorizo sausages, sliced
250 ml (1 c) grated mozzarella cheese
1 ml (pinch) cayenne pepper
1 x recipe basic egg custard (see recipe
  above)
1 large ripe tomato, peeled, seeded and
  thinly sliced
5 ml (1 t) dried oregano

Preheat the oven to 200 °C. Line a 30 cm quiche tin with the shortcrust pastry and bake blind as described on p.126.
  Stir-fry the chorizo slices in a hot pan until fragrant. Sprinkle the mozzarella cheese in the bottom of the pie crust and top with the chorizo slices. Add the cayenne pepper to the egg custard and carefully pour into the pie crust. Arrange the tomato slices on top and sprinkle with the oregano.
  Bake for 30–40 minutes or until set. Cool slightly and serve.

Serves 6.

Spinach, sweet pepper and feta quiche

1 x recipe rich shortcrust pastry
  (see p. 124)

FILLING
1 green pepper, seeded and finely
  chopped
15 ml (1 T) olive oil
250 ml x 4 (4 c) washed and shredded
  fresh spinach
salt and freshly ground black pepper
80 ml (⅓ c) crumbled feta cheese
1 x recipe basic egg custard
  (see recipe above)

Preheat the oven to 200 °C. Line a 30 cm quiche tin with the shortcrust pastry and bake blind as described on p. 126.

FILLING
  Meanwhile sauté the green pepper in the olive oil for about 1 minute or until fragrant. Add the spinach and sauté for about 1 minute or until it wilts. Remove the pan from the heat and season the spinach mixture with salt and freshly ground black pepper. Sprinkle the feta cheese over the bottom of the baked pie crust and spoon the spinach mixture on top, spreading it evenly. Carefully pour the egg custard on top. Reduce the oven temperature to 180 °C and bake for about 30–40 minutes or until set. Cool slightly and serve.

Serves 6.

Creamy cheese and onion quiche

1 x recipe rich shortcrust pastry
(see p. 124)

FILLING
2 large onions, very thinly sliced
15 ml (1 T) butter
5 chives, chopped
250 ml (1 c) finely grated mature
cheese such as Cheddar or
Emmenthaler
100 ml extra-thick cream
1 x recipe basic egg custard (see
recipe p. 138)
1 ml (pinch) ground nutmeg

Preheat the oven to 200 °C. Line a 30 cm quiche tin with the shortcrust pastry and bake blind as described on p. 126.

FILLING
Reduce the oven temperature to 180 °C. Sauté the onions in heated butter over low heat until golden brown and done. Add the chives, spoon the mixture into the pie crust and spread evenly. Add the cheese and cream to the prepared egg custard. Stir well and carefully pour the mixture over the onions. Sprinkle with the nutmeg and bake for 30–40 minutes or until set and golden brown. Remove from the oven, cool slightly and serve with a green salad.

Serves 6.

Variations
For a cheese quiche omit the onions and use piqaunté peppers instead.

Substitute 125 g chopped fried bacon, salami or ham for the onions.

Use 180 ml (¾ c) blue cheese and 60 ml (¼ c) Parmesan cheese and add 80 g rocket leaves to the onion mixture.

Add 125 ml (½ c) grated biltong if desired.

Make a vegetable quiche by roasting a variety of vegetables such as butternut, peppers and baby marrows along with plenty of chopped garlic. Spoon the mixture into the prepared pie crust along with the onion mixture and prepare as described.

For an interesting twist add about 125 ml (½ c) chopped fresh herbs such as parsley, oregano and thyme to the onion mixture.

Prepare small quiches. Use 10–12 small quiche tins (10 cm in diameter) and bake the quiches for 10–15 minutes or until set.

Tomato and basil quiche

1 x recipe rich shortcrust pastry
  (see p. 124)
9 ripe but firm tomatoes, sliced
250 g mozzarella cheese, thinly sliced
45 ml (3 T) basil pesto or tomato pesto
1 x recipe basic egg custard (see p. 138)
salt and freshly ground black pepper

Preheat the oven to 200 °C. Line a 30 cm quiche tin with the shortcrust pastry and bake blind as described on p. 126. Arrange a layer of the tomato slices in the pie crust, alternating them with layers of the mozzarella cheese so they overlap. Add the pesto to the egg custard and pour the mixture over the cheese and tomato filling. Season with salt and pepper. Bake for about 30 minutes. Reduce the oven temperature to 180 °C and bake for another 10 minutes or until set. Serve immediately.

Serves 6–8.

Variations
Substitute Roma tomatoes for the tomato slices. Bake the tomatoes beforehand. Sprinkle them with a little balsamic vinegar and sugar and bake for about 15 minutes.

Use feta cheese instead of the mozzarella cheese.

Snoek quiche

1 x recipe rich shortcrust pastry
  (see p. 124)
125 ml (½ c) grated Cheddar cheese
1 ml (pinch) cayenne pepper

FILLING
500 ml (2 c) flaked smoked snoek
2 hard-boiled eggs
125 ml (½ ml) sun-dried tomatoes
  in vinaigrette
15 ml (1 T) chopped chives
150 ml grated Cheddar cheese
1 x recipe basic egg custard (see p. 138)

Preheat the oven to 200 °C. Mix the cheese and cayenne pepper with the dry ingredients for the shortcrust pastry before adding the liquid. Proceed as described and line a 30 cm quiche tin with the pastry. Bake blind as described on p. 126.

FILLING
Mix the filling ingredients and spoon the mixture into the baked crust. Pour over the egg custard and bake for 30–40 minutes or until set.

Serves 6–8.

Variations
Substitute any other smoked fish such as mackerel or angel fish for the smoked snoek.

Add 80 ml (1/3 c) pitted black olives and 45 ml (3 T) chopped Italian parsley to the mixture.

Use feta cheese instead of Cheddar cheese.

Tomato and basil quiche

Savoury tarts and tartlets
1-2-3 tart

This savoury tart is incredibly quick to make, says Lizette Welthagen of Vanderbijlpark.
The basic tart ingredients are simply mixed and then fish, meat or vegetables are added.

1 large onion, chopped
375 ml (1½ c) grated Cheddar cheese
125 ml (½ c) cake flour
5 ml (1 t) mustard powder
10 ml (2 t) finely chopped fresh parsley
1 clove garlic, crushed
3 ml (generous ½ t) salt
3 extra-large eggs
500 ml (2 c) milk

Preheat the oven to 180 °C and grease a 30 cm x 15 cm ovenproof dish with butter, margarine or nonstick food spray. Stir together all the ingredients and add any of the variations to taste. Pour the mixture into the greased dish and bake for 30 minutes or until golden brown and set.

Serves 6.

Variations
Cooked bacon, spinach and feta cheese.
Flaked cooked haddock.
Tuna and asparagus.
Cooked mince and sweet peppers.

Mushroom phyllo tart

CRUST
6 sheets phyllo pastry, defrosted
melted butter

FILLING
40–60 ml (3–4 T) basil or sun-dried
   tomato pesto
6–8 large brown mushrooms,
   wiped clean
12 black olives, pitted and halved
sprigs fresh rosemary
125 g feta cheese
fresh pecorino or Parmesan cheese
   shavings for sprinkling on top
fresh basil leaves for sprinkling on top

Preheat the oven to 190 °C. Grease a baking sheet with melted butter.

CRUST
Brush each phyllo pastry sheet with melted butter and layer them on the baking sheet. Set aside.

FILLING
Spread a thin layer of pesto over the phyllo pastry and arrange the mushrooms, stem sides facing up, on the pastry. Arrange the olives and a few rosemary sprigs on top. Crumble the feta cheese and scatter over the olives. Bake for 15–20 minutes or until the cheese has just melted and the phyllo pastry is done and crisp. Cut into large squares, scatter pecorino cheese shavings and basil leaves on top and serve lukewarm.

Serves 6–8.

Tuna savoury tart

Lolita Munro of Uitenhage makes a cream cracker crust which she fills with a tuna and mushroom filling.

CRUST
1½ packets (300 g) cream crackers,
    crushed
180 g butter, melted

FILLING
15 ml (1 T) butter
1 onion, finely chopped
1 clove garlic, crushed
1 green pepper, finely chopped
2 cans (185 g each) tuna, drained
    and flaked
250 g (1 punnet) fresh mushrooms,
    thinly sliced
3 extra-large eggs, whisked
1 can (170 g) evaporated milk
salt and freshly ground black pepper

Preheat the oven to 180 °C and grease a 35 cm pie dish with butter, margarine or nonstick food spray.

CRUST
Mix the cream cracker crumbs and melted butter and press the mixture onto the base and against the sides of the pie dish. Chill.

FILLING
Heat the butter and gently sauté the onion, garlic and green pepper until just done. Remove from the pan and mix with the tuna. Stir-fry the mushrooms in the same pan until just done and combine with the tuna mixture. Beat the eggs and evaporated milk together and add to the tuna mixture. Season well with salt and black pepper and spoon the mixture into the prepared crust. Bake for about 30 minutes or until the filling has set. Serve hot or lukewarm.

Serves 6.

Variations
Add 250 ml (1 c) grated mature Cheddar cheese to the filling.

Substitute 300 g haddock for the tuna and cook in 250 ml (1 c) milk until done. Drain. Use the milk in which the haddock was cooked instead of evaporated milk. Proceed as described.

Mediterranean tartlets

We were treated to these tasty tartlets with their Mediterranean-inspired filling at the Langberg game farm near Kimberley.

1 x recipe rich shortcrust pastry (see
    p. 124)
410 g bottled sun-dried tomatoes,
    chopped
50 g black olives, pitted and finely sliced
375 ml (1½ c) onion marmalade
150 g feta cheese, crumbled

Preheat the oven to 180 °C and grease 10 small quiche tins (10 cm in diameter) with butter, margarine or nonstick food spray. On a floured surface roll out the dough to a thickness of 5 mm. Cut out pastry circles big enough to line the quiche tins. Line the tins with the pastry circles. Prick the pastry and chill until needed. Bake the pastry casings blind until just done as described on p. 126). Mix the sun-dried tomatoes, olives, onion marmalade and feta cheese.
  Spoon the filling into the pastry casings and bake for about 20 minutes or until the pastry is done and golden brown. Serve lukewarm.

Makes 10.

Herb and cheese tart

This tart is made with creamed cottage cheese mixed with herbs and piquanté peppers.

CRUST
8 sheets phyllo pastry
80 ml (⅓ c) melted butter or margarine

FILLING
45 ml (3 T) butter
3 large leeks, cleaned and thinly sliced
2 cloves garlic, crushed
10 piquanté peppers, finely chopped
4 extra-large eggs
125 ml (½ c) cream or yoghurt
125 ml (½ c) milk
250 g creamed cottage cheese
80 ml (⅓ c) finely grated
   Parmesan cheese
180 ml (¾ c) finely chopped fresh herbs,
   such as parsley, thyme, sage and rocket
salt and freshly ground black pepper

Preheat the oven to 180 °C and grease a 25 cm pie dish with butter, margarine or nonstick food spray.
   Brush each sheet of phyllo pastry with butter or spray with olive oil and line the pie dish with the pastry sheets, placing one layer on top of the other until the entire pie dish is lined. Roughly fold the loose ends inwards to give the tart a rustic appearance.

FILLING
Melt the butter in a heavy-bottomed saucepan and slowly sauté the leeks and garlic over low heat until soft and fragrant. Spread the leek mixture evenly over the bottom of the lined pie dish. Scatter the piquanté peppers on top. Whisk together the eggs, cream, milk and cottage and Parmesan cheeses. Stir in the herbs and season well with salt and freshly ground black pepper. Pour the egg mixture into the crust and bake for 30–35 minutes or until the filling has set. Remove from the oven and serve lukewarm.

Serves 6.

Crustless tartlets

With a basic savoury tart mixture it's easy to rustle up a selection of tartlets. Prepare the mixtures beforehand but bake the tartlets just before serving so they can be enjoyed lukewarm.

BASIC SAVOURY TART MIXTURE
500 ml (2 c) milk
5 extra-large eggs
125 ml (½ c) cake flour
1 small onion, grated
salt and freshly ground black pepper
250 ml (1 c) finely grated Cheddar
   cheese
60 ml (¼ c) finely grated Parmesan
   cheese

Preheat the oven to 200 °C and grease 2 muffin tins each with 12 hollows with butter, margarine or nonstick food spray. Whisk together the milk, eggs, cake flour, onion, salt and pepper. Add the cheeses and mix.
   Divide the mixture among 4 mixing bowls. Add the ingredients for one of the variations to each bowl. Fill the muffin tin hollows three-quarters of the way and bake for 15–20 minutes or until set. Cool slightly, remove with a pallet knife and serve lukewarm.

Makes 24.

Variations
Mushrooms and anchovies: Fry 125 g chopped mushrooms and 2 chopped anchovies until the mushrooms are tender. Add 250 ml (1 c) steamed spinach and 45 ml (3 T) chopped fresh parsley.

Baby marrows and piquanté peppers: Grate 2 baby marrows and mix them with 2 chopped piquanté peppers. Add 1 crumbled round of feta cheese.

Ham and asparagus: Mix 180 ml (¾ c) chopped ham with 180 ml (¾ c) drained asparagus tips. Add 60 ml (¼ c) crumbled blue cheese.

Basil and sun-dried tomatoes: Mix 30 ml (2 T) basil pesto, 60 ml (¼ c) chopped sun-dried tomatoes, 60 ml (¼ c) chopped cherry tomatoes and 60 ml (¼ c) chopped fresh basil.

Crustless tartlets

Upside-down tarts
Tomato tarte Tatin

This impressive tart is actually easy to make, says Mrs J Shelford of Marshalltown.

CHEESE PASTRY
200 ml cake flour
50 g cold butter, diced
50 g mature Cheddar cheese, grated
2 ml (½ t) prepared mustard
4 spring onions, chopped
ice-cold water

TOPPING
15 ml (1 T) olive oil
15 ml (1 T) butter
15 ml (1 T) caster sugar
9–10 medium-sized Roma tomatoes,
   halved

Quick tip
Use puff pastry instead of the
cheese pastry.

Preheat the oven to 200 °C.

CHEESE PASTRY
Combine the flour, butter and cheese in a food processor until the mixture resembles breadcrumbs. Alternatively rub the butter and cheese into the flour with your fingertips. Add the mustard and spring onions and mix gently. With the motor running add 30–45 ml (2–3 T) ice-cold water. Blitz until the mixture begins to form a ball. Wrap the pastry in clingfilm and chill for 20 minutes.

TOPPING
Heat the oil and butter in a 22–23 cm pan with an ovenproof handle. Add the sugar and heat until it begins to caramelise. Arrange the tomatoes in the pan and fry over high heat until glossy. Remove from the heat and cool slightly.

Gently roll out the pastry on a floured surface to a size slightly bigger than the pan. Put the pastry on top of the tomatoes and press to the inside of the pan.

Bake for 15–20 minutes or until golden brown. Leave to cool in the pan for 5 minutes. Gently loosen the crust and invert the tart on a plate. Serve the tarte Tatin with a green salad.

Serves 4.

Upside-down vegetable and bread tart

TOPPING
45 ml (3 T) olive oil
2 onions, sliced
3–4 cloves garlic, chopped
1 red pepper, seeded and diced
3–4 baby brinjals, halved
¼ small cauliflower, broken into smaller
   florets, or 250 g mushrooms
15 ml (1 T) balsamic vinegar
45 ml (3 T) grated Parmesan cheese
15 ml (1 T) chopped fresh parsley
salt and freshly ground black pepper

CRUST
250 g ready-made bread dough
fresh herbs to scatter on top

Preheat the oven to 190 °C.

TOPPING
Heat the olive oil in a frying pan with an ovenproof handle and sauté the vegetables over medium heat for 10 minutes. Remove from the heat and add the vinegar, Parmesan cheese, parsley, salt and pepper.

CRUST
Roll out the dough on a floured surface until slightly bigger than the pan. Cover the vegetables with the rolled-out dough and gently ease it down the sides of the pan. Leave the dough to rise slightly. Bake for 25–30 minutes or until a testing skewer comes out clean. Leave the tart to cool in the pan for 5 minutes. Invert it onto a serving platter and scatter sprigs of fresh herbs on top. Serve with balsamic vinegar and olive oil.

Serves 6–8.

Upside-down onion tart

Everyone at the *YOU* test kitchen loves blue cheese so whenever possible we add it to a dish.
This tart was inspired by one of Nigella Lawson's recipes – she uses red onions and Cheddar cheese.
Our variation is made with pickling onions and blue cheese.

TOPPING
10–15 pickling onions, peeled
10 ml (2 t) olive oil
15 ml (1 T) butter
salt and freshly ground black pepper
1 ml (pinch) dried or 5 ml (1 t) chopped
    fresh thyme
50 g blue cheese, crumbled
1 x recipe cheese pastry (see tomato
    tarte Tatin p.146)
sour cream to serve

Tip
Leave the inverted tin for a few
minutes before removing. This
will allow the vegetables or
fruit to sink onto the crust and
prevent them breaking when
the tin is removed.

Line a deep square cake tin with aluminium foil and grease
with butter.

TOPPING
Halve the pickling onions if fairly big. Heat the oil and butter in
a nonstick or heavy-bottomed pan. Add the onions and, stirring
continuously, braise over low heat for 20 minutes. Season with
salt, pepper and thyme. Spoon the onion mixture on the bottom
of the prepared tin and sprinkle over the blue cheese.
    Preheat the oven to 180 °C. Prepare the cheese crust as
described. Put the pastry on a bread board, shape it into
a square the size of the tin and put it on top of the onion
mixture. Bake for 30 minutes or until the pastry is done and
golden brown. Leave to stand for 5 minutes before inverting
onto a serving platter. Serve hot with a scoop of sour cream.

Serves 6.

Mediterranean upside-down tartlets

Delicious as a main course or brunch, lunch or side dish.

TOPPING
30 ml (2 T) olive oil
1 onion, halved and thinly sliced
12 button mushrooms, sliced
3 baby marrows, sliced into discs
1 red pepper, sliced into strips
1 yellow pepper, sliced into strips
5 cloves garlic, finely chopped
salt and freshly ground black pepper
8 cherry tomatoes, halved
12 black olives, pitted and halved
15 ml (1 T) chopped fresh basil
200 g feta cheese, crumbled

CRUST
400 g ready-made puff pastry,
    at room temperature

Preheat the oven to 190 °C and grease 6 small quiche tins.

TOPPING
Heat the oil in a pan and sauté the onion, mushrooms, baby
marrows, peppers and garlic until the vegetables are soft.
Season with salt and pepper. Remove from the heat and
add the tomatoes, olives, basil and feta cheese. Spoon the
vegetable mixture into the prepared tins.

CRUST
Roll out the pastry on a lightly floured surface. Cut out
circles slightly bigger than the quiche tins and place on top
of the vegetable mixture. Gently ease the pastry edges down
the inside of the tins. Bake for about 15 minutes or until the
pastry is puffed and golden.
    Leave the tartlets to cool in the tins for 5 minutes. Invert
the tins on a serving platter and leave for a few minutes
before removing them. Serve the tartlets at room temperature.

Serves 4–6.

PASTA AND PIZZA

Pasta and pizza come from Naples in the south of Italy but today they are enjoyed all over the world, including South Africa. Pasta was one of the first foreign foods South Africans took to and still enjoy experimenting with. Pasta is the perfect fast food: it takes only a few minutes to prepare, especially if mixed with a quick pasta sauce. Lasagne is also an old favourite. It's affordable and because it goes such a long way it's a regular on the menu in many homes.

Classic sauces

For our selection of pasta sauces we dipped into Paoli Liberti's book, *Bravo! The Stylish Man's Guide to Italian Cooking*. Here are some old favourites.

Spaghetti alla puttanesca
(Prostitute's spaghetti)

This is an old recipe from Naples. *Puttana* means prostitute, which has led to several explanations for the name of the sauce. Some say it's because the sauce is quick, affordable and hot. Others say the sauce was invented by the girls to enjoy an affordable, quick meal in between working.

50 ml olive oil
40 ml butter
3 cloves garlic, finely chopped
4 anchovies
150 g black olives, drained,
   pitted and halved
1 can (420 g) Italian tomatoes or 350 g
   fresh cherry tomatoes, halved
30 ml (2 T) capers, rinsed
½ red chilli, seeded and finely chopped
salt and freshly ground black pepper
500 g spaghetti
30 ml (2 T) chopped fresh parsley

Heat the oil and butter in a large pan over medium heat and sauté the garlic and anchovies until the garlic begins to change colour and the anchovies disintegrate. Add the olives, tomatoes, capers and chilli and simmer for 20 minutes. Season with salt and pepper. Meanwhile cook the spaghetti according to the packet instructions. Drain and add the cooked pasta to the sauce in the pan. Simmer for a few minutes and spoon into a warm serving dish or divide among four plates. Scatter parsley on top.

Serves 4.

WHICH PASTA TO BUY
The best quality pasta you can buy is made from 100 per cent durum wheat, a hard grain that produces an elastic yet firm pasta that doesn't easily become soggy and floury and retains its shape when cooked.

Tip
Make the sauce first and cook the pasta only when the sauce is nearly done so you can serve it immediately.

Spaghetti alla puttanesca

Pasta all'amatriciana
(Pasta tubes with bacon and tomato sauce)

This classic sauce is a speciality of the village Amatrice in the Lazio region of Italy.
The main ingredient is pancetta, an unsmoked Italian bacon. The sauce is sometimes
made without tomatoes. It's similar to hot and spicy arrabbiata sauce.

45 ml (3 T) olive oil
150 g pancetta or bacon, cut into strips
1 small onion, finely chopped
½ red chilli, seeded and finely chopped
1 can (420 g) Italian tomatoes
30 ml (2 T) capers, rinsed (optional)
salt and freshly ground black pepper
500 g penne pasta
50 g grated fresh pecorino cheese

Heat the oil in a large pan and fry the pancetta until crisp.
Remove from the pan and set aside. Stir-fry the onion and
chilli for 3–4 minutes in the same pan until the onion is lightly
browned. Add the tomatoes, reduce the heat and simmer
for 10–15 minutes over medium heat. Add the capers and
return the pancetta to the pan. Season to taste with salt and
pepper. Meanwhile cook the pasta according to the packet
instructions and drain. Gently mix the sauce with the pasta
and spoon into a warm serving dish. Serve with pecorino.

Serves 4.

Fettuccine al Pacino
(Ribbon pasta with vegetable and tomato sauce)

If you want to cook like a real Italian, commercial pesto simply won't do. It's quick and easy to make
homemade pesto in a food processor. This sauce must be cooked slowly to allow the flavours to develop.

50 ml olive oil
4 cloves garlic, crushed
1 large onion, finely chopped
1 large carrot, scraped
  and finely chopped
1 stalk celery, finely chopped
30 ml (2 T) chopped fresh basil leaves
2 cans (420 g each) Italian tomatoes
salt and freshly ground black pepper
1 x recipe basil pesto (see p. 151)
30 ml (2 T) grated Parmesan cheese
50 ml cream
500 g fettuccine pasta
fresh basil leaves to garnish

Heat the olive oil in a large pan over medium heat and
sauté the garlic until soft. Add the vegetables, herbs and
tomatoes. Season with salt and pepper to taste and simmer
for 1 hour over medium heat. Add the pesto to the tomato
mixture. Stir in the Parmesan cheese and cream. Meanwhile
cook the pasta according to the packet instructions. Drain the
pasta and toss it with the sauce.
Spoon into a warm serving dish and garnish with fresh
basil leaves if desired.

Serves 6.

SHOULD COOKED PASTA BE RINSED?
Cooked pasta has a layer of starch on the surface, making it sticky when cooled. For dishes
such as lasagne, cannelloni or cold pasta salads where the pasta will be either cooked again or
used as is, it must be rinsed. For other dishes it's best to cook the sauce in advance and to then
immediately mix it with the cooked, drained pasta which must not be rinsed. If keeping the
pasta warm stir in 15 ml (1 T) or more oil to prevent it sticking together.

Basil pesto

Pesto is a raw, finely ground green sauce originally made with basil, salt, garlic, olive oil, Parmesan cheese and pine nuts. The name comes from the word *pestâ,* which means to crush.

4 cloves garlic

coarse salt

30 ml (2 T) pine nuts, toasted

30 g fresh basil

30–40 ml (6–8 t) olive oil

60 g Parmesan cheese, grated

Blend the garlic, salt, pine nuts and basil with a little of the olive oil in a food processor until roughly chopped. Add the remaining olive oil and Parmesan cheese and blitz until well blended but still slightly coarse. Store in the fridge until needed.

Makes about 150 ml.

Coriander pesto

Coriander pesto is not an authentic Italian sauce but a jar in the fridge comes in useful when you have to rustle up a quick meal.

25 ml (5 t) chopped fresh coriander
    leaves

60 ml (¼ c) chopped fresh parsley

20 ml (4 t) pine nuts or almonds

100 ml grated Parmesan cheese

5 ml (1 t) crushed garlic

30 ml (2 T) lime juice

125 ml (½ c) olive oil

salt and freshly ground black pepper

Put the pesto ingredients in a food processor and blitz until well blended.

Makes about 250 ml (1 c).

IDEAS WITH PESTO

Serve it with your favourite pasta.

Mix pesto with mayonnaise and use it as a dressing for potato salad.

Add sun-dried tomatoes and feta cheese and use as a pasta sauce.

Mix pesto with breadcrumbs and use as a crust for chicken breasts.

HOW TO COOK PASTA

Use 3 litres water to cook 500 g pasta and 1 litre extra water per 250 g extra pasta added. Bring the water to the boil and add 15 ml (1 T) salt per 500 g pasta. Add the pasta and stir occasionally to prevent it sticking together. Cook the pasta until *al dente* and drain.

WHICH PASTA WITH WHICH SAUCE?

Spaghetti is ideal with butter sauces or sauces with a cream or tomato base, while thinner kinds of pasta such as vermicelli and linguine (thin ribbon noodles) are ideal with seafood or olive oil sauces. Stubby pasta shapes such as penne, conchiglie (shells) and fusilli (spirals) are ideal for meat sauces and rich sauces with bigger ingredients such as pieces of sausage and vegetables because the hollows in the pasta hold the ingredients better. Alternatively serve these sauces with broad ribbon noodles.

Pasta carbonara
(Pasta with pancetta and eggs)

André Brink, deputy editor at *YOU's* sister magazine *Huisgenoot,* gave us this recipe. 'Years ago when I was a political reporter there was a restaurant near parliament in Cape Town that served the most wonderful pasta,'he recalls. 'I think they used a recipe like this one – one of my own concoctions.' Steer clear of this dish if you have high cholesterol or want to avoid rich dishes. You can use yoghurt instead of cream but the result is not as good, André says.

500 g pasta (spaghetti, fettuccine,
    tagliatelle or your favourite pasta)
45 ml (3 T) olive oil
4 spring onions, chopped
3–4 mushrooms, thinly sliced
150 g pancetta or bacon, chopped
salt and freshly ground black pepper
2–3 eggs
350 ml fresh cream (or half yoghurt
    for a less rich result)
125 ml (½ c) or more grated
    Parmesan cheese

Cook the pasta according to the packet instructions. Drain and set aside. Heat the oil in a large heavy-bottomed saucepan and sauté the spring onions and mushrooms for about 1 minute. Add the pancette or bacon and stir-fry for another 3–5 minutes or until crisp. Remove the saucepan from the heat. Add the pasta to the onion and bacon mixture in the saucepan and return it to the heat to keep warm. Season with salt and pepper to taste and remove from the heat. Whisk together the eggs, cream and half the cheese until the mixture is creamy and pour it over the pasta. The heat from the pasta will cook the eggs and heat the sauce. Return the pan to the heat for about 1 minute. Serve immediately with the remaining cheese.

Serves 4.

PASTA FACT FILE
Al dente means firm to the bite and *molto al dente* means very firm to the bite. No Italian will cook pasta until it's soft; it's ready when it's still firm and offers some resistance when chewed. The *molto al dente* stage is about 30–90 seconds before the *al dente* stage, depending on the kind of pasta. If a recipe calls for pasta *molto al dente* it means it's not eaten immediately and will be cooked in the oven or in the pan until done. The best way to test if pasta is done is to taste it.

HOW TO SERVE PASTA
Transfer the pasta to a warm dish and spoon the sauce on top. Toss lightly with a fork and spoon to coat the pasta with the sauce. Alternatively you can toss the sauce and pasta in the pan if it's big enough. Do not make the common mistake of serving the sauce on top of the pasta without tossing it.

VARIOUS KINDS OF PASTA
Long pasta is mostly round: spaghettini (thin spaghetti), spaghetti and linguine (thicker than spaghetti).
Ribbons are long and flat: fettuccine (thinner than tagliatelle), tagliatelle and pappardelle (the broadest of the three).
Tubes are short, thick and hollow: macaroni (the most common), penne (the ends look like pen nibs) and rigatoni (ridged tubes).

Pasta carbonara

Quick economical sauces

Creamy olive and pilchard pasta

Heather Hall of Fish Hoek says this dish is an ideal everyday supper dish but also to serve when entertaining guests. The combination of creamy fish, green pepper, mushrooms and olives is delicious.

30 ml (2 T) butter
1 large onion, sliced
2 cloves garlic, crushed
1 green pepper, seeded and
   sliced into strips
1 punnet (250 g) button
   mushrooms, sliced
5 ml (1 t) chopped fresh or 2 ml (¼ t)
   dried oregano
250 ml (1 c) fresh cream
few black olives, pitted and halved
   (to taste)
1 can (425 g) pilchards in tomato sauce,
   roughly flaked
salt and freshly ground black pepper
500 g spaghetti or fettuccine
30 ml (2 T) chopped fresh parsley
extra chopped olives and parsley

Heat the butter in a large heavy-bottomed saucepan over medium heat and sauté the onion and garlic until soft and fragrant. Add the green pepper, button mushrooms and oregano and sauté until the mushrooms are tender and done. Add the cream, reduce the heat and simmer slowly until the sauce thickens slightly. Add the olives and flaked pilchards to the sauce and simmer until heated through. Season to taste.

Meanwhile cook the pasta according to the packet instructions until just done, drain and add the parsley. Divide the cooked pasta between warm serving platters and spoon the sauce on top. Toss and serve immediately with a scattering of olives and parsley if desired.

Serves 6.

Pasta with creamy spinach and bacon sauce

Lisa-Anne Stone of Harare, Zimbabwe loves making this delicious dish over weekends.

SAUCE
15 ml (1 T) butter
1 medium-sized onion, chopped
1 clove garlic, crushed
½ packet (125 g) back bacon, diced
large pinch dried mixed herbs
300 g fresh spinach, washed, roughly
   chopped and steamed

WHITE SAUCE
20 ml (4 t) butter
15 ml (1 T) cake flour
250 ml (1 c) hot milk
salt and freshly ground black pepper

PASTA
500 g ribbon noodles
olive oil
60 ml (¼ c) grated Cheddar cheese
extra grated cheese to serve

SAUCE
Melt the butter and sauté the onion and garlic until soft and fragrant. Add the bacon and stir-fry until just done. Add the herbs and spinach and remove the pan from the heat.

WHITE SAUCE
Melt the butter in a medium-sized saucepan and stir in the flour. Heat for 1 minute, stirring continuously. Remove from the heat and gradually whisk in the hot milk. Return the saucepan to the heat, season and, stirring continuously, simmer until the sauce thickens and is done.

PASTA
Cook the pasta according to the packet instructions, drain and stir in 15 ml (1 T) olive oil to prevent the pasta sticking together. Add the onion and bacon mixture to the cooked white sauce and heat through. Remove the saucepan from the heat, add the cheese and stir until just melted. Taste and season if necessary. Divide the pasta among warm plates, spoon the hot sauce on top, toss and sprinkle with extra grated cheese. Serve immediately.

Serves 4.

Fusilli with meatballs in tomato sauce

Pasta with a Mexican twist. We used canned Mexican tomatoes so the dish takes only
a few minutes to prepare.

SAUCE
45 ml (3 T) olive oil
1 large onion, chopped
2 cloves garlic, finely chopped
1 red chilli, finely chopped
250 ml (1 c) vegetable stock
2 cans (420 g each) whole Mexican
   tomatoes, chopped
15 ml (1 T) tomato paste
salt and freshly ground black pepper

MEATBALLS
500 g extra-lean mince
1 egg, lightly whisked
250 ml (1 c) fresh breadcrumbs
3 ml (generous ½ t) ground cumin
1 clove garlic, finely chopped
salt and freshly ground black pepper
oil for frying

TO SERVE
500 g fusilli, cooked
freshly grated Parmesan cheese

SAUCE
Heat the oil in a heavy-bottomed saucepan and stir-fry the
onion for about 5 minutes over medium heat until it begins to
brown. Add the garlic and chilli and stir-fry for another
2 minutes. Increase the heat and add the stock. Bubble hard
for 5 minutes before adding the tomatoes and tomato paste.
Turn the heat to as low as possible and season to taste with
salt and pepper. Simmer till flavoursome and no longer watery.

MEATBALLS
Mix the ingredients for the meatballs and shape into walnut-
sized balls. Stir-fry the meatballs in heated oil until brown on
the outside. Add them to the tomato sauce in the saucepan
and simmer for 10–15 minutes. Spoon the sauce over the
pasta, toss and serve with Parmesan cheese.

Serves 6.

Linguine with mussels

One of the quickest and easiest ways to rustle up a meal is to stir a can or two of smoked mussels
into pasta. Delicious!

60 g butter
60 ml (¼ c) olive oil
2 cloves garlic, crushed
30 ml (2 T) chopped fresh parsley
2 cans (170 g) smoked mussels, drained
salt and freshly ground black pepper
250 g linguine (ribbon noodles)
Parmesan cheese shavings to garnish

Heat together the butter and oil and sauté the garlic until
fragrant. Add the parsley and mussels and sauté gently for
about 2 minutes, shaking the pan. Do not stir. Season to taste
with salt and black pepper. Meanwhile cook the linguine in
rapidly boiling salted water until al dente and drain. Divide
among the plates. Spoon the mussels on top of the pasta, pour
over the oil mixture and toss gently. Garnish with Parmesan
cheese shavings and serve with crusty bread and a green salad.

Serves 4.

Marinara sauce

Another quick seafood sauce.

Fry 1 chopped onion in 15 ml (1 T) oil. Add 80 ml (⅓ c) dry white wine, 80 ml (⅓ c) tomato paste and
2 cans (420 g each) whole tomatoes. Simmer for 10 minutes or until the sauce has thickened. Add 750 g
seafood marinara mix and heat for 5 minutes. Stir frequently. Add 60 ml (¼ c) roughly chopped fresh parsley
and season with salt and pepper. Add to cooked pasta and toss gently.

Pasta with frankfurters and asparagus

Magriet Espach of Levubu devised this dish combining sausages and asparagus. Rich and delicious.

20 ml (4 t) olive oil
1 clove garlic, crushed
1 small onion, sliced into rings
1 medium-sized leek or 2 smaller leeks,
    washed and sliced into rings
4 frankfurters, sliced
15 ml (1 T) cake flour
250 ml (1 c) hot milk
100 ml cream, cream cheese
    or crème fraîche
1 punnet (125 g) fresh asparagus, steamed
500 g pasta such as penne, macaroni
    or rigatoni
grated Parmesan cheese to serve
fresh ground black or lemon pepper

Heat the oil and sauté the garlic, onion and leek until soft and fragrant. Add the sliced sausages and stir-fry until the leeks and sausages begin to brown. Sprinkle over the cake flour and stir to mix. Remove the saucepan from the heat and gradually whisk in the hot milk and cream. Return the saucepan to the stove and heat, stirring continuously until the sauce thickens and is done. Add the asparagus to the cooked sauce and keep warm.

Cook the pasta according to the packet instructions, drain and mix with a little olive oil. Divide the cooked pasta among warm plates, spoon the sauce on top and sprinkle with grated Parmesan cheese and black pepper. Serve immediately.

Serves 4.

> **Tip**
> Instead of the white sauce use the same quantity basil pesto or sun-dried tomato pesto and toss it with the pasta along with the frankfurters, asparagus and other stir-fried vegetables.

Easy pasta with chicken

We slightly adapted the recipe sent to us by Vanessa Hartley of Bellville for a less creamy but equally delicious result.

500 g chicken breast fillets, cut into strips
oil for frying
1 green pepper, seeded and
    roughly chopped
200 g baby marrows, sliced into discs
250 g (1 punnet) button mushrooms,
    roughly chopped
10 ml (2 t) chopped fresh parsley
5 ml (1 t) paprika
salt and freshly ground black pepper
500 g pasta shells
olive oil
basil pesto
balsamic vinegar

Stir-fry the chicken strips in a little heated oil until nearly done. Add the green pepper, baby marrows and mushrooms and stir-fry until done but still crisp. Add the parsley and paprika. Season to taste with salt and pepper.

Meanwhile cook the pasta in rapidly boiling salted water until *al dente*. Add the chicken mixture to the pasta and toss gently. Drizzle with a little olive oil and stir in a few spoonfuls of pesto and a splash of balsamic vinegar.

Serves 4–6.

HOW MUCH PASTA TO COOK PER PERSON?
If serving pasta as a main course allow 80–250 g per person, depending on the kind and quantity of the sauce. Use more pasta if serving it with a simple sauce such as pesto or butter and herbs and less pasta if combining it with a more satisfying sauce made with tomato, cream or mince.

Pasta with frankfurters and asparagus

Pasta with three cheeses

Perfect for supper on a cold winter's evening. The three cheeses mixed into the pasta are blue cheese, mature Cheddar cheese and Parmesan cheese.

500 g fettuccine or tagliatelle
45 ml (3 T) butter
500 g portobello mushrooms,
   thickly sliced
100 g English spinach
100 g mature Cheddar cheese, grated
125 g Simonzola or Gorgonzola
   (blue cheese), crumbled
50 g Parmesan or Gruyère cheese, grated
salt and freshly ground black pepper
150 ml cream, heated to just below
   boiling point

Cook the pasta according to the packet instructions. Meanwhile heat the butter in a pan and stir-fry the mushrooms until tender. Remove from the heat. Drain the pasta and layer it in a warm serving dish, alternating it with the mushrooms, spinach and three cheeses. End with a layer of pasta. Season each layer with salt and pepper. Pour over the hot cream and toss gently. Serve immediately.

Serves 4.

Lite 'n creamy mushroom pasta

We used low-fat cream cheese and low-fat milk to make the sauce – it's still creamy but lower in kilojoules.

500 g fusilli (pasta spirals)
60 ml (¼ c) vegetable stock
1 clove garlic, crushed
500 g button mushrooms, thickly sliced
4 spring onions, roughly chopped
80–100 ml low-fat cream cheese
125 ml (½ c) low-fat milk
60 ml (¼ c) roughly chopped Italian parsley
20 ml (4 t) wholegrain mustard
125 ml (½ c) grated Edam cheese
45 ml (3 T) finely chopped fresh chives

Cook the pasta according to the packet instructions, drain and set aside. Bring the stock to the boil in a saucepan, add the garlic and mushrooms and stir-fry until tender and all the liquid has evaporated. Add the spring onions and stir-fry until soft. Add the cream cheese and milk and heat, stirring continuously until the sauce thickens slightly. Remove from the heat and stir in the pasta, parsley, mustard and cheese. Scatter the chives on top just before serving.

Serves 4.

Quick nut and herb sauce

This is another light sauce made with walnuts and ricotta cheese.

Heat 60 g butter in a heavy-bottomed saucepan. When the butter starts foaming add 250 ml (1 c) chopped walnuts and 200 ml pine nuts and stir-fry for 5 minutes. Add 30 ml (2 T) chopped fresh parsley, 10 ml (2 t) chopped fresh thyme, salt and pepper. Whisk together 60 ml (¼ c) ricotta cheese and 60 ml (¼ c) milk and add the mixture to the nut mixture. Season with salt and pepper and mix the sauce with the pasta.

Serves 4.

Baked pasta
Macaroni and brinjal cake

2–3 brinjals, sliced lengthways
salt
about 60 ml (¼ c) olive oil
1 clove garlic, crushed
1 onion, chopped
500 g chicken breast fillets, finely
  chopped OR 250 g back bacon
1 can (420 g) chopped tomatoes
30 ml (2 T) tomato paste
salt and freshly ground black pepper
125 g macaroni, cooked
250 ml (1 c) grated mozzarella cheese
125 ml (½ c) grated Cheddar cheese
1 egg, whisked
125 ml (½ c) grated Parmesan cheese

Preheat the oven to 180 °C. Grease a 23 cm nonstick spring-form cake tin. (An aluminium tin will react with the brinjal.)

Arrange the brinjal slices on a work surface, sprinkle with salt and leave for 20 minutes. Rinse well and pat dry with paper towels. Heat 30 ml (2 T) oil in a large saucepan and fry the brinjal slices a few at a time until brown on both sides. Add more oil as needed. Drain and set aside. Sauté the garlic and onion in the same pan until soft. Add the chicken, tomatoes, tomato paste, salt and pepper and simmer for 15–20 minutes. Using a wooden spoon mix the chicken mixture, cooked macaroni, mozzarella and Cheddar cheeses, egg and half the Parmesan cheese.

Line the bottom and sides of the tin with the brinjal slices, overlapping them slightly. Sprinkle half the remaining Parmesan cheese over the brinjal slices. Spoon the macaroni mixture into the tin, pressing it down firmly. Arrange the remaining brinjal slices on top and sprinkle over the remaining Parmesan cheese. Bake uncovered for 25–30 minutes or until golden brown. Leave to rest for 5 minutes before transferring the cake to a platter. Slice and serve hot.

Serves 6–8.

WHAT'S THE DIFFERENCE BETWEEN PARMESAN AND PECORINO CHEESES?
Parmesan is the common name for Parmigiano-Reggiano, the king of Italian cheeses. This cheese, which has been made according to the same method for the past 700 years, is unrivalled in quality, taste and texture. The production of authentic Parmigiano-Reggiano is limited by law to a fairly small region in the Emilia-Romagna region of Italy where the milk has a characteristic taste. Strict regulations require that each cheese be matured for at least 18 months before it is sold. Each cheese also bears a stamp of approval.

Parmesan and pasta go well together. The cheese can be added to sauces or grated on top of pasta. The strong flavour of the cheese combines well with meat, tomato, vegetable and cream sauces but is not recommended for use with mushroom or seafood sauces. Freshly grated Parmesan cheese is vastly superior to ready-grated cheese sold in sachets.

If buying a large chunk of Parmesan cheese cut it into smaller pieces, wrap each piece in clingfilm and then in aluminium foil and store in the fridge. The cheese will keep for several months. Use one piece at a time and grate it just before using.

Pecorino Romano is a hard sheep's milk cheese which is aged for about a year. It is sharper in flavour than Parmigiano-Reggiano so use less when grating it onto pasta. It also keeps for a long time.

Pasta cake

This is the ideal way to use leftover pasta such as macaroni and cheese. A pasta dish with a plain tomato or bolognese sauce also works well. Add egg and cook the pasta mixture in a frying pan to make a firm cake. Slice and serve hot or cold.

100 ml olive oil
50 g Parmesan cheese, grated
salt and freshly ground black pepper
4 eggs, lightly whisked
250 g of any cooked pasta dish

Heat half the oil in a large, deep frying pan. Add the Parmesan cheese, salt, pepper and eggs to the cooked pasta dish and mix. Spread the mixture evenly in the pan. Cook over medium heat until a crust forms at the bottom. Invert the cake onto a plate. Add the remaining oil to the pan and fry the other side of the cake until a crust forms. Turn out onto a plate. Slice and serve hot or cold.

Serves 4–6.

Spinach and tagliatelle bake

This baked pasta dish consists of layers of brinjal and spinach interspersed with ricotta cheese and olives mixed with tomato. Satisfying but not too rich.

45 ml (3 T) olive oil
1 brinjal, unpeeled, diced
200 g baby leaf spinach, roughly torn
salt and freshly ground black pepper
2 cans (420 g each) Italian chopped
    tomatoes
1 packet (250g) black olives, drained,
    pitted and roughly chopped
5 ml (1 t) sugar
500 g crumbly cottage or ricotta cheese
350 ml crumbled feta cheese
30 ml (2 T) chopped fresh parsley
500 g tagliatelle

Preheat the oven to 180 °C and grease a deep ovenproof dish with butter, margarine or nonstick food spray.
   Heat the olive oil in a large frying pan and stir-fry the brinjal until brown. Remove from the pan and set aside. Put the spinach in the same pan and cover it for a few minutes or until the spinach has wilted. Season with salt and pepper. Return the brinjal to the pan. Mix the tomatoes and olives and season to taste with salt, pepper and sugar. Set aside.
   Blend the cottage or ricotta cheese in a food processor until smooth and mix with the brinjal mixture. Add a third of the feta cheese and mix. Add the parsley and season with salt and pepper. Cook the tagliatelle in salted water until *molto al dente* and drain. Spread a third of the tomato mixture in the bottom of the greased dish. Cover the sauce with a third of the tagliatelle and spoon half the brinjal mixture on top. Sprinkle with a little feta cheese but reserve some for a final sprinkling on top. Repeat the layers, ending with a layer of the tomato mixture. Cover the dish with aluminium foil and bake for 20 minutes. Remove the aluminium foil and sprinkle over the remaining feta cheese. Bake uncovered for another 20 minutes. Leave to rest for 20 minutes before serving.

Serves 6.

WHAT ARE BOCCONCINI?
Bocconcini are small fresh, pale-white mozzarella balls packed in brine. They are delicious in salads or with vegetables. Use the yellowish mozzarella for dishes where the cheese is grated and melted, such as pizza.

Pasta cake

Quick macaroni bake

It's hard to believe this delicious dish is made with so few ingredients.

375 ml (1½ c) soft fresh breadcrumbs
4 extra-large eggs, separated
250 ml (1 c) milk or thin cream
375 ml (1½ c) grated Cheddar cheese
30 ml (2 T) chopped fresh parsley
375 ml (1½ c) cooked macaroni
salt and freshly ground black pepper
2 large ripe tomatoes, sliced

Preheat the oven to 180 °C and grease a medium-sized ovenproof dish with butter, margarine or nonstick food spray. Mix the breadcrumbs and egg yolks and add the milk, three-quarters of the cheese, parsley and cooked macaroni. Season generously. Whisk the egg whites with a clean, dry beater until soft peaks form and fold them into the mixture. Spoon into the prepared dish and arrange the tomato slices on top. Sprinkle with the remaining cheese and bake for 25–30 minutes or until set and golden brown on top. Serve hot with homemade tomato sauce (see p. 165 at tip).

Serves 6.

Variation
Add fried bacon or sausages to the dish if desired.

Basic cannelloni

This pasta bake with tuna, tomatoes and ricotta or cottage cheese makes a satisfying meal.

2 cans (185 g each) tuna chuncks in oil
1 large onion, chopped
3 cloves garlic, crushed
2 red peppers, seeded and diced
1 bunch spring onions,
    chopped (optional)
500 ml (2 c) ricotta cheese
salt and freshly ground black pepper
16 cannelloni tubes
3–4 cans (420 g each) whole tomatoes
    in their juice
1 ml (pinch) mixed dried herbs or fresh
    herbs such as chopped parsley
sugar
torn fresh basil leaves or
    5 ml (1 t) dried basil
125 ml (½ c) freshly grated Parmesan
    cheese

Preheat the oven to 180 °C and lightly grease a large, shallow ovenproof dish with butter, margarine or nonstick food spray.
    Drain the tuna and reserve the oil. Flake the tuna and set it aside. Heat 15 ml (1 T) of the drained tuna oil in a medium-sized saucepan. Sauté the onion and garlic until soft and fragrant. Add the red peppers and spring onions and sauté for another few minutes. Remove from the heat, add the ricotta, flaked tuna and season generously with salt and pepper.
    Cook the cannelloni tubes according to the packet instructions and stuff with the tuna mixture.
    Chop the tomatoes into small pieces and bring to the boil in a saucepan along with the juice and all the remaining ingredients except the Parmesan cheese. Simmer for 10 minutes or until the mixture is fragrant and has thickened slightly. Stir occasionally.
    Spoon half the sauce in the bottom of the ovenproof dish and arrange the stuffed cannelloni tubes on top. Spoon the remaining sauce over the tubes and scatter the basil leaves on top. Sprinkle with the Parmesan cheese and bake for 30–35 minutes or until heated through. Leave to rest for a few minutes before serving. Garnish with extra basil and serve with extra Parmesan cheese, bread rolls and a salad.

Serves 6.

Budget-beating tip
Roll up the filling in
lasagne sheets.

Variation
For an authentic Mediterranean flavour add a handful of pitted black olives.

Lasagne
Butternut and ricotta cheese lasagne

A delicious vegetarian lasagne that's quick and easy to make because you don't first have to make meat and white sauces.

PASTA
2 butternuts, peeled, seeds removed
    and cut into 5 mm slices
salt and freshly ground black pepper
50 ml olive oil
500 g lasagne sheets
500 g ready made pasta sauce (creamy
    sun-dried tomato and pecorino)

CHEESE LAYER
450 g ricotta cheese, pressed
    through a sieve
2 egg yolks, whisked
500 ml (2 c) grated mozzarella cheese
200 ml grated Parmesan cheese

Variation
Substitute a selection of vegetables, such as baby marrows and red and yellow peppers for the butternut. Substitute creamed cottage cheese for the ricotta cheese and stir in about 60 ml (¼ c) mayonnaise.

Preheat the oven to 180 °C and grease a deep ovenproof dish with butter, margarine or nonstick food spray.

PASTA
Arrange the butternut slices on a large baking tray. Season with salt and pepper and drizzle with olive oil. Bake for 20–30 minutes or until just soft. Cook the lasagne sheets according to the packet instructions. Carefully remove from the saucepan with a slotted spoon and transfer them to a dish filled with cold water. Drain and arrange the pasta sheets on a lightly oiled tray.

CHEESE LAYER
Mix the ricotta cheese, egg yolks and three-quarters of the mozzarella and Parmesan cheeses. Spoon a layer of the pasta sauce on the bottom of the prepared ovenproof dish. Cover with a layer of lasagne sheets. Arrange half the butternut slices on top. Spoon half the cheese mixture on top of the butternut layer. Repeat the layers of lasagne sheets, pasta sauce, butternut and cheese mixture, ending with a layer of lasagne sheets. Spoon over the remaining pasta sauce and sprinkle with the remaining mozzarella and Parmesan cheeses. Bake the lasagne in the preheated oven for 30–40 minutes or until golden brown on top.

Serves 8.

Tip
When using ready-made pasta sauces, check the ingredients list on the jar to determine the quality: the more natural ingredients and the fewer preservatives, colorants, flavour enhancers and binding agents it contains, the better.

Delicious chicken lasagne

Chicken, garlic and white wine are a winning combination, especially if baked in a creamy sauce between soft pasta sheets. The perfect dish to make when entertaining family and friends.

60 ml (¼ c) olive oil
1 medium-sized onion, finely chopped
2 cloves garlic, crushed
250 g (1 punnet) brown
  or button mushrooms, sliced
7 ml (1½ t) fresh thyme
45 ml (3 T) cake flour
600 ml hot milk
150 ml dry white wine
salt and freshy ground black pepper
25 ml (5 t) sweet sherry (optional)
750 ml (3 c) cooked, shredded chicken
300 g fresh spinach, shredded
  and steamed
8 lasagne sheets (see tip)
grated Parmesan cheese

Tips
Substitute 2 cans (185 g each) tuna for the chicken. Use milk instead of wine and add a few spoonfuls of basil or sun-dried tomato pesto to the sauce.
  Use tagliatelle instead of lasagne sheets.

Preheat the oven to 180 °C and lightly grease a large, shallow ovenproof dish with butter, margarine or nonstick food spray. Heat the oil in a large saucepan and slowly sauté the onion and garlic until soft and fragrant. Add the mushrooms and sauté until tender and all the liquid has evaporated. Sprinkle over the thyme and cake flour, stir well and remove from the heat. Gradually add the milk, stirring until the mixture is smooth. Add the white wine, return the saucepan to the stove and heat while stirring continuously. Simmer slowly until the sauce thickens and is done. Season with salt and pepper and add the sherry. Leave to simmer for another few minutes, then remove from the heat. Cool slightly before adding the chicken. Spoon a little of the sauce in the bottom of the ovenproof dish and scatter over a third of the spinach. Arrange the lasagne sheets on top (do not let them overlap – rather break them into smaller sheets). Repeat the layers of sauce, spinach and pasta twice more and cover the top layer of pasta sheets with a final layer of sauce. Sprinkle generously with grated Parmesan cheese and bake for 30–35 minutes or until golden brown and done.

Serves 6–8.

Pizza

Pizza originates from the back streets of Naples where it was served as takeaway food. Today there's hardly a city or town in the world where you can't buy pizza. I like a pizza with a crisp, thin base and a generous topping, which is how it's made in Italy. If you prefer a thicker base bake the pizza a little longer.

Basic pizza

This is a basic recipe for a pizza base with a various toppings.

DOUGH
500 ml (2 c) cake flour
1½ packets (15 g) instant yeast
2 ml (½ t) sugar
1 ml (pinch) salt
160 ml (²/₃ c) lukewarm water

TOPPING
100 ml tomato and onion mixture (see tip)
20 black olives
12 slices salami, halved
salt and freshly ground black pepper
150 ml grated Cheddar cheese
150 ml grated mozzarella cheese

Combine the flour, instant yeast, sugar and salt in a bowl.

Add the lukewarm water and mix well to form a soft, manageable dough. It must be soft but not sticky. Add more flour if the dough is too slack.

Knead the dough for 5 minutes or until it is smooth and elastic and no longer sticks to your fingers. It's not necessary to knead the dough for too long as it contains a fair amount of yeast. Cover the bowl with a damp cloth or clingfilm and leave the dough to rest in a warm place for 30 minutes.

Preheat the oven to 220 °C and lightly grease a large baking sheet with oil.

Divide the dough into two equal parts. Sprinkle mealie meal or flour on a clean surface and flatten the dough with the palms of your hands or a rolling pin.

Put the dough circles on the prepared baking sheet and spread with a little of the tomato mixture. Bake for 5 minutes, then carefully remove from the oven.

Arrange the olives and salami on the pizzas and season with salt and pepper. Scatter over the Cheddar and mozzarella cheeses and return the pizzas to the oven. Bake for another 5–7 minutes or until the cheese has just melted.

> **Tip**
> Use ready-made canned tomato and onion mix or make it yourself: Stir-fry 2 chopped cloves garlic in 60 ml (¼ c) olive oil. Add 1 can (420 g) chopped, peeled tomatoes, season with salt and pepper and simmer for 10 minutes. Add 12 fresh basil leaves and simmer for another 5 minutes.

More pizza toppings

Arrange any of the following combinations on the tomato-covered pizza bases after they come out of the oven the first time. Sprinkle with mozzarella cheese and bake until the cheese has melted. Stack rocket leaves on top if desired. You can also sprinkle over extra Parmesan or pecorino cheese.

Combinations
Halved cherry tomatoes, chopped salami, asparagus pieces.
Diced ham or bacon, green pepper and banana.
Ham, salami or bacon, mushrooms and gherkins.
Anchovies, olives, halved cherry tomatoes and mushrooms.
Mince, green peppers and piquanté peppers.
Chorizo, cherry tomatoes, mushrooms and pineapple.
Olives, capers and mozzarella cheese.
Artichokes, salami and mushrooms.

Pan pizza with tuna topping

When you're short of time make a quick pan pizza instead of a yeast base.

DOUGH
500 ml (2 c) cake flour
15 ml (1 T) baking powder
2 ml (½ t) salt
30 ml (2 T) sugar
45 ml (3 T) cold butter or margarine,
    coarsely grated
180–200 ml mixture of buttermilk
    and 1 egg

TOPPING
tomato purée
2 cans (185 g each) tuna in brine, drained
100 g (1 packet) black olives, pitted
    and roughly chopped
a few gherkins, chopped
125 g (½ punnet) mushrooms, sliced
375 ml (1½ c) grated mozzarella cheese
oregano

Preheat the oven to 220 °C and grease a baking sheet with butter, margarine or nonstick food spray. Sift together the dry ingredients and rub in the butter with your fingertips until the mixture resembles breadcrumbs. Add the liquid a little at a time and cut it in with a spatula. (Do not overhandle the dough.) Put the dough on a floured surface and roll out gently to a thickness of 1 cm. Press the dough onto the baking sheet so it covers the base and forms a slight lip.

Spread the dough with the tomato purée and scatter the tuna, olives, gherkins and mushrooms on top. Sprinkle the cheese on top and season with salt, black pepper and oregano. Bake for 15–20 minutes or until the dough has risen and the cheese has melted.

Makes 1 large pizza.

> **Tip**
> To make a pizza in a large roasting tin make 1½ times the dough.

Pan pizza with pesto

Roll out 500 g ready-made bread dough until thin and press it down on a baking sheet. Peel 4 plum tomatoes and chop them roughly. Mix the tomatoes with 45 ml (3 T) basil pesto and spread the mixture over the dough base. Arrange a few rashers back bacon on top and sprinkle with grated mozzarella cheese. Bake at 200 °C for 10–12 minutes or until the base is done. Drizzle with olive oil and sprinkle with Parmesan cheese. Serve immediately.

Serves 4–6.

INTERESTING IDEAS WITH PIZZA

Pizza bites
Bake your favourite pizza and leave it to rest until lukewarm. Cut it into small triangles with a pizza cutter. Skewer a pitted olive and fresh basil leaf onto a cocktail stick and insert it into a pizza triangle.

Mexican bites
Substitute ready-made tortillas for conventional pizza bases. Cover with cooked leftover mince, onions and garlic. Scatter olives, loose-kernel sweet corn, kidney beans, chillies and mozzarella cheese on top and bake at 180 °C until the cheese has melted and the tortillas begin to change colour. Serve immediately.

Savoury wedges
Generously brush pizza bases with olive oil and sprinkle with ground cumin, sesame seeds, salt and black pepper. Bake until golden brown and crisp, cut into wedges and serve with a variety of dips.

Basic pizza

RICE AND NOODLES

With a good supply of rice and noodles (the Asian equivalent of Italian pasta) it's quick and easy to rustle up a meal. Dishes such as jambalaya, risotto and pilaf sound as good as they taste. Glass or cellophane noodles, rice noodles and egg noodles are great for making a quick Asian stir-fry.

Rice as a meal

Affordable rice is the ideal way to make a dish go further.

Rice brensie

On the Cape Flats rice brensie is often made for large family get-togethers.

oil
1 onion, chopped
1 kg mutton shanks, cut into pieces
3 cloves garlic, chopped
1 green pepper, seeded and chopped
3 cardamom pods
2 pieces stick cinnamon
1 red chilli, seeded and chopped
250 ml (1 c) water
1 can (410 g) peas
salt and freshly ground black pepper
1 can (340 g) whole-kernel corn
500 g prepared fragrant yellow rice
(see p. 176)

Heat a little oil in a large saucepan and fry the onion until soft. Add the meat and brown all over. Add the garlic, green pepper, cardamom pods, cinnamon and chilli and fry for a few minutes. Add the water, bring the mixture to the boil, cover and simmer for 1½–2 hours or until the meat is tender. Season with salt and pepper. Stir in the peas and corn and mix with the yellow rice.

Serves 8–10.

Rice brensie

Jambalaya

This Creole dish can be made in advance and reheated before serving. The prawns must, however, be added only when reheating.

45 ml (3 T) olive oil
225 g Russian sausages or salami
    or bacon, sliced
15 ml (1 T) paprika
8 cloves garlic, chopped
1 medium-sized onion, chopped
2 red peppers, seeded and chopped
4 stalks celery, chopped
3 red chillies, seeded and finely
    chopped (optional)
450 g chicken breast fillets, cut into
    bite-sized pieces
450 g long-grain rice
salt and freshly ground black pepper
2 bay leaves
few sprigs fresh thyme
1,25 litres (5 c) chicken stock
450 g large frozen prawns, defrosted
    at room temperature
chives and parsley to garnish

Heat the oil in a large pan and fry the sausages until nearly done. Add the paprika and stir-fry for 1 minute. Add the garlic, onion, red peppers, celery and chillies. Sauté until the onion is soft. Add the chicken pieces and stir-fry slightly. Add the rice, stirring to coat the rice with the oil. Season generously with salt and black pepper. Add the bay leaves, thyme and chicken stock. Bring to the boil, cover and reduce the heat. Simmer gently for 15–20 minutes or until the rice is done and all the liquid has been absorbed. Add the prawns about 10 minutes before the end of the cooking time. Season to taste and garnish with a sprinkling of chives and parsley. Serve hot.

Serves 6.

Couscous jambalaya

100 g frozen prawns, defrosted at
    room temperature
2 chicken breast fillets, cut into
    small pieces
15 ml (1 T) Creole spice (see recipe)
45 ml (3 T) olive oil
2 Russian sausages, sliced
1 onion, chopped
½ green pepper, seeded and sliced
    into strips
2 stalks celery, chopped
3 cloves garlic, crushed
2 tomatoes, peeled, seeded and chopped
3 bay leaves
10 ml (2 t) Worcestershire sauce
5 ml (1 t) chilli sauce
250 ml (1 c) chicken stock
5 ml (1 t) salt
3 ml (generous ½ t) freshly ground
    black pepper
250 ml (1 c) couscous

Mix the prawns, chicken and Creole spice. Heat 30 ml (2 T) of the olive oil over high heat in a large pan and stir-fry the prawns and chicken for 1 minute. Add the sausages, onion, green pepper, celery and garlic and stir-fry for another 1 minute. Add the tomatoes, bay leaves, Worcestershire sauce, chilli sauce, stock, salt and pepper and bring the mixture to the boil. Reduce the heat and simmer for 10 minutes over low heat.

Stir in the couscous, cover and remove the pan from the heat. Leave for 7 minutes or until the couscous is fluffy. Stir in the remaining olive oil with a fork to fluff the couscous and serve immediately.

Serves 3–4.

CREOLE SPICE
Mix 15 ml (1 T) paprika, 10 ml (2 t) salt, 10 ml (2 t) garlic powder, 5 ml (1 t) black pepper, 5 ml (1 t) onion salt, 5 ml (1 t) cayenne pepper, 5 ml (1 t) dried oregano and 5 ml (1 t) dried thyme and store the mixture in an airtight container.

Mushroom risotto

To make a perfect risotto simply follow this recipe carefully. The secret to making a risotto is that it needs your undivided attention: it must be stirred continuously. It must also be made with butter and homemade stock.

25 ml (5 t) olive oil
25 g butter
2 onions, finely chopped
20 dried porcini mushrooms, soaked in
    water and chopped
100 g button mushrooms, chopped
150 g Arborio rice
1 litre (4 c) chicken stock
salt and freshly ground black pepper
60 ml (¼ c) white wine
60 ml (¼ c) cream or butter
50 g grated Parmesan cheese
chopped spring onions to garnish

Heat the oil and butter in a large saucepan with straight sides (not a wok or pan with sloping sides). Add the onions and sauté until soft. Add the mushrooms and sauté until buttery and caramelised. Remove the onion and mushroom mixture from the saucepan and set aside. Add the rice to the same saucepan and sauté, stirring to coat it with the butter. Using a 150 ml soup ladle add 1 ladleful of stock to the rice. Stir continuously over low heat until all the liquid has been absorbed and the rice is nearly dry before adding the next ladleful of stock. Repeat the process and do not add more than one ladleful of stock at a time. The risotto is done when the rice is tender but still firm to the bite. The mixture must be moist and creamy but not runny. The process will take about 40 minutes. Season with salt and pepper. Stir in the onion and mushroom mixture, white wine, cream and Parmesan cheese. Garnish with chives and serve immediately.

Serves 4.

WHAT IS RISOTTO?
It's an Italian rice dish made with Arborio rice. Onions are usually sautéed in butter and oil. The rice is then added and sautéed to coat the grains with the butter mixture. The hot stock or mixture of stock and wine is added a little at a time so the rice can absorb it. Almost any ingredient can be added to the risotto. At the end of the cooking time extra butter and freshly grated Parmesan cheese is stirred into the mixture. The rice must be tender but still firm to the bite. When cooked the risotto should be rich, fragrant and creamy.

Variations
Substitute any of the following for the mushrooms:

Use spring onions instead of the onion and add 1 chopped clove garlic.

Stir in fresh peas and asparagus towards the end of the cooking time.

Add leftover chicken or smoked chicken breasts.

Stir in a sachet of sun-dried tomatoes in vinaigrette.

Add roasted butternut.

Use red wine instead of white wine and add chorizo or Russian sausages.

Apricot and nut pilaf

Dried apricots and nuts mixed with a savoury rice mixture are delicious.
This affordable dish makes an ideal vegetarian meal.

2 ml (½ t) turmeric
850 ml chicken or vegetable stock
125 g dried apricots
olive oil
100 g (1 packet) mixed nuts
2 onions, sliced
2 large cloves garlic, crushed
5 cm piece fresh ginger, grated
6 cardamom seeds, crushed
2 pieces stick cinnamon
4 whole cloves
250 g white rice
grated rind of 1 orange
salt and freshly ground black pepper
15 ml (1 T) honey
chopped fresh coriander leaves

Mix the turmeric with the stock and pour the mixture over the apricots. Heat a little olive oil in a pan and stir-fry the nuts until golden brown. Remove from the pan and set aside. Add a little more oil to the pan and sauté the onions, garlic, ginger and whole spices until the onions are soft. Remove the cardamom seeds and cloves and add the rice, stirring to coat the grains with oil. Add the stock with the apricots and orange rind. Cover and simmer for 10–12 minutes or until the liquid has been absorbed and the rice is done but not soggy. Season to taste with salt, pepper and honey. Scatter the nuts and chopped coriander leaves on top.

Serves 4.

HOW MUCH WATER?
When cooking rice always add twice as much water as rice. For couscous use equal quantities of water and couscous (do not guess, measure the quantities exactly).

Variations
Substitute cumin for the spices and omit the apricots and orange rind. Fry brinjal and spicy sausages and add them to the rice. Proceed as described.
   Fry chicken strips with a variety of vegetables such as green, red or yellow peppers, carrots and celery and add the rice. Proceed as described and scatter chives and feta cheese on top instead of the nuts.

KINDS OF RICE
Brown rice
This is rice where the husks have been removed from the grains. Brown rice is more nutritious than white rice.

White rice
Long-grain white rice retains its separate grains after cooking and is ideal for use in salads and as a side dish.

Medium-grained white rice such as **Arborio rice** is plump, moist and sticky when cooked. It is usually used to make risotto or Spanish paella.

Short-grain white rice such as **sushi rice** contains plenty of starch and the grains stick together after cooking. It's ideal for sushi, stir-fries and puddings.

Bonnet rice is a popular, affordable long-grain rice with a mild flavour and soft texture when cooked, making it extremely versatile. Serve it with spicy dishes.

Basmati rice is an aromatic long-grain white rice with a distinctive flavour and texture. The grains are longer and thinner than other long-grain rice types. Basmati means fragrant in Hindu. The rice works well with curries or in breyani, pilaf and puddings. Basmati rice must be soaked before cooking it for 5–10 minutes and then steaming it.

Jasmin rice is a long-grain rice with a delicate flavour and fairly sticky texture when cooked. It comes from Thailand.

Apricot and nut pilaf

Stir-fried rice

Stir-fry leftover rice to rustle up a quick, light meal. When my children were younger it was their favourite evening meal – they loved eating it with chopsticks.

Vegetable rice with egg

This is the most basic rice stir-fry.

30 ml (2 T) oil
2 large eggs, lightly whisked
30 ml (2 T) crushed garlic and
    fresh ginger
1 small red chilli, chopped (optional)
1–2 bunches spring onions, chopped
2 large carrots, scraped and
    coarsely grated
250 ml (1 c) frozen peas
5 x 250 ml (5 c) cold cooked white rice
250 ml (1 c) cooked brown lentils
    (optional)
20 ml (4 t) white grape vinegar
    or rice wine
oyster or soy sauce
5 ml (1 t) sesame oil

TO SERVE
60 ml (¼ c) chopped toasted peanuts
60 ml (¼ c) chopped fresh coriander
    leaves or parsley

Heat a little oil in a fairly large pan and pour in the eggs. Heat slowly without stirring until the eggs have set. Remove with a spatula. Heat the remaining oil and stir-fry the garlic, ginger, chilli and spring onions for a few seconds or until fragrant. Add the carrots and peas and stir-fry until the carrots begin to soften. Add the rice and lentils and stir-fry for another 1 minute or until heated through. Add the vinegar, a dash or two of oyster or soy sauce and sesame oil and mix gently. Cut the omelette into thin strips and add to the stir-fry. Heat through, sprinkle the peanuts and coriander over and serve immediately.

Serves 4.

> **Variation**
> You can add any other vegetables to the rice, including small broccoli florets or shredded spinach. You can also add a little lean bacon.

Tips
- Ensure the rice is chilled before stir-frying it or it will become soggy.
- Heat a large wok or pan and add the oil – this ensures you use less. Stir-fried rice must not be oily.
- Reduce the heat while stir-frying.
- The vegetables must still be firm to the bite and not soft. Try covering the pan for a few minutes to let the vegetables steam until just done.
- The basic seasonings for vegetable stir-fries are garlic, fresh ginger and spring onions, onions or leeks.
- White grape vinegar or rice vinegar, soy sauce, fish sauce or Worcestershire sauce add extra flavour.

Stir-fried rice with spicy sausages and vegetables

30 ml (2 T) oil
10 ml (2 t) crushed garlic
1 medium-sized onion, thinly sliced
200 g spicy sausages, sliced
375 ml (1½ c) broccoli florets
500 ml (2 c) cauliflower florets
60 ml (¼ c) boiling water
5 x 250 ml (5 c) cold cooked white rice

SEASONING
25 ml (5 t) soy sauce
Worcestershire sauce
15 ml (1 T) white grape vinegar
   or rice vinegar
salt and freshly ground black pepper
30 ml (2 T) chopped fresh parsley

Heat the oil in a fairly large pan until hot and rapidly stir-fry the garlic and onion until fragrant. Add the sausages and stir-fry until lightly browned. Add the broccoli and cauliflower, stir-fry slightly and pour over the boiling water. Cover and heat until the vegetables just begin to soften but are still firm to the bite. Remove the lid and heat until the liquid has evaporated.
   Add the rice and heat through. Add the seasoning and mix. Serve immediately.

Serves 4.

Stir-fried rice with mushrooms and spinach

30 ml (2 T) oil
6–8 cloves garlic, thinly sliced
125 g (½ punnet) button
   mushrooms, sliced
125 g (½ punnet) brown
   mushrooms, sliced
45 ml (3 T) white grape or rice vinegar
green tops of 2–3 bunches
   spring onions, chopped
200 g spinach (washed and white
   stems removed), shredded
5 x 250 ml (5 c) cold cooked brown
   or white rice
125–250 ml (½–1 c) cooked brown
   lentils (optional)
50 ml soy sauce
45 ml (3 T) finely chopped fresh
   coriander leaves
salt and freshly ground black pepper
2 rounds feta cheese, crumbled

Heat the oil in a large, deep pan and stir-fry the garlic for a few seconds over high heat until fragrant. Add the mushrooms and stir-fry for 1–2 minutes or until they begin to soften. Add the vinegar, green spring onion tops and spinach and stir-fry until most of the liquid has evaporated. Add the rice and lentils and stir until heated through. Add the soy sauce and coriander and season with salt and pepper. Heat for another 1 minute, add the feta cheese and serve immediately. Garnish with extra spring onion tops.

Serves 4.

Rice as a side dish

Most of us are familiar with rice as a side dish. Give it extra interest with spices or vegetables.

Fragrant yellow rice

Perfect with bobotie.

500 ml (2 c) white rice
2 pieces stick cinnamon
2 ml (½ t) turmeric
1 litre (4 c) water
salt
250 ml (1 c) seedless raisins or sultanas
30 g butter
sugar (optional)

Bring the rice, spices, water and salt to the boil in a saucepan. Cook until the rice is done. Drain and rinse under running water. Return the rice to the saucepan and add the raisins, butter and sugar. Cover and steam over low heat until heated through.

Serves 6.

Coconut rice

This Indian rice dish is especially good with hot curries.

500 ml (2 c) basmati rice
45 ml (3 T) oil
1 piece cassia
2 cardamom pods
2 whole cloves
250 ml (1 c) coconut milk
250 ml (1 c) water
5 ml (1 t) black mustard seeds
1 sprig curry leaves
200 ml desiccated coconut
salt

Rinse the rice and soak in clean water for 30 minutes. Heat 30 ml (2 T) of the oil in a large saucepan and fry the whole spices until fragrant. Add the coconut milk and water and bring the mixture to the boil. Add the rice and simmer for about 15 minutes or until most of the liquid has been absorbed. Cover and simmer over very low heat for another 10 minutes or until just done. Do not overcook the rice or it will be soggy. Heat the remaining 15 ml (1 T) oil in a pan and fry the mustard seeds and curry leaves until the mustard seeds begin to pop. Add the coconut and mix with the rice. Season with salt and serve hot

Serves 6.

Savoury pearl wheat

Black South Africans add chopped peppers and onion to rice to give it extra flavour. Try it with pearl wheat – it's delicious.

2 cloves garlic, crushed
1 onion, chopped
1 yellow pepper, seeded and chopped
1 red pepper, seeded and chopped
15 ml (1 T) olive oil
300 g raw pearl wheat, soaked in water
    for at least 1 hour
750 ml (3 c) hot chicken stock
5 ml (1 t) salt
60 ml (¼ c) chopped fresh parsley
25 ml (5 t) butter

In a large saucepan sauté the garlic, onion and peppers in the oil. Drain the pearl wheat and add to the saucepan along with the stock. Bring the mixture to the boil and simmer until the stock has been absorbed and the pearl wheat is soft. Season with salt and add the parsley and butter just before serving.

Serves 4.

Savoury pearl wheat

Braised rice

A typical spicy Malay dish. Delicious with mild curries.

1 large onion, chopped
5 ml (1 t) cumin seeds
3 cardamom pods (optional)
2 pieces stick cinnamon
3 allspice berries
3 whole cloves
60 ml (¼ c) oil
500 ml (2 c) white rice
10 ml (2 t) salt
1 litre (4 c) water
15 ml (1 T) butter

Sauté the onion and spices in the oil until the onion is soft and fragrant. Add the rice and stir-fry for 2 minutes. Add the salt and water. Cover, reduce the heat and simmer for 20–25 minutes or until the rice is done and all the water has been absorbed. Stir the butter into the hot rice just before serving.

Serves 6.

Spicy rice cake with vegetables

Shape rice into a cake and serve with fragrant vegetables.

RICE CAKE
625 ml (2½ c) water
3 cardamom pods
2 whole allspice berries
1 bay leaf
5 ml (1 t) salt
250 ml (1 c) basmati rice
125 ml (½ c) dried lentils, cooked
    and drained
15 ml (1 T) butter
3 medium-sized onions, thinly sliced

SPICY VEGETABLES
10 ml (2 t) oil
1 clove garlic, crushed
6 baby marrows, cut into 5 cm matchsticks
2 medium-sized carrots, cut into
    5 cm matchsticks
10 ml (2 t) mild curry powder
5 ml (1 t) turmeric
2 ml (½ t) ground ginger
2 ml (½ t) ground coriander
2 ml (½ t) ground cumin
2 cans (420 g each) whole tomatoes
    in tomato purée, chopped with
    their juice
15 ml (1 T) soft brown sugar
salt and freshly ground black pepper
fresh coriander leaves or parsley to
    garnish

RICE CAKE
In a large saucepan bring the water, spices, salt and rice to the boil and cook according to the packet instructions until just done. Remove the whole spices. Mix the rice and lentils. Meanwhile preheat the oven to 200 °C and grease a 23 cm cake tin with butter.

Melt the butter and slowly sauté the onion rings for about 15 minutes or until a deep golden brown. Season to taste and spoon the onions into the prepared cake tin. Spoon the rice mixture on top and press down firmly with the back of a large spoon. Cover with a double layer of aluminium foil and bake for 25 minutes.

SPICY VEGETABLES
Heat a medium-sized saucepan and add the oil. Sauté the garlic and matchstick vegetables until the vegetables just begin to soften. Reduce the temperature, add the spices and sauté for another 1 minute. Add the remaining ingredients and cook rapidly for 10–15 minutes or until the sauce thickens slightly and the vegetables are just done. Season to taste.

Remove the rice cake from the oven at the end of the baking time, remove the aluminium foil and leave to stand for a few minutes. Put a plate on top and invert the cake tin and plate. Scrape any onion rings that stick to the bottom of the tin on top of the rice.

Spoon the hot vegetable mixture on top of the rice and garnish with coriander leaves or parsley. Serve as part of a buffet with salads and chutney.

Stir-fries and Asian noodles
Asian stir-fry

Chicken breast fillets and/or pork are ideal for stir-fries. Add vegetables such as sweet peppers, carrots and shredded cabbage as desired. Dolores Bezuidenhout of Wentworth also uses turkey to make this stir-fry.

SAUCE
30 ml (2 T) soy sauce
80 ml (⅓ c) rice vinegar
30 ml (2 T) sugar
8–10 drops fish sauce
30 ml (2 T) sweet chilli sauce
　or a little honey

STIR-FRY
oil
1 onion, chopped
15 ml (1 T) finely grated fresh ginger
3–4 cloves garlic, crushed
250 g (1 punnet) button mushrooms,
　sliced
500 g pork or chicken breast fillets, cut
　into strips
125 g young green beans, cut into
　short pieces
1 bunch spring onions, chopped
125 ml (½ c) bean sprouts

SAUCE
Mix together the ingredients for the sauce and set aside.

STIR-FRY
Heat a little oil in a wok or pan and stir-fry the onion, ginger, garlic and mushrooms until done but still crisp. Add the meat strips and stir-fry for 2–3 minutes or until just done. Add the beans and half the spring onions. Add the sauce and heat for 2 minutes. Remove from the heat and mix in the remaining spring onions and bean sprouts.
　Serve with Asian noodles or rice.

Serves 4.

> **Tips**
> To make crispy meat strips: Dip the meat strips in a little whisked egg white and then in cornflour. Fry a few strips at a time in heated oil until golden brown.
> 　Thicken and clarify the stir-fry sauce by stirring in a little cornflour.

Basic tips for making stir-fries
Ensure all the ingredients are prepared and sliced before you start cooking.
Do not cook too many ingredients at once. To make a perfect stir-fry cook the meat in small batches and add the vegetables a little at a time.
To ensure the vegetables remain crisp cook them for a short period over very high heat.
If one ingredient looks as if it's going to stick to the pan add the next ingredient as this will reduce the heat. Add the soy sauce at the end because it's very salty and will extract moisture from the other ingredients.
Heat the wok or pan over high heat before adding the oil.

Asian noodles

For years you could buy only ordinary pasta but now that Asian cuisine has become so popular you can get all the ingredients to prepare the dishes at home, including Asian noodles.

THE ABC OF ASIAN NOODLES
A variety of noodles are used in Asian cooking, the most commonly available ones being rice noodles, wheat (Hokkein) noodles, egg noodles and mung bean noodles. Most of these noodles come dried.

RICE NOODLES
Rice noodles are made from rice flour, salt and water and are available as rice vermicelli and rice stick noodles. They should preferably be soaked in water until they separate and become flexible before boiling for no longer than a few seconds. Alternatively they can be soaked in boiling water for a few minutes.

Rice vermicelli
These thin, transparent white strands come packed in bundles. Rice vermicelli is usually used in soups and salads or is wrapped around raw vegetables and herbs and served as a salad. It is are also used to wrap around cooked meat and shellfish and is added to Vietnamese spring rolls. To make an impressive garnish deep-fry rice vermicelli until puffed up and white.

Rice stick noodles
Like rice vermicelli these noodles are also white but are flat in shape like linguine or fettuccine. They come in various widths, from 2 mm to 10 mm, and are usually used in salads and stir-fries.

MUNG BEAN NOODLES

These noodles are also called glass or cellophane noodles or bean vermicelli. They look like rice vermicelli but are made from mung beans. They have a firmer texture than rice vermicelli when soaked. Mung bean noodles are soaked in hot water until soft and then boiled for a short period until soft and translucent. They can be cut into more manageable lengths with a scissors after soaking. The noodles are used mostly in salads, spring rolls and soup.

FRESH NOODLES

Instant, fresh Japanese noodles require no soaking or cooking. Add them directly to stir-fries and stir until heated through. These noodles are made from wheat.

WHEAT AND EGG NOODLES

Wheat noodles are made with or without eggs. Wheat noodles are firmer and denser than rice noodles and are mostly used in soups and stir-fries. Boil them for 4–5 minutes, depending on their thickness. Always check the packet instructions.

Wheat noodles without egg
These straw-coloured noodles can be either round and thin or flat like linguine. The flat noodles are generally used in soup, while the thin round noodles are used in stir-fries. Two-minute noodles are a type of wheat noodle.

Wheat noodles with egg
These noodles are generally called egg, Hokkein or stir-fry noodles. They vary in thickness from fine strands to strands the thickness of shoelaces.

Beef stir-fry with cumin

The cumin imparts a wonderful flavour to this quick stir-fry that can be served with any kind of noodles.

350 g boneless steak
15 ml (1 T) rice wine (mirin)
2 ml (½ t) salt
10 ml (2 t) soy sauce
15 ml (1 T) cornflour
oil
10 ml (2 t) finely chopped fresh ginger
15 ml (1 T) crushed garlic
2 red chillies, seeded and finely chopped
10 ml (2 t) ground cumin
100 g bok choy, tatsoi, spinach or
   cabbage, shredded
2 spring onions, cut into strips
30 ml (2 T) peanuts
15 ml (1 T) sesame oil

Cut the steak into strips against the grain. Mix the rice wine, salt, soy sauce and cornflour in a mixing bowl. Add the meat strips and mix well to coat with the cornflour mixture. Heat a little oil in a wok or large pan and stir-fry the meat strips until they separate and are nearly done. Remove from the wok.

Heat a little more oil in the wok and stir-fry the ginger, garlic, chillies and cumin until fragrant. Return the meat strips to the wok and add the cabbage. Mix well and heat through – the cabbage should still be crisp. Season to taste with salt. Scatter spring onions and peanuts over and drizzle with sesame oil. Serve with noodles.

Serves 3–4.

Beef stir-fry with fresh noodles

Fresh Asian noodles are already cooked and come vacuum-packed.
Available from large branches of Woolworths and Pick n Pay.

15 ml (1 T) vegetable oil
300 g rump steak, cut into strips
3 ml (generous ½ t) grated fresh ginger
10 ml (2 t) sesame oil
1 small onion, thinly sliced
1 red pepper, seeded and thinly sliced
150 g broccoli florets
10 ml (2 t) lime juice
60 ml (¼ c) satay sauce
20 ml (4 t) hoisin sauce
80 ml (⅓ c) soy sauce
20 ml (4 t) ketjap manis (see tip)
150 g snow peas
2 packets (200 g each) fresh
   Asian noodles
20 ml (4 t) chopped fresh
   coriander leaves
60 ml (¼ c) unsalted roasted peanuts,
   roughly chopped
extra fresh coriander leaves to serve

Heat the vegetable oil in a large wok or pan. Mix the meat strips with the ginger and fry in small batches in the hot wok until brown. Remove from the wok and set aside. Heat the sesame oil in the same wok and stir-fry the onion, red pepper and broccoli until just tender but not soft.

Return the meat strips to the wok, add the lime juice, satay, hoisin and soy sauces and ketjap manis and stir-fry until the mixture comes to the boil. Add the snow peas and noodles and stir-fry until heated through. Stir in the chopped coriander, scatter over the peanuts and garnish with fresh coriander leaves. Serve immediately.

Serves 4.

Tips
Ketjap manis is a type of thick, sweet soy sauce of Indonesian origin. It's available at most supermarkets and Asian stores. If unavailable use thick, sweet soy sauce instead.
If fresh noodles are unobtainable use wheat noodles or egg noodles for this stir-fry.

Egg noodles with chicken and coconut milk

The chicken for this fragrant noodle dish is cooked in a spicy coconut mixture and is topped with crispy deep-fried noodles.

CURRY PASTE
3 red chillies, seeded and chopped
4 shallots, chopped
4 cloves garlic, crushed
5 cm fresh ginger, grated
60 ml (¼ c) fresh coriander leaves
2 ml (½ t) turmeric
5 ml (1 t) curry powder
5 ml (1 t) fish sauce

NOODLES
75 ml (5 T) coconut cream
30 ml (2 T) brown sugar
30 ml (2 T) soy sauce
4 chicken drumsticks and 4 chicken
   thighs, with skin and bone
500 ml (2 c) chicken stock or water
1 can (400 ml) coconut milk
oil for deep-frying
400 g dried egg noodles
chopped spring onions to garnish
fresh coriander leaves to garnish
lime or lemon slices to serve

CURRY PASTE
Blitz the chillies, shallots, garlic, ginger and coriander in a food processor until smooth. Add the turmeric, curry powder and fish sauce and blend once more in a food processor.

NOODLES
Simmer the coconut cream in a wok or saucepan for 5 minutes or until it separates and forms a layer of oil on the surface. Stir occasionally. Stir in the curry paste. Add the sugar, soy sauce and chicken and mix well. Add the stock or water and coconut milk and bring the mixture to the boil. Reduce the heat and simmer for about 30 minutes or until the chicken is done and tender. Meanwhile heat the oil in a saucepan and deep-fry 100 g of the noodles until puffed up. Remove with a slotted spoon and drain on paper towels.

Cook the remaining noodles in boiling water according to the packet instructions. Drain well and transfer to a large serving bowl. Spoon the chicken mixture on top of the noodles and garnish with the deep-fried noodles, spring onions and coriander. Garnish with a large handful of fresh coriander leaves and serve with lime or lemon slices.

Serves 4–6.

> **Tip**
> The curry paste is stir-fried in coconut cream instead of butter or oil. The cream separates and forms an oil layer for frying.

Tips
Dried noodles tend to fly all over the place when handled. Avoid this by putting them in a large paper or plastic bag.
Flat noodles are used mostly in soups while round noodles are ideal for stir-fries.

Egg noodles with chicken stir-fry

Green beans and carrots impart colour to this delicious chicken stir-fry that's served with crispy stir-fried Asian noodles and peanuts.

1 packet (375 g) thin egg noodles
60 ml (¼ c) peanut oil
500 g chicken breast fillets,
    cut into strips
5 ml (1 t) chilli flakes
175 g young green beans,
    halved diagonally
2 medium-sized carrots, cut into
    matchsticks
2 cm piece ginger, cut into
    matchsticks
2 cloves garlic, crushed
60 ml (¼ c) soy sauce
juice of 1 lemon
125 ml (½ c) peanuts
lemon wedges

Cook the noodles according to the packet instructions. Pat dry with paper towels and set aside. Heat 20 ml (4 t) of the oil in a wok or large pan over high heat. Add the noodles and stir-fry for 10 minutes or until they begin to brown and are crisp. Remove from the wok and set aside.

Mix the chicken and chilli flakes.

Heat another 20 ml (4 t) oil over high heat and stir-fry the chicken in two batches until brown and done. Remove the chicken and set aside. Heat the remaining oil over high heat and stir-fry the green beans, carrots, ginger and garlic for 2 minutes. Add the noodles, chicken and soy sauce and stir-fry until heated through. Sprinkle over the lemon juice and peanuts and serve with lemon wedges.

Serves 4.

Tip
Make crispy Japanese tempura chicken for a change: Mix 40 ml iced water, 10 ml (2 t) cornflour and 10 ml (2 t) soy sauce. Dip the chicken strips in the mixture and stir-fry them in hot oil over high heat. Shelled prawns can also be dipped in the tempura batter and fried.

Rice noodles with meat and prawns

Flat rice noodles, which take only seconds to cook, are stirred into this quick stir-fry made with pork, chicken and prawns.

250 g flat rice noodles
20 ml (4 t) sesame oil
250 g pork strips
10 ml (2 t) mild curry paste
1 ml (pinch) turmeric
2,5 cm piece fresh ginger, grated
2 red chillies, seeded and chopped
2 cooked chicken breasts,
    cut into strips
250 g prawns, cleaned
150 g baby leaf spinach (optional)
1 handful bean sprouts
4 spring onions, chopped
few drops fish sauce
about 15 ml (1 T) soy sauce
125–250 ml (½–1 c) coconut milk
    (optional)

Prepare the noodles according to the packet instructions and set aside. Heat the oil in a wok and stir-fry the pork strips until just done. Add the curry paste, turmeric, ginger, chillies and chicken and stir-fry for about 5 minutes or until the chicken is just done.

Add the prawns, spinach, sprouts and spring onions and stir-fry for 3–4 minutes.

Add the noodles and fish and soy sauces. Stir in the coconut milk if the mixture is too dry for your taste. Serve immediately.

Serves 4–6.

Egg noodles with chicken stir-fry

Stir-fry sauces

Here are a few quick ideas for sauces to add to the stir-fry at the end of the cooking period.

Basic sauce

30 ml (2 T) soy sauce
30–45 ml (2–3 T) oyster sauce
5 ml (1 t) sugar or 15 ml (1 T) sherry

Mix all the ingredients and pour the sauce over stir-fried vegetables, lamb or beef strips.

Sweet chilli sauce

Delicious with seafood or even chicken.

30 ml (2 T) honey
15–30 ml (1–2 T) sweet chilli sauce
15 ml (1 T) soy sauce

Mix all the ingredients and pour over the stir-fry. Add a little lemon juice just before serving.

ASIAN FLAVOURS

Essential ingredients
Fish sauce, sesame oil, soy sauce, rice vinegar, hoisin sauce, peanuts, Chinese five -spice powder, star anise, turmeric, coconut milk, rice paper, basmati rice, rice, cellophane and egg noodles and fresh seasonings such as ginger, garlic, chillies, coriander leaves, mint, Asian or ordinary basil, lemon grass and limes. Many recipes call for tamarind but you can use lemon juice instead to impart tartness to a dish.

BECOME A CONNOISSEUR OF EASTERN SAUCES

Oyster sauce
This thick, intensely flavoured sauce is used often (but cautiously) in Chinese cuisine. It is made of dried oysters and soy sauce and it adds colour, flavour and a salty taste to stir-fries and fried dishes.

Fish sauce
This has a sharp, salty taste and aroma. It's made of dried salted fish and is used like soy sauce or as a salt replacement to flavour dishes.

Plum sauce
A sweetish sauce often used in Chinese cuisine. It's also served as a dip with chicken, pork and vegetables.

Black bean sauce
This rich, robust sauce made of black beans and fermented soya is seasoned with smoked chilli, garlic and spices. It is delicious with steamed food and in stir-fries; it also complements vegetables, noodles, seafood and meat.

Teriyaki sauce
A Japanese sauce that can be used as a marinade or dip. It usually contains soy sauce, mirin (a type of Japanese rice wine) and ginger and is spread on fish, meat or chicken before grilling.

Satay sauce
This sweet sauce hails from South East Asia. The base of peanuts and coconut is seasoned with curry and other spices. Delicious with chicken kebabs.

Soy sauce
Supermarket shelves are groaning under the weight of a wide variety of soy sauces these days but only a handful are really great. Soy sauce is made from soybeans, water, wheat and salt fermented together. Some are natural, others are chemically produced. The golden rule is to avoid artificially made soy sauce. Naturally fermented soy sauce is wonderfully aromatic and salty and emphasises the natural flavour of food without overwhelming it. Good soy sauce has a dark, deep, red-brown colour. Our favourite is the well-known Kikkoman Soy Sauce. You also get several specialised versions. Remember the sauces of various manufacturers can differ a lot.

Dark soy sauce
This is slightly thicker and darker than light sauce because it's fermented longer. Usually caramel or molasses is added too. It's ideal for stews or meat where you need good flavour and a deep colour. Suitable for cooking and table use.

Light soy sauce
This version is clearer and slightly saltier than ordinary soy sauces and is usually used only for cooking. The lighter, clearer colour ensures the ingredients retain their natural colour while being cooked. Suitable for seafood, white meat dishes and soups.

Tamari soy sauce
This is fermented according to the original Japanese method. It's thicker and darker and tastes stronger than light soy sauce. Suitable for cooking and table use.

Sweet soy sauce
This gives a subtle sweet taste to dishes and can be used instead of sugar. It also gives a crispy glaze to grilled food and is ideal for exotic spicy dishes. Ketjap manis is an example.

Thick soy sauce
Thickened with starch and sugar and sometimes also molasses, this sauce is often used for stir-fries and as a dipping sauce.

WHOLESOME VEGETABLES

Crisply stir-fried, fragrantly roasted or simply steamed, no matter how you prepare them vegetables make a delicious meal on their own. And with the growth in fresh-produce markets you can now pick and choose from a wonderful array of freshly picked vegetables and herbs. Even better, you can start your own vegetable patch.

Spicy vegetable stew with chickpeas

The ideal vegetarian dish. Use your favourite vegetables.

30 ml (2 T) tomato paste
250 ml (1 c) plain yoghurt
5 ml (1 t) paprika
salt and freshly ground black pepper
30 ml (2 T) olive oil
1 piece stick cinnamon
2 cardamom pods, crushed
1 bay leaf
2 medium-sized onions, finely chopped
2 cloves garlic, finely chopped
5 ml (1 t) grated fresh ginger
250 ml (1 c) cubed butternut
1 large potato, peeled and cubed
500 ml (2 c) cauliflower florets
15 young green beans, cut into 5 cm pieces
4 baby marrows, sliced into discs
1 red pepper, seeded and diced
30 ml (2 T) finely chopped fresh
    coriander leaves
125 ml (½ c) water
2 ml (½ t) ground cumin
1 can (400 g) chickpeas, rinsed and drained
10 ml (2 t) toasted sesame seeds

Blend the tomato paste, yoghurt and paprika and season to taste with salt and black pepper. Set aside. Heat the oil and stir-fry the cinnamon, cardamom, bay leaf, onions, garlic and ginger for 5 minutes. Stir in the yoghurt mixture. Add the vegetables, coriander and water, season with cumin and leave the mixture to simmer slowly until the vegetables are just done.

Add the chickpeas just before the end of the cooking time and heat through until hot and fragrant. Season with salt and pepper and sprinkle over the sesame seeds. Serve with savoury couscous (see recipe) if desired.

Serves 6.

Budget-beating tip
Mix 250 ml (1 c) breadcrumbs with the rind of 1 lemon and 30 ml (2 T) chopped parsley and stir-fry the mixture in a little butter until brown. Sprinkle over the vegetables instead of the sesame seeds.

SAVOURY COUSCOUS
Prepare the couscous according to the packet instructions. Add a spoonful of olive oil and crushed dried chillies. Season with paprika and ground cumin and ginger to taste. Mix gently with a fork to loosen the grains. Microwave on 100 per cent power (high) for 2 minutes and fluff again. Add chopped fresh coriander leaves, parsley and a knob of butter and stir.

Spicy vegetable stew with chickpeas

Delicious stir-fry

The secret to making a perfect stir-fry is to rapidly cook the vegetables over high heat – they must still be crunchy and colourful. Mushy stir-fries don't do justice to vegetables so take care not to overcook them.

60 ml (¼ c) oil
5 ml (1 t) mustard powder
15 ml (1 T) grated fresh ginger
3 cloves garlic, crushed
1–2 chillies, seeded and finely chopped
5 ml (1 t) turmeric
5 ml (1 t) ground cumin
1 medium-sized onion, thinly sliced
750 g vegetables of your choice,
    cut into bite-sized pieces
80 ml (⅓ c) vegetable stock
5 ml (1 t) soy sauce
3 spring onions, chopped

Heat the oil in a wok or large frying pan. Add the mustard powder, ginger, garlic, chillies and spices and stir-fry for 30 seconds over medium heat. Add the onion and vegetables and stir-fry for 3–5 minutes or until the vegetables are tender but still crisp. Add the stock and simmer for 2 minutes. Season with soy sauce. Sprinkle over the spring onions and serve immediately.

Serves 4–6.

Variation
For a creamier stir-fry add 1 can (400 ml) of coconut milk or a few spoonfuls of plain yoghurt.

VEGETABLES SUITABLE FOR STIR-FRYING
Baby marrows, patty pans, mushrooms, baby sweet corn, young green beans, sweet peppers, cauliflower and broccoli florets, carrot strips and shredded cabbage.

Tips
If desired scatter seeds such as pumpkin, sunflower and sesame seeds and chopped nuts over the vegetables for extra crunch.
Use two chopsticks to stir-fry the vegetables.

Caponata

Caponata is an Italian vegetable dish made with brinjals, onions and tomatoes.
For a South African twist serve it on mealie meal wedges or enjoy as a side dish
with roasts or smoked fish. It's also delicious on bread served with cheese and olives.

MEALIE MEAL WEDGES
1 litre (4 c) chicken or vegetable stock
5 ml (1 t) salt
500 ml (2 c) maize meal

CAPONATA
250 g small brinjals, halved
salt and freshly ground black pepper
olive oil
2 large red onions, cut into wedges
    OR 8 pickling onions,
    peeled and halved
4 cloves garlic, crushed
2 red or yellow peppers, seeded and
    diced (optional)
30 ml (2 T) sun-dried tomato pesto
1–2 anchovies
5 ml (1 t) capers
ssugar and paprika
125 g small Roma tomatoes
60 ml (¼ c) chopped fresh flat-leaf
    parsley
60 ml (¼ c) torn basil leaves
50 g butter, melted
Parmesan cheese shavings

MEALIE MEAL WEDGES
Bring the stock and salt to the boil in a large saucepan.
Add the maize meal and stir rapidly to blend. Cover and cook
for about 20 minutes over low heat without stirring. Spread
a 2 cm thick layer of the maize meal mixture on a greased
baking sheet and leave it to cool.

CAPONATA
Put the brinjal halves in a colander, sprinkle with salt and
leave for 15 minutes. Rinse off the salt and pat dry the brinjal
halves (this will ensure they brown more easily and absorb
less oil). Heat a little olive oil in a large saucepan and fry the
onions and garlic until golden brown. Add the brinjal halves
and peppers and stir-fry until lightly browned. Add the tomato
pesto, anchovies and capers and season with salt, pepper,
sugar and paprika.
   Cover and simmer slowly for about 10 minutes or until the
vegetables are soft. Add the Roma tomatoes, parsley and basil
and heat through.
   Cut the maize meal layer into neat wedges, brush
generously with melted butter and grill until hot, brown and
crisp. Put the wedges on a warm plate, spoon the caponata
on top and serve immediately with Parmesan shavings.

Serves 6.

Sweet 'n sour onions

This is a version of the popular Italian dish, *agrodolce* (*agro* means sour and *dolce* means sweet). It's the perfect side dish to serve with pies and game.

5 large red onions OR 500 g pickling
    onions, peeled
75 ml (5 T) olive oil
125 ml (½ c) red muscadel or port
125 ml (½ c) good quality wine vinegar
    or apple cider vinegar
30 ml (2 T) moist brown sugar
125 ml (½ c) seedless raisins
salt
cayenne pepper to taste

Quarter the onions. Heat 45 ml (3 T) of the oil in a heavy-bottomed saucepan and fry the onions for 5 minutes or until halfway soft. Remove from the saucepan and set aside. Add the remaining olive oil to the pan along with the muscadel, vinegar and sugar. Bring to the boil and, stirring continuously, bubble hard until the mixture is dark and syrupy. Take care that it doesn't burn. Add the raisins and onions to the syrup, season with salt and pepper and boil for another 2 minutes or until fragrant. Spoon into a dish and serve lukewarm or cold.

Serves 4–6.

Variation
Provençale tomato and onion dish
Put 12 halved small pickling onions, 5 unpeeled cloves garlic, 4 quartered plum tomatoes, 2 sprigs rosemary and 3 sprigs thyme in a dish, drizzle with 40 ml oil and bake at 160 °C for 1–1½ hours. Pour the pan juices into a saucepan, squeeze out the garlic purée and add it to the pan juices along with 40 ml olive oil, 60 ml (¼ c) red wine vinegar and 20 ml (4 t) brown sugar. Simmer for 10 minutes and pour over the onions and tomatoes.

Serves 4.

Onion marmalade

2 large onions
250 ml (1 c) red wine
125 ml (½ c) balsamic vinegar
125 ml (½ c) soft brown sugar

Halve and slice the onions. Heat the red wine, balsamic vinegar and soft brown sugar in a saucepan over medium heat, stirring until the sugar has dissolved. Add the onions and cook until they are soft and caramelised. Delicious with a cheese platter or beef and ham.

Serves 4.

Tip
English mustard powder will remove the flavour of chillies or garlic from your hands or chopping board. Wash your hands thoroughly after handling chillies and don't touch your eyes or the delicate skin of a baby. It will burn!

Sweet 'n sour onions

Gnocchi with brown butter

This Italian speciality is like homemade potato dumplings. Serve it with browned butter.

GNOCCHI
500 g floury potatoes such as Up-to-date
2 ml (½ t) salt
30 g butter
1 egg, whisked
325 ml (1½ c) cake flour

BROWN BUTTER
150 g unsalted butter
1 handful fresh sage leaves
Parmesan cheese to sprinkle on top

GNOCCHI
Cook the potatoes in water until very soft, drain well and remove the skins. Press the potatoes through a sieve. Add the salt, butter, egg and 250 ml (1 c) of the flour while the potatoes are still warm. Mix gently and turn out on a floured surface. Add just enough of the remaining flour to make a smooth, soft dough and knead for about 5 minutes. Divide the dough into 4 equal parts and roll each quarter into a long sausage. Cut the sausages into 2 cm pieces. Press the pieces onto the tines of a fork to make ridges and place the gnocchi on a floured cloth.

Bring a large saucepan of salted water to the boil and cook a few gnocchi at a time for 2–3 minutes – they are done when they float to the top. Remove the gnocchi from the water with a slotted spoon and keep warm.

BROWN BUTTER
Heat the butter over medium heat. Add the sage and fry until slightly brown and crisp. Pour the butter mixture over the gnocchi and serve with Parmesan cheese.

Serves 6.

Variation
Fry 75 g bacon with the sage in the butter until crisp. Substitute basil leaves for the sage leaves.

Potato cakes

These delicious potato cakes are made with cheese and sun-dried tomatoes.
Serve them with a salad as a light vegetarian meal.

500 g potatoes, peeled and quartered
15 ml (1 T) butter
2 ml (½ t) salt
1 ml (pinch) white pepper
1 ml (pinch) nutmeg
1 whole egg, lightly whisked
1 egg yolk, lightly whisked
10 ml (2 t) finely chopped fresh parsley
100 g Cheddar cheese, cut into 1 cm cubes
1 round feta cheese, roughly crumbled
50 ml roughly chopped sun-dried tomatoes
about 100 ml cake flour
1 egg, whisked
about 125 ml (½ c) dried breadcrumbs
oil for deep-frying

Cook the potatoes in salted water until soft. Drain, return to the saucepan and shake over low heat until the potatoes are dry. Mash the potatoes, then beat with a wooden spoon until very smooth. Add the butter, salt, pepper, nutmeg, egg, egg yolk and parsley and mix well. Add more salt if necessary. Gently stir in the cheeses and tomatoes and leave to cool.

Divide the mixture into 5–6 uniform pieces and shape into neat cakes. Dust with the flour, dip them in the whisked egg and then in the breadcrumbs. Cover and chill in the fridge for at least 2 hours.

Heat enough oil for deep-frying in a saucepan. When medium-hot fry the cakes a few at a time until golden brown. Drain on paper towels and serve hot.

Serves 5–6.

Ethiopian mashed potatoes

1 kg potatoes
250 ml (1 c) spicy butter (see recipe)
300 ml milk

Cook the potatoes, drain and remove the skins. Mash the potatoes. Heat the spicy butter with the milk until the butter has melted. Mix with the mashed potatoes and serve warm.

Serves 4.

Spicy butter

1 kg butter
1 onion, chopped
3 cloves garlic, crushed
2 cm piece fresh ginger, grated
1 piece stick cinnamon
2 whole cloves
1 ml (pinch) grated nutmeg

Clarify the butter (see tip) and add the onion, garlic, ginger, cinnamon stick, cloves and grated nutmeg. Simmer for about 50 minutes or until most of the solids have sunk to the bottom. Drain and used as needed.

HOW TO CLARIFY BUTTER
Heat butter slowly until a white foam forms on the surface. Skim the foam. Line a sieve with a double layer of damp muslin cloth. Put the sieve over a bowl and strain the butter. Repeat a few times. Pour the clarified butter into a screw-top jar, leave to cool and seal.

Pumpkin fritters

These fritters are delicious as a side dish or served simply with cinnamon sugar or maple syrup. The batter is made according to the choux pastry method.

250 ml (1 c) mashed cooked pumpkin
100 ml water
thick strip of orange rind
1 ml (pinch) salt
10 ml (2 t) sugar
15 ml (1 T) butter
15 ml (1 T) brandy
80 ml (⅓ c) cake flour, sifted
2 extra-large eggs
5 ml (1 t) baking powder
oil for deep frying
cinnamon sugar or maple syrup

Put the mashed pumpkin in a sieve and leave to drain and cool slightly. Meanwhile put the water, orange rind, salt, sugar, butter and brandy in a saucepan and heat slowly until the sugar has dissolved and the butter has melted. Bring to the boil and remove from the heat.

Remove the orange rind and add all the cake flour at once. Stir with a wooden spoon until a ball of dough forms and it no longer sticks to the sides of the saucepan. Leave to cool. Add the eggs one by one, beating well with a wooden spoon after each addition until the mixture is smooth and shiny. Add the mashed pumpkin and baking powder and mix well.

Heat enough oil for deep-frying in a saucepan and fry spoonfuls of the batter until the fritters are puffed up, golden brown and done. Drain on paper towels. Sprinkle with cinnamon sugar or drizzle with maple syrup and serve warm.

Makes 20–25.

Isabella's pumpkin fritters

This is her mom's recipe for pumpkin fritters, says Isabella Niehaus of Langebaan. She always steamed the pumpkin instead of cooking it in water as she believed this preserved the flavour.

500 ml (2 c) peeled pumpkin, butternut
   or sweet potato
125 ml (½ c) cake flour or more if necessary
1 ml (pinch) salt
5 ml (1 t) baking powder
2 eggs, whisked
oil and butter for frying
brown sugar and ground cinnamon
   for sprinkling on top

Steam the pumpkin until cooked and soft. Mash it and add flour, salt, baking powder and eggs. Heat a little oil and butter in a pan and drop spoonfuls of the mixture in the pan. Fry until golden brown on both sides. Arrange on a plate and sprinkle with brown sugar and cinnamon.

Makes 10–12.

HOW TO STEAM VEGGIES
Put the wire rack of a pressure cooker in the bottom of the cooker. Add enough water to come to just below the rack. Put the vegetables in containers (preferably with holes) and arrange them on the rack. Cover the cooker with the lid (do not put it under pressure) and steam until the vegetables are soft. Alternatively the vegetables can be steamed in a waterless saucepan.

Zulu cabbage

1 small cabbage
1 onion
1 green pepper
15 ml (1 T) oil
mild curry powder
1 ml (pinch) cumin
1 can (420 g) chopped tomatoes
salt, freshly ground black pepper
   and sugar

Roughly chop the cabbage, onion and green pepper. Heat a little oil in a pan and stir-fry the onion and green pepper with the curry powder and cumin until soft. Add the cabbage and stir-fry until it just begins to wilt. Add the tomatoes and simmer for 7 minutes. Season with salt, pepper and a pinch of sugar to taste.
   Serve with maize meal porridge and a sprinkling of peanuts.

Serves 4.

Beetroot with caper dressing

Young beetroot served with a lemony dressing and a scattering of capers. Delicious.

1 bunch young beetroot
500 ml (2 c) water
10 ml (2 t) salt
grated rind of ½ lemon
15 ml (1 T) balsamic vinegar
15 ml (1 T) olive oil
10 ml (2 t) finely chopped chives
10 ml (2 t) finely chopped fresh parsley
freshly ground black pepper
20 ml (4 t) capers

Wash and scrub the beetroot well. Remove the leaves 5 cm from the bulbs. Cook the beetroot in the water with the salt until soft. Remove the skins under running water but keep the stems intact. Halve the beetroot and keep warm. Blend the lemon rind, vinegar, olive oil, herbs and pepper. Pour the dressing over the beetroot and transfer them to a serving dish. Scatter the capers on top and serve.

Serves 4.

Isabella's pumpkin fritters

Asparagus with mustard cream

500 g fresh asparagus
15 ml (1 T) oil
1 clove garlic, crushed
15 ml (1 T) wholegrain mustard
5 ml (1 t) honey
180 ml (¾ c) cream
salt and freshly ground black pepper

Break off the hard, woody ends of the asparagus stalks at the first joint. Cut the asparagus into pieces or keep them whole. Heat the oil in a pan or wok and sauté the garlic for a few seconds over fairly low heat until fragrant. Add the asparagus and stir-fry for 3–4 minutes or until soft. Take care not to overcook the asparagus. Remove them from the pan and keep warm.

Whisk together the mustard, honey and cream and pour the mixture into the pan. Bring the mixture to the boil and reduce until slightly thick. Return the asparagus to the pan, season with salt and pepper, heat through and serve with meat.

Serves 3–4.

Butternut with cashew nuts

The butternut is seasoned with cumin, mustard seeds and coriander before it's cooked in a sweet orange sauce. A delicious side dish with braaivleis or for a buffet.

250 ml (1 c) raw cashew nuts
oil
1 leek, sliced into thin rings
10 ml (2 t) ground coriander
10 ml (2 t) ground cumin
10 ml (2 t) brown mustard seeds
2 cloves garlic, crushed
1 kg butternut, peeled and cubed
180 ml (¾ c) orange juice
5 ml (1 t) soft brown sugar

Heat a wok and stir-fry the cashew nuts until golden brown. Do not add any oil but take care the nuts don't burn. Remove the nuts from the wok. Heat a little oil in the wok and stir-fry the leek for 2–3 minutes or until soft. Remove from the wok and set aside.

Heat the wok again and add 15 ml (1 T) oil. Stir-fry the coriander, cumin, mustard seeds and garlic for about 2 minutes or until fragrant and the mustard seeds start popping. Add the butternut and stir-fry for about 7 minutes or until golden brown. Reduce the heat, cover the wok and steam the butternut until nearly soft.

Add the orange juice and sugar, bring the mixture to the boil and simmer until the butternut is slightly caramelised. Remove from the wok and scatter over the leeks and cashew nuts.

Serves 3–4.

> **Tip**
> For a more rustic dish do not peel the butternut. I first steam the butternut in the microwave oven until nearly soft.

Tomato and brinjal bake with feta cheese

Cherry tomatoes, pickling onions and brinjal slices are roasted before being baked in a fragrant tomato sauce.

2 large brinjals, sliced
16 pickling onions, halved
150 ml olive oil
12 cherry tomatoes
5 cloves garlic
1 can (420 g) chopped tomatoes
45 ml (3 T) basil pesto (optional)
30 ml (2 T) balsamic vinegar
salt and freshly ground black pepper
10 ml (2 t) chopped fresh rosemary
250 ml (1 c) roughly crumbled white
    or brown bread
4 rounds feta cheese, crumbled

Preheat the oven to 220 °C and grease an ovenproof dish with butter, margarine or nonstick food spray.

Put the brinjal slices and pickling onions on a baking sheet and drizzle with 60 ml (¼ c) of the olive oil. Shake gently to coat the vegetables with the oil. Roast for about 20 minutes, shaking the baking sheet occasionally. Add the cherry tomatoes and garlic and drizzle with 30 ml (2 T) of the olive oil. Roast for another 10–15 minutes or until the tomatoes begin to soften. Remove from the oven and transfer the vegetables to the greased ovenproof dish. Mix the canned tomatoes, pesto, vinegar, salt, pepper and remaining olive oil and pour the mixture over the vegetables. Sprinkle over the rosemary, breadcrumbs and feta cheese and bake for 20–25 minutes or until golden brown. Serve with crusty bread.

Serves 4–6.

Variations
Dip the brinjal slices in flour and fry them in a pan before putting them in the ovenproof dish along with the other roasted vegetables.
You can also add a sprinkling of mozzarella or Parmesan cheese.

Creamy potato bake

This rich and creamy dish goes a long way. Omit the asparagus if desired or use cooked chopped vegetables instead. You can also add sausages and salami for extra flavour.

30 ml (2 T) oil
2 large onions, cut into wedges
2 cloves garlic, crushed
250 g (1 packet) bacon, chopped
6–8 large potatoes, boiled in
    their jackets until soft
1 can (410 g) asparagus tips
1 packet (60 g) white onion soup powder
250 ml (1 c) milk
250 ml (1 c) mayonnaise
salt and freshly ground black pepper
250 ml (1 c) grated Cheddar cheese

Preheat the oven to 190 °C and grease a large ovenproof dish with butter, margarine or nonstick food spray.

Heat the oil and sauté the onions and garlic until fragrant. Remove from the pan and set aside.

Fry the bacon in the same pan until done. Cut the potatoes into slices or wedges or make fanned potato (see tip). Arrange the potatoes in the ovenproof dish and spoon over the onion mixture. Drain the asparagus tips but reserve the liquid. Spoon the bacon and asparagus tips over the onion mixture.

Blend the soup powder, milk, mayonnaise and asparagus liquid and pour over the potatoes. Season with salt and black pepper and sprinkle over the cheese. Cover with aluminium foil and bake for 20 minutes. Remove the foil and bake for another 10 minutes or until golden brown and heated through.

Serves 6–8.

Tip
To make fanned potato put a potato on a spoon and slice it from the top. The spoon stops you cutting all the way through the potato.

Vegetable lasagne

A meat- and pasta-free lasagne: vegetable slices are used instead of pasta sheets. Perfect for vegetarians.

10 baby marrows, sliced lengthways
3 small brinjals, sliced lengthways
1 large butternut, peeled,
    seeds removed and sliced
4 red peppers, seeded and sliced
5 ripe tomatoes, sliced
4 cloves garlic, crushed
salt and freshly ground black pepper
100 ml olive oil
10 ml (2 t) brown sugar
20 ml (4 t) chopped fresh parsley
100 g butter or margarine
200 ml cake flour
6 x 250 ml (6 c) milk
15 ml (1 T) wholegrain mustard
8–10 large potatoes, boiled,
    skins removed and sliced
250 ml (1 c) grated Cheddar cheese
50 ml grated Parmesan cheese

Switch on the oven grill. Grease an oven dish with butter, margarine or nonstick food spray.

Arrange the baby marrows, brinjals, butternut, peppers and tomato slices in a single layer in a roasting tin. Sprinkle over the garlic, season with salt and pepper and drizzle generously with olive oil. Sprinkle the brown sugar over the tomatoes and roast the vegetables until golden brown and just soft. Scatter over the parsley as soon as the vegetables come out of the oven. Reduce the oven temperature to 200 °C.

Make a white sauce: Melt the butter in a saucepan and gradually stir in the flour to make a thick paste. Heat slowly for 1 minute and, stirring continuously, gradually add the milk. Add the mustard and season to taste with salt and pepper.

Layer the roasted vegetables in the oven dish, alternating them with the potatoes and white sauce. Sprinkle Cheddar cheese over each layer. End with a layer of white sauce and sprinkle over the Parmesan cheese. Bake for 20–30 minutes and serve lukewarm.

Serves 8–10.

Cheese and vegetable pie

Sue Erasmus of Scottsville in Pietermaritzburg says this is one her favourite vegetarian recipes. Add fresh cheese to the mixture and it becomes like a vegetable cheesecake.

6 extra-large eggs, lightly whisked
125 ml (½ c) cream or full-cream milk
250 g ricotta cheese or creamed
    cottage cheese (optional)
5 ml (1 t) dried basil
5 ml (1 t) dried thyme
salt and freshly ground black pepper
500 g baby marrows, finely grated
250 g sweet potatoes or potatoes,
    peeled and grated
1 bunch chives, finely chopped
250 g cherry tomatoes, halved
250 ml (1 c) finely chopped, cooked
    spinach
2 cloves garlic, crushed
40 g freshly grated Parmesan cheese

Preheat the oven to 180 °C and grease a 26 cm square ovenproof dish with butter, margarine or nonstick food spray. Blend the eggs, cream, ricotta cheese, herbs and seasoning and set aside.

Mix the vegetables, add the egg mixture and mix well. Spoon the mixture into the prepared dish, sprinkle with the Parmesan cheese and bake for 35–40 minutes or until the pie has set. Leave to cool slightly before cutting into neat squares.

Serve warm or at room temperature with wholewheat rolls.

Serves 8–10.

> Ricotta cheese is a fresh, soft low-fat cheese that must be used within at least five days of purchase. It loses its creamy freshness thereafter.

> **Variation**
> Add finely chopped red pepper to the mixture.

Baked pumpkin

Pumpkin doesn't always have to be sweet. The sage enhances the flavour of these baked pumpkin slices.

salt
25 ml (5 t) olive oil
30 ml (2 T) butter, melted
25 ml (5 t) honey
15 ml (1 T) lemon juice
1,5–2 kg pumpkin with skin,
    cut into 3 cm thick slices
1 handful fresh sage leaves

Preheat the oven to 180 °C.
    Mix the salt, olive oil, butter, honey and lemon juice in a mixing bowl. Drizzle the mixture over the pumpkin slices and mix well to coat them. Arrange the pumpkin slices on a baking sheet and drizzle the remaining oil mixture on top. Roast for 20–30 minutes or until golden brown. Scatter the sage leaves over the pumpkin halfway through the baking time.

Serves 6.

Spinach strudel

Deborah Goldberg of Great Brak River says you can use any combination of ingredients for the filling. She also likes adding preserved sweet peppers and pepperoni sausage to the filling.

8 sheets phyllo pastry
45 ml (3 T) olive oil
4 slices mozzarella cheese
15 slices salami (optional)
125 ml (½ c) ready-made tomato salsa
6 large spinach leaves, washed
    and shredded
1 egg, whisked
20 pitted black olives, chopped

Preheat the oven to 180 °C and lightly grease a baking sheet with olive oil. Lightly brush each sheet of phyllo pastry with oil and stack them on top of each other. Arrange the cheese slices lengthways on the pastry sheets, about 5 cm from the edges. Arrange the salami on top and spread with the salsa. Spread the spinach on top of the salsa and spoon over the whisked egg. Finally scatter the olives on top.
    Roll the pastry up firmly and tuck the ends under the roll. Put the roll on the baking sheet and brush lightly with olive oil again. Bake for 30 minutes or until pale brown. Slice the roll and serve it with a salad.

Serves 6.

> **Budget-beating tip**
> Substitute tomato and onion mix for the tomato salsa.

Sweet potato wheels

Sweet potatoes wrapped in puff pastry are a hit on the menu at Langberg game farm near Kimberley.

1,5 kg sweet potatoes, peeled and
    cut into 2 cm thick slices
5 ml (1 t) salt
250 ml (1 c) white sugar
2 rolls (400 g each) frozen puff pastry,
    defrosted
250 ml (1 c) brown sugar
250 g butter
20 ml (4 t) ground cinnamon

Preheat the oven to 180 °C and grease an ovenproof dish with butter, margarine or nonstick food spray. Cook the sweet potatoes in salted water until soft and add the white sugar. Roll out the puff pastry until slightly thinner. Spoon the sweet potatoes on a third of the pastry, roll up and cut the roll into 4 cm thick slices.
    Arrange the sweet potato rounds in the prepared dish. Heat together the brown sugar and butter until melted and pour over the sweet potato slices. Sprinkle with cinnamon and cover with aluminium foil. Bake the slices for 30 minutes. Remove the foil and bake for another 10 minutes or until golden brown and done.

Serves 6–8.

Stuffed peppers

Food writer Nettie Pikeur grows her own vegetables in Montagu. I adapted the original recipe for her stuffed peppers, which are now a firm family favourite.

6 large peppers, preferably 3 red
   and 3 yellow
1 onion, finely chopped
1–2 baby marrows, finely chopped
3 spinach leaves, shredded
45 ml (3 T) finely chopped fresh herbs
   such as oregano, parsley and chives
750 ml (3 c) cooked rice, preferably
   brown basmati rice
45 ml (3 T) olive oil
60 ml (¼ c) chopped pecan nuts
salt and freshly ground black pepper
45 ml (3 T) freshly grated Parmesan cheese

Preheat the oven to 180 °C.
   Carefully remove the bottom and top of each pepper and remove the seeds and white pith. Set the whole peppers aside and finely chop the removed pepper tops and bottoms. Sauté the chopped peppers and other vegetables along with the herbs until soft. Mix with the rice, olive oil and nuts and season to taste with salt and pepper. Generously stuff each pepper with the mixture and sprinkle with the Parmesan cheese.
   Put the peppers on a oiled baking sheet and bake for 30–40 minutes or until the peppers begin to soften. Serve hot or cold.

Serves 6.

Jamie's onions

Jamie Oliver of *The Naked Chef* fame is a great source of inspiration for many cooks, especially guys. Niël Burger of Melkbosstrand treated us to his onions à la Jamie.

6 large onions, peeled
250 g (1 packet) streaky bacon
6 rosemary sprigs
10 ml (2 t) butter
10 ml (2 t) finely chopped garlic
10 ml (2 t) finely chopped rosemary
60 ml (¼ c) freshly grated Parmesan cheese

Preheat the oven to 180 °C.
   Cook the whole onions in slowly boiling water for 10 minutes. Make a 2–3 cm deep hollow in the top of each onion. Wrap each onion in a rasher of bacon and secure it with a rosemary sprig. Finely chop the remaining bacon and scooped out onion and fry in butter along with the garlic and finely chopped rosemary until the bacon is done.
   Remove from the heat, add three-quarters of the cheese and stir until the cheese has melted. Fill the hollowed-out onions with the bacon mixture and sprinkle over the remaining cheese. Bake for 30–40 minutes or until the onions are soft.

Serves 6.

> **Tip**
> You can also use red onions.

Cauliflower bake

This dish looks attractive prepared in individual dishes.

1 cauliflower, cut into fairly
   large pieces
4 extra-large eggs, whisked
250 ml (1 c) sour cream OR crème
   fraîche
90 ml (6 T) freshly grated Parmesan cheese
salt and freshly ground black pepper

Preheat the oven to 180 °C and grease a medium-sized ovenproof dish or 4 small ovenproof dishes with butter or margarine. Steam the cauliflower until tender but still crisp. Transfer it to the dish(es).
   Lightly whisk together the eggs and sour cream. Add 60 ml (¼ c) of the Parmesan cheese and pour the mixture over the cauliflower. Season with salt and black pepper. Sprinkle the remaining Parmesan cheese on top and bake for about 35–40 minutes or until golden brown and the sauce has set.

Serves 4.

Stuffed peppers

Mushrooms with mustard and cheese sauce

A delicious variation on Welsh rarebit.

200 g Stilton or blue cheese, crumbled
80 ml (⅓ c) beer or milk
60 ml (¼ c) cake flour
100 ml fresh breadcrumbs
5 ml (1 t) English mustard
salt and freshly ground black pepper
    to taste
3 ml (generous ½ t) Worcester sauce
Tabasco sauce to taste
1 whole egg
1 egg yolk
20 ml (4 t) olive oil
4 large brown mushrooms,
    stems trimmed short

Heat the cheese and beer over low heat until the cheese has melted – do not allow the mixture to come to the boil. Add the flour, breadcrumbs and mustard and simmer until the mixture forms a thick paste. Season with salt, pepper and Worcester and Tabasco sauces and leave to cool. Whisk in the egg and egg yolk and leave the mixture in the fridge. Switch on the oven grill. Heat the oil in a frying pan. Season the mushrooms with salt and pepper and fry in the oil until tender. Transfer the mushrooms to a small baking sheet. Shape the cold cheese paste into 4 small rounds and put them on top of the mushrooms. Grill the mushrooms until the cheese topping is golden brown and starts to bubble. Serve immediately.

Serves 4.

Budget-beating stuffing for brown mushrooms
Mix 250 g ricotta cheese with 30 ml (2 T) basil or sun-dried tomato pesto and 2 crushed cloves garlic and spoon on top of each mushroom. Drizzle with a little oil, cover and bake at 200 °C for 20 minutes or until the mushrooms are tender. Serve with a scoop of pesto on toasted bread circles.

Moroccan roast potatoes

2 kg baby potatoes
olive oil
20 ml (4 t) Moroccan rub (see recipe)
sea salt flakes
lemon slices to serve

Preheat the oven to 190 °C.
Scrub the baby potatoes and rub with olive oil. Arrange them in a roasting tin and sprinkle with the Moroccan rub. Roast in the preheated oven until done and soft. Sprinkle with salt and serve with lemon slices.

Serves 6.

MOROCCAN RUB
Using a mortar and pestle, pound together 4 bay leaves, 15 ml (1 T) ground cinnamon, 15 ml (1 T) coriander seeds, 15 ml (1 T) cumin seeds, 15 ml (1 T) black peppercorns, 2 ml (½ t) aniseed, 2 ml (½ t) cardamom seeds, 2 ml (½ t) whole cloves, 2 ml (½ t) mixed spice, 15 ml (1 T) ground ginger and 5 ml (1 t) ground nutmeg.

Tip
The Moroccan rub can also be used to add flavour to carrot purée or sweet potatoes.

Baked sweet potatoes with brinjal and peppers

Sweet potatoes are no longer regarded as fattening. Their low glycemic index makes them the ideal carbohydrate vegetable.

5 small brinjals
200 g sweet potatoes
   OR potatoes, peeled
60 ml (¼ c) olive oil
1 red pepper, seeded and quartered
1 green pepper, seeded and quartered
20 ml (4 t) balsamic vinegar
1 clove garlic, crushed
30 ml (2 T) chopped sun-dried tomatoes
60 ml (¼ c) fresh basil leaves, torn
30 ml (2 T) toasted and chopped
   blanched almonds
6 pitted black olives, chopped

Preheat the oven to 180 °C and grease a large roasting tin with a little of the oil.
   Halve the brinjals lengthways. Cut the sweet potatoes into 1 cm thick slices. Heat about 15 ml (1 T) of the olive oil in a griddle pan and lightly brown the brinjals, sweet potatoes and peppers in batches. Transfer the vegetables to the roasting tray, drizzle over the remaining olive oil, cover and bake for 45 minutes or until done.
   Blend the vinegar and garlic and pour the mixture over the vegetables. Scatter over the sun-dried tomatoes, basil, almonds and olives and serve hot or cold.

Serves 6.

Roasted sweet potatoes with harissa

Harissa (see recipe) is a hot and spicy paste that's often used in African cuisine.

1 kg redskin sweet potatoes
olive oil

Rub unpeeled sweet potatoes with olive oil and arrange them in a roasting tray. Roast at 190 °C until soft and done. Cut a cross in each sweet potato, press gently to open and spoon a little harissa inside.

HARISSA
Blitz together 8 chillies, 4 cloves garlic and 5 ml (1 t) salt to make a paste. Mix in 10 ml (2 t) caraway seeds, 5 ml (1 t) coriander seeds and 5 ml (1 t) cumin seeds. Add the seeds and a big bunch of chopped mint to the chilli paste and blend. Add 125 ml (½ c) olive oil and blitz until well blended.

Roasted vegetables with ginger

Ginger and orange juice are delicious with sweet vegetables such as sweet potatoes, butternut and carrots. Serve with ham, roasts or baked fish.

150 g sweet potatoes, peeled and cut
   into thick strips
1 butternut, peeled and cut into
   thick strips
2 carrots, scraped and cut into thick strips
40 ml olive oil
60 g butter
25 ml (5 t) brown sugar
3 cm piece fresh ginger, grated
60 ml (¼ c) orange juice

Preheat the oven to 210 °C and grease a large roasting tin with a little of the oil. Arrange the vegetables in a single layer in the prepared tin and brush with the remaining oil. Dot with butter. Mix the brown sugar, ginger and orange juice and pour evenly over the vegetables. Roast for about 1 hour or until the vegetables are tender and done and slightly caramelised.

Serves 6.

GARDEN-FRESH SALADS

It's hard to believe that an ordinary green salad can be served in so many different ways and that salad dressings come in so many different flavours. Mix and match the flavours so they complement each other or provide contrast. Some of these deliciously wholesome salads are satisfying enough as a meal on their own, while others make the perfect starter, side dish or snack.

Green salad

A mixed salad needn't be a mixture of all the leftovers in the fridge. Nor are you limited to only using iceberg lettuce. You can now choose from a wonderful variety of salad leaves in various colours and flavours. So combine iceberg, cos, butter and oak-leaf lettuce with other leaves. One of my favourite salad ingredients is baby leaf spinach. Give your imagination free rein and combine sweet and savoury flavours. While pineapple definitely doesn't go with olives or tomatoes, strawberries with blue cheese and pears with bacon are sensational.

> **Tip**
> Check what ingredients you have on hand and make a salad dressing to complement them.

Basic vinaigrette

Make enough to keep in the fridge to use later. This vinaigrette makes a delicious salad dressing but can also be used to marinate fish, prawns, chicken and fillet steak.

juice of 1–2 lemons OR
    15 ml (1 T) balsamic, grape or
    red wine vinegar
1 clove garlic (optional)
30–45 ml (2–3 T) oil (mixture of canola
    and olive oils)
salt OR 5 ml (1 t) soy sauce
freshly ground black pepper
1 ml (pinch) sugar

Squeeze out the lemons if using and grate the rind. Bruise the garlic clove with the flat side of a knife blade. Pour the oil into a measuring jug and add the lemon juice, garlic and remaining ingredients. Whisk together and leave the dressing to stand for at least 30 minutes so the flavour of the garlic can permeate the mixture. Remove the garlic.

> **Variations**
> **Herb vinaigrette:** Add 45 ml (3 T) fresh herbs such as parsley, oregano, basil, thyme or chives to the basic vinaigrette.
>   For a creamier dressing stir 30 ml (2 T) plain yoghurt into the salad dressing.

Tips
- The garlic can be crushed and added to the vinaigrette but take care that it doesn't dominate the dressing. Use only the best quality ingredients when making a salad dressing.
- Choose a green olive oil (South African olive oil is excellent). Check that it is extra-virgin olive oil. Price is a good indication of quality. The flavour of olive oil varies from green to peppery; choose the one you like best.
- Cold-pressed oil is healthier. Canola and avocado oils have a neutral flavour and combine well with olive oil.
- Sesame oil, which is delicious in Asian salad dressings, has a strong flavour and should be used sparingly.
- Vinegar is an equally important ingredient. Choose a natural vinegar that's easy on the palate such as grape, wine or apple cider vinegar. Balsamic vinegar is ideal for making Mediterranean dressings, while rice vinegar imparts an exotic flavour to dressings.

Green salad with dried pears and bacon

A good example of sweet and savoury flavours in harmony.

selection of salad leaves,
    including watercress
125 g bacon rashers, fried
6 dried pears, sliced into thin strips
toasted sunflower seeds or chopped
    pecan nuts
1 x basic vinaigrette (see recipe p. 206)

Arrange the salad leaves on a serving platter and stack the fried bacon and dried pear strips on top. Sprinkle over the sunflower seeds or nuts just before serving. Serve the vinaigrette separately.

Serves 6.

> **Variation**
> Use fresh instead of dried pears.

Green salad with tomato, olives and feta

This is a classic mixed salad. The Mediterranean salad dressing, made with herbs, garlic, capers and olive oil, imparts a wonderful flavour. Don't even think of adding pineapple or other sweet ingredients to this savoury salad.

MEDITERRANEAN SALAD DRESSING
125 ml (½ c) in total of: finely chopped
    green, red and yellow peppers
    and olives
60–80 ml (¼–⅓ c) parsley, oregano,
    garlic chives, spring onions, chives
    and basil, roughly chopped
1 anchovy, finely chopped
1 clove garlic, crushed
15 ml (1 T) capers
80 ml (⅓ c) olive oil
60 ml (¼ c) wine vinegar or lemon juice
15 ml (1 T) French mustard
1 ml (pinch) sugar
salt and freshly ground black pepper

SALAD
selection of salad leaves, including baby
    leaf spinach and basil
few black olives, pitted and halved
125 g cherry tomatoes, halved
few quail eggs, hard-boiled
1–2 rounds feta cheese, broken
    into pieces or fresh Parmesan
    cheese shavings

SALAD DRESSING
Blend all the ingredients and season to taste with salt and pepper.

SALAD
Arrange the ingredients in small dishes or one deep salad bowl or on a large platter and serve the Mediterranean salad dressing on the side so guests can help themselves.

Serves 6.

> **Tip**
> The salad dressing is delicious tossed with salad leaves and avocado or with beetroot salad.

> **FLAVOUR COMBOS: Contrasting or complementary**
> When mixing ingredients it's important to ensure they go together. Keep these two simple guidelines in mind: Allow flavours to complement each other, for instance combine savoury ingredients such as feta cheese, tomato and olives with a savoury salad dressing. Alternatively, use contrasting flavours. This is a typically South African culinary tradition, for instance savoury snoek with sweet potatoes and grape jam. When making a salad with contrasting flavours try sweet strawberries with savoury blue cheese or sweet dried pears with savoury bacon.

Green salad with strawberries and blue cheese

Mustard-flavoured mizuna leaves go well with strawberries and blue cheese.
Serve with a basic mustard vinaigrette.

MUSTARD VINAIGRETTE
15 ml (1 T) Dijon mustard
30 ml (2 T) honey
salt and freshly ground black pepper
45 ml (3 T) red wine or grape vinegar
45 ml (3 T) sherry vinegar
125 ml (½ c) canola or olive oil

SALAD
selection of salad leaves, including mizuna
125 g strawberries, sliced
60 g blue cheese, broken into small pieces
toasted sunflower seeds (optional)

VINAIGRETTE
Whisk together all the ingredients and chill until needed.

SALAD
Arrange the leaves on a serving platter or individual plates
or in bowls. Top with the strawberries and scatter over the
cheese and seeds. Moisten with a little of the salad dressing
and serve the remaining dressing separately.

Serves 8.

> **Tip**
> Vinegar flavoured with, for instance, raspberries imparts a special flavour to salad dressing.
> You can also substitute fragrant oils such as walnut or peanut oil for half the oil. If desired
> add 125 ml (½ c) chopped fresh strawberries or raspberries to the vinaigrette; blitz in a food
> processor until smooth.

Green salad with roasted butternut and chickpeas

Pumpkin, butternut and beans are typical African fare. Serve as a salad by moistening them with a
fragrant salad dressing flavoured with African spices such as cumin, coriander, cinnamon and paprika.

AFRICAN SALAD DRESSING
45 ml (3 T) sunflower oil
30 ml (2 T) lemon juice
5 ml (1 t) paprika (smoked if desired)
5 ml (1 t) ground cumin
2 ml (½ t) ground coriander
1 ml (pinch) ground cinnamon
3–5 ml (generous ½–1 t) honey
    or brown sugar
salt and freshly ground black pepper
5 ml (1 t) grated lemon rind
45 ml (3 T) chopped fresh parsley,
    coriander leaves and/or mint

SALAD
1 butternut, peeled, seeded
    and sliced into thin fingers
oil
selection of salad leaves,
    including rocket
1 can (410 g) chickpeas, drained
pumpkin seeds

SALAD DRESSING
Whisk together the salad dressing ingredients and set aside so
the flavours can develop.

SALAD
Preheat the oven to 200 °C. Arrange the butternut in a single
layer in a roasting tin, drizzle with oil and roast for about
20 minutes or until done. Drizzle over a little of the salad
dressing while cooling. Arrange the leaves on a salad platter
and pile the butternut and chickpeas on top. Moisten with a
little of the salad dressing and scatter pumpkin seeds on top.
Serve the remaining salad dressing separately.

Serves 6.

> **Tip**
> Add feta or goat's cheese and/or slices of green apple
> to the salad.

Green salad with cucumber and avocado

Rice vinegar, sesame oil, fish or oyster sauce and fresh ginger impart a typically Asian flavour to this salad made with cucumber, avocado and peanuts.

ASIAN SALAD DRESSING
60 ml (¼ c) sunflower or canola oil
60 ml (¼ c) rice vinegar
juice and rind of 2 lemons
15 ml (1 T) soy sauce
5–10 ml (1–2 t) fish or oyster sauce
5–15 ml (1–3 t) sesame oil
15 ml (1 T) sugar
25 ml (5 t) water
5–10 ml (1–2 t) finely grated fresh
    ginger
2 cloves garlic, crushed
1 chilli, seeded and finely chopped
30 ml (2 T) chopped fresh coriander leaves
15 ml (1 T) chopped fresh mint leaves

SALAD
selection of salad leaves, including fresh
    coriander leaves
1 avocado, peeled and sliced
1 red pepper, seeded and sliced
    into thin strips
1 small cucumber, halved, seeded
    and sliced into rings
1 handful peanuts

SALAD DRESSING
Whisk together the salad dressing ingredients and chill until needed.

SALAD
Arrange the leaves on a serving platter and stack the remaining ingredients, except the peanuts, on top. Drizzle over the salad dressing and chill until ready to serve. Scatter the peanuts on top.

Serves 6.

> **Tip**
> Toast a handful of sesame or mustard seeds in a dry pan and add to the salad dressing.

Pear and blue cheese salad

This is chef Mike Bassett of Cape Town restaurant Ginja's take on pears in red wine: he combines them with blue cheese and serves them as a salad.

4 pears, peeled and quartered
250 ml (1 c) red wine
125 ml (½ c) balsamic vinegar
125 ml (½ c) brown sugar
500 ml (2 c) salad leaves (mixture of
    lettuce, rocket and watercress)
60 ml (¼ c) Gorgonzola cheese, crumbled
30 ml (2 T) toasted sunflower seeds OR
    walnuts
mustard vinaigrette (see recipe p. 209)
deep-fried leeks

Put the pears, wine, balsamic vinegar and brown sugar in a saucepan and slowly bring the mixture to the boil. Simmer gently until the pears are just soft. Remove the pears from the saucepan and increase the heat. Reduce the liquid until slightly syrupy. Return the pears to the saucepan and leave to cool. Put the salad leaves in a large dish and moisten with the sauce. Arrange the leaves, Gorgonzola cheese and pear quarters on plates and scatter sunflower seeds on top. Drizzle with a little of the vinaigrette and garnish with deep-fried leeks.

Serves 4.

Pear and blue cheese salad

Lowdown on salad leaves

Rocket leaves with their indented, wavy edges are similar to oak leaves in appearance. The leaves have a piquant, peppery flavour and are delicious in salads made with sharp cheeses and olives, roasted vegetables and dried or fresh fruit.

Wild rocket leaves have deeper indentations and are more jagged than ordinary rocket leaves. They also have a more intense flavour and go well with goat's cheese, fish, meat and pasta.

Basil
This soft-leaf herb with its hint of cloves is synonymous with Mediterranean cooking and goes perfectly with tomatoes.

Lollo rosso and lollo biondo
Lollo rosso (with a wavy red edge) and lollo biondo (with a wavy green edge) have a mild flavour and delicate texture. Lollo rosso wilts rapidly. Use with other salad leaves.

Mizuna is also called mustard lettuce and is sometimes confused with wild rocket because of its jagged leaves. It has a mustardy rather than peppery flavour.

Watercress has small, round leaves with a slightly peppery taste. It's ideal for salads and delicious in sandwiches, soup and pesto.

Swiss chard and spinach
Often called spinach in South Africa Swiss chard is in fact a member of the beetroot family and is far removed in appearance and flavour from English spinach.

Swiss chard has large, firm, curly leaves with prominent white veins and thick white stems and is ideal in dishes that are heated. English spinach has smaller, more delicate leaves with green stems. It is also called baby leaf spinach and is excellent in salads. English spinach is also grown with purple stems for effect. Marog is a typically African spinach.

Citrus salad

Use the rich abundance of winter citrus fruit to make this refreshing salad.

SALAD
4 oranges OR red grapefruit,
  thickly peeled
juice of 2 oranges or as needed
selection of baby salad leaves
2 avocados, sliced into strips
1 red onion, sliced into rings
toasted seeds such as sunflower,
  sesame and pumpkin seeds
pickled ginger to garnish (optional)

SALAD DRESSING
180 ml (¾ c) freshly squeezed orange
  juice (see method)
45 ml (3 T) plain yoghurt
30 ml (2 T) olive oil
5 ml (1 t) Dijon mustard
15 ml (1 T) finely grated fresh ginger
5 ml (1 t) honey
10 ml (2 t) each finely chopped chives,
  mint and coriander leaves

SALAD
Using a small sharp knife cut the oranges into segments by cutting on both sides of the membranes. Work over a bowl to catch the juice. Set the segments aside. Squeeze out the juice from the membranes into the bowl and add enough squeezed out orange juice to make up 180 ml (¾ c) for the salad dressing.

SALAD DRESSING
Blend the orange juice with the remaining ingredients and set aside.
  Put the salad leaves in a bowl just before serving. Arrange the orange segments, avocado and onion rings on top. Scatter over the seeds and add the salad dressing or serve it separately. Garnish with pickled ginger if desired.

Serves 6.

> **Variation**
> Add apple slices.

> **Tip**
> Add a scattering of mixed toasted seeds or use fresh figs and pepper ham instead of the orange, avocado and onion.

Goat's cheese salad with basil oil

Fried goat's cheese adds an interesting twist to this caprese salad. Flavoured oils such as basil oil are very popular.

cake flour for dusting
250 ml (1 c) dried breadcrumbs
240 g goat's cheese, sliced
2 eggs, lightly whisked
30 ml (2 T) olive oil
4 cherry tomatoes, halved
250 ml (1 c) fresh basil leaves
100 g (1 packet) rocket leaves
basil oil for salad dressing (see recipe)

Put the flour and breadcrumbs on separate plates. Dip the goat's cheese in the flour, then in the whisked eggs and finally in the breadcrumbs. Heat the oil in a nonstick frying pan and fry the cheese for 1–2 minutes on each side or until golden brown and crisp. Divide the cheese, tomatoes, basil and rocket among the plates and drizzle with basil oil.

Serves 6.

BASIL OIL
Blanch 250 ml (1 c) fresh basil leaves and 125 ml (½ c) fresh parsley in boiling water and drain. Blitz the blanched leaves and 1 clove garlic in a food processor until smooth. Season with salt and pepper to taste. Slowly add 80 ml (⅓ c) olive oil while the machine is running.

Makes 200 ml.

Green salad with halloumi

Halloumi cheese must be eaten immediately after frying or it becomes rubbery. To make the salad dressing fried onion and ginger are blended with oil and vinegar to impart flavour to the dressing. The onion and ginger are discarded before using the dressing.

SALAD DRESSING
½ small onion
   (preferably a red onion)
1 cm piece fresh ginger, peeled
80 ml (⅓ c) canola oil
125 ml (½ c) brown sugar
180 ml (¾ c) washed and chopped
   coriander leaves
125 ml (½ c) olive oil
150 ml white wine vinegar

SALAD
selection of salad leaves
250 g cherry tomatoes, halved
1 cucumber, thinly sliced
½ red onion, finely sliced
1 avocado, thinly sliced
1 packet (about 250 g) halloumi
   cheese, sliced
cake flour
olive oil

SALAD DRESSING
Blitz the onion and ginger in a food processor until smooth. Heat the canola oil and braise the onion mixture until soft. Add the sugar and heat until melted and the onion mixture has caramelised slightly, about 5–10 minutes. Add the coriander, remove the pan from the heat and leave the mixture for about 1 minute to allow the flavours to blend. Add the olive oil and vinegar, leave to cool and strain the mixture. Discard the onion mixture and chill the salad dressing until needed.

SALAD
Arrange the salad ingredients, except the cheese, on a platter. Gently roll the slices of cheese in cake flour and fry rapidly in a little heated olive oil until lightly browned. Arrange on the salad, pour over a little of the salad dressing and serve immediately.

Serves 6.

> **Tip**
> **Crisply fried herbs:** Deep-fry large-leaf herbs such as basil and sage in very hot oil for a few seconds or until crisp. Scatter over a fresh mixed salad.

Green salad with walnut dressing

Walnuts fried in oil impart a wonderful flavour to this dressing. The salad is made with asparagus, olives and a selection of salad leaves.

WALNUT SALAD DRESSING
50 ml olive oil
100 ml walnuts, chopped
3 sprigs rosemary
30 ml (2 T) fresh lemon juice
salt and freshly ground black pepper

SALAD
18 baby asparagus, blanched
100 g rocket leaves
50 g watercress
100 g baby leaf spinach
200 g black olives, pitted

SALAD DRESSING
Gently heat together the olive oil, walnuts and rosemary for 5 minutes so the flavours can infuse the oil. Remove from the heat and stir in the lemon juice, salt and pepper. Remove the sprig of rosemary.

SALAD
Combine the asparagus and leaves and arrange the mixture on a salad platter. Scatter the olives on top and drizzle over the lukewarm salad dressing.

Serves 4–6.

Green salad with walnut dressing

Caesar salad

This classic salad is as popular as ever.

3 slices day-old white bread,
   crusts removed
90 ml (6 T) olive oil
5 ml (1 t) paprika
pinch cayenne pepper
3 cloves garlic, peeled
50 g anchovies, soaked in milk
   and drained
15 ml (1 T) Dijon mustard
15 ml (1 T) balsamic vinegar
Worcestershire sauce
Tabasco sauce
salt and freshly ground black pepper
30 ml (2 T) mayonnaise
1 packet (100 g) mixed salad leaves
Parmesan cheese shavings

Preheat the oven to 220 °C and keep a baking sheet on hand. Cube the bread and drizzle with 30 ml (2 T) of the olive oil. Season with the paprika and cayenne pepper and shake the bread cubes to coat them well with the oil and seasoning. Spread the bread cubes on the baking sheet and bake until crisp. Set aside. Slowly heat the whole garlic cloves and two of the anchovies in the remaining oil for about 5 minutes. Remove the garlic and anchovies. Set the oil aside. Mash together the garlic, fried anchovies, mustard, vinegar, Worcestershire and Tabasco sauces, salt and pepper. Whisk in the mayonnaise and flavoured oil. Mix the salad leaves and bread cubes. Finely chop the remaining anchovy and mix it with the salad leaves. Spoon over the salad dressing and scatter Parmesan cheese shavings on top.

Serves 4.

Lentil and apricot salad

Make this salad well in advance to allow the flavours to develop. Make extra and keep leftovers in the fridge to serve the next day.

SALAD
150 g soft dried apricots
juice and finely grated rind of
   2 small oranges
625 ml (2½ c) cooked brown lentils
1 large bunch flat-leaf parsley,
   finely chopped
salt and freshly ground black pepper

SALAD DRESSING
60 ml (¼ c) olive oil
30 ml (2 T) white wine vinegar
2 ml (½ t) cumin
2 ml (½ t) mustard seeds
5 ml (1 t) roasted curry powder
1 ml (pinch) sugar
30 ml (2 T) finely chopped fresh
   coriander

SALAD
Soak the apricots in the orange juice for at least 30 minutes. Add the orange rind, lentils and parsley and mix well. Season with salt and pepper.

SALAD DRESSING
Whisk together the salad dressing ingredients and pour over the apricot mixture. Adjust the seasoning and leave to stand for 1 hour before serving.

Serves 6–8.

Coriander and bean salad

A new variation of an old stand-by: three-beans salad. Fresh coriander leaves are a must with this salad.

SALAD DRESSING
80 ml (⅓ c) fresh coriander leaves
45 ml (3 T) cider vinegar
10 ml (2 t) Dijon mustard
3 ml (generous ½ t) ground cumin
2 cloves garlic, crushed
3 ml (generous ½ t) freshly ground
   black pepper
2 ml (½ t) salt
80 ml (⅓ c) olive oil
juice of ½ lemon

SALAD
1 can (420 g) red kidney beans, drained
1 can (420 g) butter beans, drained
1 can (420 g) whole-kernel sweet corn,
   drained
1 medium-sized red onion, chopped
lemon or lime slices or lemon pickle,
   finely chopped

SALAD DRESSING
Blitz the salad dressing ingredients in a food processor until smooth.

SALAD
Mix the beans, sweet corn and onion in a large bowl and pour over half the salad dressing. Adjust the seasoning if necessary. Pour over the remaining salad dressing just before serving and toss lightly. Garnish with citrus slices and serve at room temperature.

Serves 6–8.

Chickpea salad

Chickpeas and butter beans make a wholesome salad. Frances Grethé of Cramerview moistens them with a mustard vinaigrette.

1 can (420 g) chickpeas, drained
250 ml (1 c) cooked lentils or brown rice
1 can (420 g) butter beans, drained
1 green chilli, seeded and finely chopped
1 stalk celery, finely chopped
6 chives, finely chopped
60 ml (¼ c) chopped fresh parsley
mustard vinaigrette (see recipe p. 209)
15 ml (1 T) chopped fresh coriander
   leaves

Mix all the salad ingredients except the vinaigrette and coriander leaves. Pour over the vinaigrette and scatter the coriander leaves on top. Chill before serving.

Serves 4–6.

Creamy pasta salad

Ideal with a light lunch or braai.

500 g (1 packet) pasta shells
30 ml (2 T) olive oil
1 bunch chives, chopped
1 cucumber, peeled, seeded and
   cut into pieces
few black olives
few small cherry tomatoes
salt and freshly ground black pepper
30 ml (2 T) chopped parsley or basil
30 ml (2 T) wholegrain mustard
250 ml (1 c) low-oil mayonnaise
250 ml (1 c) plain yoghurt
10 ml (2 t) lemon juice
coarsely chopped fresh chives to garnish

Cook the pasta in rapidly boiling salted water until done but firm to the bite. Drain and pour over the olive oil. Toss lightly and leave to cool. Add the chives, cucumber, olives and tomatoes. Season with salt and pepper. Mix together the herbs, mustard, mayonnaise, yoghurt and lemon juice and pour over the pasta. Toss lightly and garnish with fresh chives.

Serves 6–8.

Couscous salad

Couscous takes only a few minutes to prepare and is delicious in salads.

375 ml (1½ c) couscous
250 ml (1 c) boiling water
125 ml (½ c) white wine
salt and freshly ground black pepper
½ English cucumber, diced
2 red peppers, seeded and diced
2 red onions, diced
20 g flat-leaf parsley, finely chopped
20 g fresh mint, finely chopped
60 ml (¼ c) olive oil
juice and rind of 1 large lemon

Put the couscous in a large bowl. Bring the boiling water and wine to the boil and pour over the couscous. Leave to stand until all the liquid has been absorbed. Fluff with a fork. Microwave on 100 per cent power for 2 minutes and fluff again with a fork to separate the grains. Season with salt and pepper and add the vegetables and herbs. Whisk together the olive oil, lemon juice and rind and pour the dressing over the salad. Toss and leave to stand for about 1 hour to allow the flavours to develop.

Serves 6–8.

Variations

To make a more filling salad add a 185 g tin flaked tuna or 3 hard-boiled eggs and sprinkle over feta cheese.

Substitute roasted butternut and pumpkin seeds for the cucumber.

Add left-over chicken and sun-dried tomato pesto.

Add a few black olives and/or small tomatoes if desired. Grate over lemon rind and stack a handful of rocket leaves on top.

Creamy pasta salad

Rice salad with dried fruit

Nuts and dried fruit are delicious mixed with rice and served as a salad.

SALAD DRESSING
60 ml (¼ c) fresh orange juice
45 ml (3 T) finely chopped onion
45 ml (3 T) balsamic vinegar
10 ml (2 t) Dijon mustard
5 ml (1 t) crushed garlic
125 ml (½ c) olive or canola oil
salt and freshly ground black pepper

SALAD
300 g brown basmati rice, cooked
    according to the packet instructions
125 ml (½ c) coarsely chopped toasted
    pecan or pine nuts
375 ml (1½ c) coarsely chopped
    fresh parsley
180 ml (¾ c) thinly sliced soft dried
    peaches, apricots or pears
60 ml (¼ c) sultanas or
    dried cranberries

SALAD DRESSING
Whisk together all the ingredients, except the oil, salt and
pepper. Gradually whisk in the oil. Season with salt and pepper.

SALAD
Drain the cooked rice and mix it with the salad dressing,
nuts, parsley and dried fruit. Leave to cool and serve at
room temperature.

Serves 8.

> **Variation**
> Add 125 ml (½ c) chopped piquanté peppers.
> Use couscous instead of the brown basmati rice.

Lemon potato salad

If you like food that's light and easy to make you'll love this potato salad.
I first had it at Isabella Niehaus's Langebaan home and now it's become a family favourite.

750 g baby potatoes, scrubbed
    and halved
finely grated rind of 2 lemons
olive oil
sea salt flakes
fresh rocket leaves

Boil the potatoes until soft and put them in a dish. Break them
gently with a wooden spoon and scatter over the lemon rind.
Drizzle generously with olive oil and sprinkle over sea salt
flakes. Leave to cool. Put rocket leaves in a dish and stack the
potatoes on top.

Serves 4.

Coleslaw with pickled ginger

This salad goes well with pork and fish.

15 ml (1 T) peanut or sesame oil
250 ml (1 c) shredded red cabbage
250 ml (1 c) shredded green cabbage
60 ml (¼ c) strips of pickled ginger
5 ml (1 t) crushed garlic
60 ml (¼ c) rice wine vinegar
20 ml (4 t) chopped fresh coriander leaves
salt and freshly ground black pepper
peanuts to sprinkle on top
extra fresh coriander leaves to garnish

Heat the oil in a large pan or wok and stir-fry the cabbage for 2 minutes or until done but still crisp. Add the ginger, garlic, vinegar and coriander leaves and sauté for another 1 minute. Remove from the heat and leave to cool. Season with salt and pepper, scatter over the peanuts and garnish with fresh coriander leaves.

Serves 4.

> **Variation**
> Add banana slices to the salad.

Chakalaka

A salad out of Africa. Delicious as a side dish with any meat or stew.

1 onion, sliced
2 cloves garlic, crushed
1–2 chillies, seeded and finely chopped
125 ml (½ c) olive oil
1 green pepper, seeded and sliced into strips
1 red pepper, seeded and sliced into strips
1 yellow pepper, seeded and sliced
   into strips
500 g cabbage, shredded
500 g carrots, scraped and grated
15 ml (1 T) cayenne pepepr
15 ml (1 T) paprika
1 can (410 g) peas
salt and freshly ground black pepper

Sauté the onion, garlic and chilli in half the oil until soft. Add the peppers and stir-fry for another 2–3 minutes. Add the cabbage, carrots, cayenne pepper, paprika and remaining oil and stir-fry until the vegetables are soft but still crisp. Add the peas and mix. Season with salt and pepper. Remove from the heat and set aside so the flavours can develop. Serve hot or cold.

Serves 6.

> **Budget-beating tip**
> Make the salad go further by adding a can of beans in tomato sauce to the mixture.

Broccoli and cauliflower salad

This delicious salad can be served separately as a starter or with the meal as a side dish.
This recipe comes from Frances Grethé of Cramerview.

SALAD
250 ml (1 c) broccoli florets
250 ml (1 c) cauliflower florets
1 red apple, cored and diced (do not peel)
2 stalks celery, chopped
1 small onion, thinly sliced into rings
80 ml (⅓ c) seedless raisins, sultanas
    or dried cranberries

SALAD DRESSING
60 ml (¼ c) mayonnaise
60 ml (¼ c) plain yoghurt
honey
2 ml (½ t) Dijon mustard
salt and freshly ground black pepper

SALAD
Steam the broccoli and cauliflower florets until just soft.
Drain and refresh under cold water. Pat dry gently and mix
with the remaining salad ingredients.

SALAD DRESSING
Blend the salad dressing ingredients and pour over the salad
ingredients. Toss gently and spoon into small bowls. Serve as
a starter.

Serves 4.

Beetroot salad with goat's cheese

Award-winning chef Nic van Wyk of Stellenbosch treated us to this salad. Goat's cheese, especially
feta, beetroot and orange are Nic's favourite ingredients and they go together beautifully in this
salad. I discovered a similar salad at Simonsig wine estate's stunningly beautiful restaurant, Cuvée.

ORANGE SALAD DRESSING
juice of 2 lemons
juice of 2 oranges, strained, and rind
    of 1 orange
50 ml verjuice or grape vinegar
5 ml (1 t) Dijon mustard or 2 ml (½ t)
    ground cumin
a little brown sugar
125 ml (½ c) canola or olive oil

SALAD
16 baby beetroot (stems removed), washed
olive oil
salt and freshly ground black pepper
180 g goat's feta or chevin
125 ml (½ c) shelled pistachio
    and pecan nuts
chopped spring onions
rocket leaves

Preheat the oven to 200 °C.

SALAD DRESSING
Mix together all the salad dressing ingredients except the oil.
Slowly add the oil and mix well.

SALAD
Rub each beetroot with olive oil and season with salt and
pepper. Arrange them in a roasting tin and roast until soft
and done. Remove the skins and pour over a little of the salad
dressing while they're still hot. Cool the beetroot in the salad
dressing. Arrange the beetroot on a serving platter or individual
plates and crumble the cheese around them. Drizzle with a little
of the salad dressing and scatter the nuts and spring onions on
top. Garnish with rocket leaves.

Serves 4–6.

Budget-beating tip
Roast 125 g carrots in a separate dish until done.
Mix lightly with the beetroot, pour over the salad
dressing and serve without the cheese and nuts.

Beetroot salad with goat's cheese

Asian salmon and noodle salad

Serve this salad with a glass of crisp, dry white wine such as sauvignon blanc.

250 g vermicelli glass noodles
80 ml (⅓ c) pickled ginger
500 ml (2 c) watercress
45 ml (3 T) roughly chopped fresh
   coriander leaves
45 ml (3 T) soy sauce
30 ml (2 T) sesame seeds, toasted
200 g smoked salmon
wasabi and soy sauce to serve
caper berries with stems
oil

Soak the vermicelli glass noodles in boiling water for 2 minutes. Drain and pat dry. Gently mix the noodles, pickled ginger, watercress, coriander leaves, soy sauce and sesame seeds. Spoon the mixture on plates and top with slices of salmon. Mix a little wasabi with soy sauce and serve with the salad. Deep-fry the caper berries in oil until crisp and scatter over the salad.

Serves 3–4.

Budget-beating tip
Use smoked trout instead of smoked salmon.

WHAT IS WASABI? It's a kind of horseradish paste usually served with sushi and is extremely hot. Use only a tiny bit with each bite.

Asian chicken salad

Chicken breast fillets take only a few minutes to cook and are ideal for making quick, filling salads. They also go with a variety of fruit (see variation).

SALAD DRESSING
125 ml (½ c) soy sauce
60 ml (¼ c) sesame oil
30 ml (2 T) rice vinegar
½ red chilli, finely chopped
10 ml (2 t) grated fresh ginger

SALAD
500 g chicken breast fillets
30 ml (2 T) sunflower oil
1 head butter lettuce, broken into pieces
125 ml (½ c) fresh coriander leaves
½ red onion, thinly sliced
1 mango, sliced
60 ml (¼ c) sesame seeds, toasted
60 ml (¼ c) peanuts

SALAD DRESSING
Mix all the ingredients in a small bowl.

SALAD
Cut the chicken breast fillets crossways into 5 mm wide strips and put them in a medium-sized bowl. Add 60 ml (¼ c) of the salad dressing to the chicken and marinate for 30 minutes. Heat the sunflower oil in a large heavy-bottomed frying pan over medium heat and stir-fry the chicken strips for about 2 minutes or until just done. Remove from the pan and leave to cool. Mix the lettuce, coriander leaves, onion and mango in a large bowl and arrange the mixture on a salad platter. Spoon the chicken strips on top and scatter over the sesame seeds and peanuts. Spoon a little of the salad dressing over the salad and serve the rest separately.

Serves 4.

Budget-beating tips
Soak instant noodles in boiling water until soft. Drain and add to the salad to make it go further.
   For a creamier salad dressing add 30 ml (2 T) plain yoghurt to the dressing.

Variation
Mix a little cake flour with 1 ml (pinch) each cayenne pepper and ground cumin and coriander. Add 30 ml (2 T) toasted sesame seeds and roll the chicken strips in the mixture before stir-frying.
   Add extra sliced fruit such as nectarines, peaches, melon, grapes and litchis.

Rice salad with smoked chicken

Smoked chicken is freely available in supermarkets but it's quick and easy to smoke chicken breast fillets at home.

CREAMY SALAD DRESSING
2 cloves garlic, crushed
45 ml (3 T) white wine vinegar
60 ml (¼ c) fresh lemon juice
45 ml (3 T) chopped mango atjar
  or hot chutney
salt and freshly ground black pepper
25 ml (5 t) mild curry powder or
  15 ml (1 T) Dijon mustard
125 ml (½ c) oil
125 ml (½ c) mayonnaise
60 ml (¼ c) plain yoghurt
45 ml (3 T) water
60 ml (¼ c) chopped fresh coriander
  or parsley leaves

SALAD
250 g brown basmati rice, cooked
  according to the packet instructions
15 ml (1 T) white wine vinegar
30 ml (2 T) oil
salt and freshly ground black pepper
1 bunch spring onions, chopped
250 ml (1 c) gold sultanas
6 smoked chicken breast fillets

SALAD DRESSING
Whisk together the garlic, vinegar, juice, chutney and seasoning. Gently heat together the curry powder and oil and gradually whisk into the salad dressing. Add the mayonnaise, yoghurt and water and whisk well. Add the coriander leaves, cover and chill.

SALAD
Drain the cooked rice and add the vinegar, oil, salt and pepper to taste. Stir in the chopped spring onions and sultanas and leave to cool. Cut the chicken breast fillets into strips and add to the rice mixture. Moisten with the salad dressing. Serve with the extra salad dressing.

Serves 8–10.

Variation
Substitute cherry tomatoes, cucumber and avocado for the rice mixture and season the salad dressing with mustard, not curry powder.

Tip
Don't smoke the meat for too long or it will become bitter.

HOW TO SMOKE CHICKEN BREAST FILLETS

Smoking mixture
125 ml (½ c) raw rice
60 ml (¼ c) rooibos leaves
60 ml (¼ c) Earl Grey tea leaves
3 cloves garlic, crushed
60 ml (¼ c) brown sugar
4 bay leaves, crushed

Mix all the ingredients and set aside.

How to prepare the smoker
Line the base of an old saucepan with three layers of heavy-duty aluminium foil. Put the smoking mixture in the saucepan and put an old colander or any dish with holes on top of the smoking mixture. Put the chicken breasts in the colander in a single layer, leaving enough room in between for the smoke to come through. Cover the saucepan with a double layer of aluminium foil. Ensure no smoke can escape through the sides. Prick a small hole in the foil with a cocktail stick.
  Put the saucepan on the stove plate and heat until very hot. When smoke starts coming through the hole, reduce the heat to medium and smoke the meat for 15–20 minutes. Remove from the heat and leave the meat in the smoker to cool down.

Chicken liver salad

Use affordable chicken livers to make this delicious salad. Serve it as a light meal with strawberries and cucumber.

MARINADE
125 ml (½ c) soy sauce
30 ml (2 T) honey
60 ml (¼ c) olive oil
60 ml (¼ c) sherry or sweet wine
1 handful fresh coriander leaves,
    chopped
1 ml (pinch) Cajun spice
30 ml (2 T) sweet chilli sauce
salt and freshly ground black pepper

SALAD
30 ml (2 T) olive oil
500 g chicken livers, cleaned
10 strawberries, washed and quartered
1 handful rocket leaves
mixed salad leaves
12 cucumber slices, halved
30 ml (2 T) sesame seeds, toasted

MARINADE
Blend the marinade ingredients.

SALAD
Heat the olive oil in a pan over high heat and fry the livers until brown on the outside but still pink inside. Transfer the livers to the marinade and leave them in the fridge for 1 hour. Drain and pour the marinade into a saucepan. Simmer the marinade over low heat until syrupy. Arrange the strawberries, rocket, salad leaves and cucumber on 4 plates or a large platter. Rapidly reheat the livers in a very hot pan and pile them on the salad ingredients. Moisten with the sauce and scatter over toasted sesame seeds. Serve immediately.

Serves 4.

Biltong carpaccio salad

Wet biltong sliced into paper thin slices as for carpaccio and served with rocket leaves, an avocado salsa and mustard vinaigrette makes an elegant salad.

20 ml (4 t) coriander seeds
1 beef fillet (about 1 kg)

SALTPETRE MIXTURE
20 ml (4 t) coarse salt
5 ml (1 t) brown sugar
1 ml (pinch) saltpetre
2 ml (½ t) bicarbonate of soda
2 ml (½ t) freshly ground black pepper
50 ml brown vinegar
white wine vinegar and water to rinse

AVOCADO AND FETA SALSA
200 g feta cheese, diced
2 firm avocados, peeled and diced
2 spring onions, finely chopped
30 ml (2 T) mixed bean sprouts

TO SERVE
2 handfuls rocket leaves
mustard vinaigrette (see recipe p. 209)
bean sprouts to garnish

Toast the coriander seeds in a dry pan over medium heat until fragrant. Grind until fine.
    Remove all visible fat and sinews from the fillet.

SALTPETRE MIXTURE
Mix the dry ingredients and rub the mixture into the meat. Put the meat in a plastic or enamel container and evenly sprinkle the brown vinegar over the fillet. Chill in the fridge for 18–24 hours. Mix 1 part vinegar with 10 parts water and bring the mixture to the boil. Rinse the biltong with the hot vinegar mixture to remove excess salt. Hang the biltong in a cool, well-ventilated room for 3–4 days.

AVOCADO AND FETA SALSA
Lightly mix the salsa ingredients.

Line a pretty salad platter with fresh rocket leaves. Cut the biltong into slices about 1,5 mm thick. Arrange them close together on the rocket leaves. Spoon the salsa in the centre of the platter and moisten with the vinaigrette. Scatter the bean sprouts on top.

Serves 6–8.

ABC of herbs

HERBS	IN FOOD
Parsley	Probably the most popular and best-known herb. Use to make herbed butter to serve with steak or to add to omelettes, soup and stews. Ordinary parsley has curly leaves, while Italian parsley has flat, serrated leaves.
Mint	Mint is delicious in tea, especially iced tea and other drinks. It also goes with fruit salad. Mint sauce is a classic accompaniment with leg of lamb. Cook peas and baby potatoes with mint or finely chop mint leaves and add them to butter and cottage cheese. Mint also adds flavour to chocolate puddings, ice cream and cakes.
Rosemary	Rosemary has a strong resin flavour. Rub sprigs to remove the leaves and chop them finely. Rosemary goes well with leg of lamb, stews, soup and fruit. Use sparingly unless roasting meat when whole sprigs can be used. It's also a good flavouring for oil, vinegar, bread, scones and biscuits.
Thyme	Thyme has a strong, piquant or lemony flavour. Strip the leaves from the stems and use with chicken (add lemon), meat and fish. Chop thyme and mix into batter for dumplings, scones and bread.
Sage	Sage has a potent flavour and is ideal with fatty meats and poultry. Use chopped leaves to impart flavour to bread and scone dough, oil and vinegar. Sprinkle chopped leaves over vegetables or deep-fry whole leaves and stack them on top of pasta or meat dishes.
Fennel	Fennel has a sweet aniseed flavour. The bulbs can be stir-fried and served as a salad with a light vinaigrette dressing. Add the chopped leaves to chicken, meat and fish. Wrap a whole fish in fennel leaves before cooking over a fire. Use to season butter, cheese, oil, vinegar, mayonnaise and egg dishes.
Dill	Dill is similar in appearance to fennel but has a more delicate flavour Wthat goes with fish.
Coriander	Also called dhania, Chinese parsley or cilantro. The leaves are similar in appearance to Italian flat-leaf parsley. This herb has a characteristic taste that not everyone likes. The leaves are used in curries and Malay and North African dishes. They also add flavour to salads, salsas and Asian dishes made with rice vinegar, sesame oil and fish sauce.

SWEET ENDINGS

Classic desserts such as malva pudding, dumplings and rice pudding are given an interesting new twist. There are recipes for creamy chocolate cups or mousse, fruity baked puddings or fruit cooked in a wine syrup. Also treat guests to a Pavlova, roulade or ice-cream bombe – there's something to satisfy every food-lover's craving for something sweet and delicious.

Bread pudding with Amarula

This bread pudding is simply sublime.

50 g sultanas
50 ml whisky
60 g butter
12 slices day-old white bread
6 eggs, lightly whisked
125 ml (½ c) caster sugar
250 ml (1 c) cream or 1 can (410 g)
   evaporated milk
400 ml milk
5 ml (1 t) vanilla essence
150 ml Amarula liqueur
nutmeg
brown caramel sugar to sprinkle on top

> **Variations**
> Substitute dried fruitcake mix for the sultanas. You can also add banana.
>
> Substitute Van der Hum liqueur for the Amarula liqueur.

Preheat the oven to 180 °C. Grease a medium-sized ovenproof dish that fits into a roasting tin with butter, margarine or nonstick food spray.

Soak the sultanas in the whisky. Butter one side of the bread slices and remove the crusts. Cut the bread slices into triangles and arrange them in the prepared dish so they overlap slightly. Whisk together the eggs and caster sugar until just blended – the mixture must not be foamy. Bring the cream, milk and vanilla essence just to the boil. Remove from the heat and strain the mixture. Add the Amarula liqueur to the milk mixture and add to the egg mixture.

Drain the sultanas and sprinkle a few over the bread layer. Sprinkle over a little nutmeg and pour over three-quarters of the egg custard. Repeat the bread, sultana and custard layers until all the ingredients have been used, ending with a bread layer without sultanas and nutmeg which is inclined to burn. Put the dish in a large roasting tin filled halfway with boiling water. Bake the pudding for 30–35 minutes or until the egg custard has set and the corners of the bread slices are golden brown. Sprinkle over a little caramel sugar and grill rapidly until the sugar has caramelised slightly. Serve hot.

Serves 6–8.

Bread pudding with Amarula

Malva pudding with red wine sauce

Sweet, rich baked puddings always go down a treat and what could be more satisfying than a malva pudding. This one is moistened with a delicious red wine sauce reminiscent of glühwein. Serve it with frozen yoghurt instead of ice cream. This recipe was specially developed for *YOU* by Cape Town foodie Susina Jooster.

BATTER
1 egg
100 ml sugar
250 ml (1 c) cake flour
5 ml (1 t) baking powder
5 ml (1 t) bicarbonate of soda
1 ml (pinch) salt
25 ml (5 t) smooth apricot jam
30 ml (2 T) red wine
250 ml (1 c) milk

SYRUP
100 ml sugar
150 ml boiling water
150 ml milk
50 g butter
2 ml (½ t) vanilla essence

RED WINE SAUCE
250 ml (1 c) red wine such as pinotage
100 ml sugar
rind and juice of 1 lemon
2 pieces stick cinnamon
2 star anise
10 ml (2 t) cornflour or arrowroot

Preheat the oven to 180 °C. Grease a medium-sized ovenproof dish or 6 individual ramekins with butter, margarine or nonstick food spray.

BATTER
Whisk together the egg and sugar until light and fluffy. Sift together the dry ingredients and mix into the egg mixture. Add the jam, red wine and milk, mixing to form a smooth batter. Turn the batter into the prepared dish or ramekins and bake for 20–40 minutes, depending on the size of the dish(es), or until a testing skewer comes out clean.

SYRUP
Bring the syrup ingredients to the boil and pour over the hot pudding as it comes out of the oven. Serve lukewarm with the red wine sauce and frozen yoghurt.

RED WINE SAUCE
Bring the wine, sugar, lemon rind and juice and spices to the boil and bubble for about 2 minutes. Blend the cornflour with a little cold water to make a paste and add to the wine mixture. Cook for about 1 minute. Serve the sauce with the pudding.

Serves 6.

Variation
Add 125 ml (½ c) chopped dates and nuts if desired.

Date dumplings *(souskluitjies)*

Dumplings conjure up aromas of your grandma's kitchen. This recipe from colleague
Esti Robinson is a delicious variation of traditional *souskluitjies*.

SAUCE
400 ml sugar
1 litre (4 c) water
30 ml (2 T) cold butter, diced
30 ml (2 T) smooth apricot jam
1 piece stick cinnamon
2 ml (½ t) salt
40–50 ml rum

DUMPLINGS
500 ml (2 c) cake flour
15 ml (1 T) bicarbonate of soda
2 ml (½ t) ground cinnamon
5 ml (1 t) mixed spice
30 ml (2 T) butter
125 ml (½ c) finely chopped dates
250 ml (1 c) milk

SAUCE
Slowly heat the sauce ingredients in a large heavy-bottomed
saucepan, stirring until the sugar has dissolved. Bring the
sauce to the boil, reduce the heat and cook for 5 minutes.

DUMPLINGS
Sift together the flour, bicarbonate of soda and spices. Rub
in the butter with your fingertips until the mixture resembles
coarse breadcrumbs. Add the dates and mix well. Slowly add
the milk, stirring continuously. Bring the sauce to the boil once
more.
  Use a dessertspoon dipped in water and, working rapidly,
drop spoonfuls of the batter into the boiling sauce.
Leave enough room between the dumplings for them to rise.
Dip the spoon into water frequently while working. Cover
the saucepan with a tight-fitting lid, reduce the heat slightly
and simmer for 15–20 minutes. Do not remove the lid before
the end of the cooking time. Serve hot with cream, ice cream
or custard.

Serves 4–6.

Rice dumplings in cinnamon sauce

This recipe, sent in by Jolene Mallet of Mondeor, is a cross between rice pudding and dumplings.
The dumplings can be spiced with cardamom instead of cinnamon.

DUMPLINGS
150 g white rice
500 ml (2 c) water
1 ml (pinch) salt
4 cardamom pods
15 ml (1 T) butter
15 ml (1 T) sugar
15 ml (1 T) cake flour
2 eggs

SAUCE
375 ml (1½ c) water
125 ml (½ c) sugar
5 ml (1 t) ground cinnamon
1 ml (pinch) salt
30 ml (2 T) margarine
15 ml (1 T) cake flour

TO SERVE
ground cinnamon
cream (optional)

DUMPLINGS
Bring the rice, water, salt and cardamom pods to the boil.
Reduce the heat, cover and simmer until the rice is cooked
and all the liquid has evaporated. Remove the cardamom pods
and add the butter and sugar. Mash the rice with a potato
masher. Whisk together the flour and eggs and add to the
mashed rice. Simmer over low heat, stirring until the mixture
thickens. Remove from the heat and set aside.

SAUCE
Bring the sauce ingredients to the boil in a saucepan, stirring
until the mixture is smooth and thick. Simmer for 5 minutes.
Pour the sauce into a bowl and drop spoonfuls of the rice
mixture into the sauce. Sprinkle with cinnamon, cover and
keep warm. Serve warm with cream if desired.

Serves 4–6.

Super sago pudding

180 ml (¾ c) sago
250 ml (1 c) full-cream milk
250 ml (1 c) cream
1 ml (pinch) salt
1 can (397 g) condensed milk
3 ml (generous ½ t) baking powder
3 extra-large eggs, separated
80 ml (⅓ c) soft brown sugar
7 ml (1½ t) ground cinnamon

Preheat the oven to 200 °C. Grease a medium-sized oven-proof dish with butter, margarine or nonstick food spray.
Bring the sago, milk, cream and salt to the boil over low heat. Stirring continuously, simmer gently for about 30 minutes. Remove from the heat, cool slightly and add the condensed milk, baking powder and egg yolks. Mix well. Whisk the egg whites until stiff peaks form and gently fold into the sago mixture. Spoon into the prepared dish. Mix the brown sugar and cinnamon and sprinkle on top. Bake for 20–30 minutes or until puffed and golden brown. Serve with custard.

Serves 4.

Variation
Substitute apricot or strawberry jam for the brown sugar and cinnamon and spread over the pudding when it's done. Whisk together 2 egg whites and 30 ml (2 T) caster sugar until stiff and spoon on top of the cooked pudding. Bake until the meringue is lightly browned.

Fruity rice pudding

Jill van Graan of Benoni makes a fragrant rice pudding with dried apricots, raisins, dates and almonds and serves it with cinnamon cream.

250 ml (1 c) rice, preferably Bonnet
125 ml (½ c) sugar
5 ml (1 t) ground cinnamon
1 ml (pinch) nutmeg
45 ml (3 T) butter or margarine
1 litre (4 c) milk
4 egg yolks
5 ml (1 t) vanilla essence
125 ml (½ c) dried apricots, chopped
125 ml (½ c) sultanas
125 ml (½ c) finely chopped dates
125 ml (½ c) chopped flaked almonds
125 ml (½ c) apricot jam, slightly heated

Preheat the oven to 180 °C. Grease a 25 cm ovenproof dish with butter or nonstick food spray. Stirring continuously, bring the rice, sugar, cinnamon, nutmeg, butter and milk to the boil over low heat. Simmer slowly for 5 minutes or until the mixture thickens and the rice is done. Cool slightly and whisk in the egg yolks and vanilla essence. Stir in the fruit and almonds, spoon the mixture into the prepared dish and bake for 20–25 minutes or until firm.
Brush the pudding with the warm apricot jam as soon as it comes out of the oven. Serve with custard or cinnamon cream (see recipe).

Serves 6.

CINNAMON CREAM
Whisk together 250 ml (1 c) cream, 15 ml (1 T) caster sugar, 5 ml (1 t) ground cinnamon and 5 ml (1 t) vanilla essence until thick.

Super sago pudding

Economical rice pudding

Use leftover rice to make this delicious pudding which is flavoured with marmalade and whisky.

350 ml milk
250 ml (1 c) cream
500 ml (2 c) cooked rice
75 ml (5 T) brown sugar
5 ml (1 t) vanilla essence
60 ml (¼ c) marmalade
30 ml (2 T) whisky
3 extra-large eggs
15 ml (1 T) butter

Preheat the oven to 180 °C. Grease a 20 cm x 27 cm ovenproof dish with butter, margarine or nonstick food spray.
Heat together the milk, cream, rice, 45 ml (3 T) of the brown sugar and vanilla essence until the sugar has dissolved. Bring to the boil and cook gently for 5 minutes. Remove from the heat and add the marmalade and whisky. Leave to cool slightly. Whisk the eggs and add. Spoon the mixture into the prepared ovenproof dish and sprinkle with the remaining 30 ml (2 T) brown sugar. Dot with the butter and bake for 20–25 minutes or until set. Serve warm with thin custard.

Serves 4–6.

Hot coconut pudding

Bettie Eksteen of Strand sent us the recipe for this deliciously moist pudding with an exotic coconut flavour.

125 g butter
250 ml (1 c) sugar
3 extra-large eggs
250 ml (1 c) cake flour
1 ml (pinch) salt
3 ml (generous ½ t) baking powder
500 ml (2 c) desiccated coconut
250 ml (1 c) milk

SYRUP
250 ml (1 c) sugar
250 ml (1 c) water
125 ml (½ c) cream or evaporated milk
5 ml (1 t) vanilla essence

Preheat the oven to 180 °C. Grease a 30 cm x 16 cm ovenproof dish with butter, margarine or nonstick food spray.
Cream together the butter and sugar and add the eggs one by one, beating well after each addition. Sift together the flour, salt and baking powder and add the coconut. Add the dry ingredients to the butter mixture, alternating with the milk. Spoon the mixture into the prepared dish and bake for 35 minutes or until done and a testing skewer comes out clean.

SYRUP
Bring the sugar, water and cream to the boil. Simmer for 5 minutes and add the vanilla essence. Pour over the hot pudding as soon as it comes out of the oven.

Serves 6–8.

Fruit and almond clafoutis

This classic French dessert is quick and easy to make.

400 g mixed blackberries, blueberries
and raspberries

BATTER
50 g ground almonds
30 ml (2 T) self- raising flour
125 ml (½ c) caster sugar
2 ml (½ t) baking powder
2 extra-large eggs
2 egg yolks
250 ml (1 c) cream, milk or buttermilk

Preheat the oven to 190 °C. Grease a 23 cm pie dish with butter, margarine or nonstick food spray.
Evenly spread the berries in the bottom of the dish. Whisk together the ingredients for the batter until smooth and pour over the fruit. Bake for 20–25 minutes or until puffed and golden brown. Serve hot.

Serves 6.

Variation
Use guava halves instead of the berries.

Upside-down citrus and almond cake

The bottom of the tin is layered with slices of grapefruit or orange before the batter is spooned on top. The cake is turned upside down when it comes out of the oven and moistened with the remaining syrup in which the fruit was cooked.

CITRUS SAUCE
250 ml (1 c) caster sugar
125 ml (½ c) water
5 ml (1 t) vanilla essence
1 grapefruit and 2 large oranges,
   with rind and thickly sliced

CAKE
4 eggs
250 ml (1 c) caster sugar
5 ml (1 t) vanilla essence
250 ml (1 c) self-raising flour
150 ml melted unsalted butter
250 g ground almonds

TO SERVE
mascarpone cheese

Preheat the oven to 180 °C. Grease 2 x 20 cm square cake tins with butter, margarine or nonstick food spray.

SAUCE
Slowly heat the sugar, water and vanilla essence in a saucepan, stirring until the sugar has dissolved. Bubble the syrup hard for about 3 minutes or until syrupy. Cut the grapefruit and orange slices into quarters and put them in the syrup. Simmer for another 10–15 minutes. Remove from the heat and set aside.

CAKE
In a large mixing bowl whisk together the the eggs, caster sugar and vanilla essence for 8–10 minutes or until light and fluffy. Sift the self-raising flour on top and fold in. Add the butter and almonds and fold in. Arrange the citrus slices in the greased tins and spoon the batter on top. Bake for 45 minutes or until done and a testing skewer comes out clean. Pour the remaining syrup over the cake as soon as it comes out of the oven. Turn the cake upside down on a serving platter and cut into squares. Serve with mascarpone cheese.

Makes 2 cakes.

Variation
Substitute the following for the citrus sauce: Bring to the boil 1 bottle (750 ml) rosé wine, 100 ml sugar, 10 ml (2 t) vanilla essence and the rind of 1 lemon. Peel 6 pears and gently simmer them in the syrup until soft. Remove the pears from the syrup and halve them. Use as described for the upside-down citrus and almond cake.

Peach pudding

A layer of peach halves and almonds coated in a syrup is topped with a cake layer. The wholewheat flour gives the cake layer a lovely crumbly texture. This recipe was sent in by Fynn Stathmore of Cape Town.

25 ml (5 t) soft brown sugar
10 walnuts, chopped
1 can (420 g) peach halves, drained
500 ml (2 c) wholewheat flour
   (Nutty Wheat)
6 ml (generous 1 t) bicarbonate of soda
10 ml (2 t) ground cinnamon
15 ml (1 T) ground ginger
250 ml (1 c) soft brown sugar
2 eggs
230 ml milk
100 ml oil

Preheat the oven to 180 °C and grease a 26 cm loose-bottomed cake tin with butter, margarine or nonstick food spray.
   Mix the 25 ml brown sugar and chopped walnuts and sprinkle over the base of the tin. Arrange the peach halves on top, cut side facing down. Set aside. Mix the flour, bicarbonate of soda, cinnamon and ginger. Add the 250 ml (1 c) brown sugar. Make a well in the centre. Whisk together the eggs, milk and oil and pour the mixture into the well. Mix well and carefully spoon the batter on top of the peaches. Bake for 35–40 minutes – the pudding is done when springy to the touch. Serve with custard.

Serves 8.

Berry crumble

This pudding is a winner. The berries form a wonderful syrupy purée below the oat crumble. The nuts in the crumble go beautifully with the tart flavour of the fruit.

OAT CRUMBLE
125 ml (½ c) brown sugar
5 ml (1 t) baking powder
125 ml (½ c) oats
250 ml (1 c) cake flour
100 g butter, diced
1 packet (100 g) mixed nuts or
   a mixture of almonds and hazelnuts,
   finely chopped

FRUIT MIXTURE
250 ml (1 c) brown sugar
80 ml (⅓ c) lemon juice
1 banana, chopped
1 apple, diced
250 ml (1 c) frozen berries

Preheat the oven to 180 °C. Grease 6 ramekins with butter, margarine or nonstick food spray.

OAT CRUMBLE
Mix the dry ingredients for the crumble. Rub in the butter with your fingertips until crumbly and add the nuts.

FRUIT MIXTURE
Heat the brown sugar and lemon juice over low heat, stirring until the sugar has dissolved. Cook for 5–10 minutes or until the mixture forms a syrup. Add the fruit to the syrup and simmer slowly for another 3 minutes. Pour the fruit mixture into the greased ramekins and sprinkle over the crumb topping. Bake for 20–25 minutes or until the topping is slightly crisp and pale brown. Serve with custard.

Serves 6.

Almond and apple tart

Judy Munthree of Phoenix sent us this recipe for an apple tart with a delicious almond flavour.

APPLE LAYER
700 g (about 3–4 large) Granny Smith
   apples, peeled, cored and cut
   into wedges
5 ml (1 t) ground cinnamon
75 ml (5 T) brown sugar

TOPPING
125 g butter, at room temperature
160 ml (⅔ c) brown sugar
2 extra-large eggs
225 ml self-raising flour
3 ml (generous ½ t) almond essence
30 ml (2 T) milk
30 ml (2 T) flaked almonds
icing sugar

Preheat the oven to 180 °C. Grease a 27 cm ovenproof dish with butter, margarine or nonstick food spray.

APPLE LAYER
Arrange the apple wedges in the prepared dish. Mix the cinnamon and brown sugar and sprinkle over the apples.

TOPPING
Cream together the butter and brown sugar. Add the eggs one by one, beating well after each addition. Add the self-raising flour, almond essence and milk and mix. Spoon the batter on top of the apples, spreading it evenly. Sprinkle the almonds on top and bake for 50–60 minutes or until risen and golden brown. Blend the icing sugar with a little water and drizzle over the tart. Cut into squares and serve with a little cream or ice cream if desired.

Serves 8.

Berry crumble

Chocolate and plum pan cake

The chocolate flavour of this heavenly moist, sticky cake is complemented by the tartness of the fruit. Bake the cake in a pan with an ovenproof handle.

CAKE
125 g butter
100 ml caster sugar
3 egg yolks
250 ml (1 c) self-raising flour
80 ml (⅓ c) cocoa powder
125 ml (½ c) milk
50 g (½ slab) chocolate, melted
100 g pecan nuts, chopped
4 plums, pitted and halved

BUTTER CARAMEL SAUCE
200 ml soft brown sugar
80 g butter
300 ml cream

Preheat the oven to 180 °C. Grease an 18 cm ovenproof pan with butter, margarine or nonstick food spray.

CAKE
Cream together the butter and sugar until light and fluffy. Add the egg yolks one by one, beating well after each addition. Sift together the self-raising flour and cocoa powder and beat into the butter mixture, alternating with the milk. Add the melted chocolate and pecan nuts and turn the batter into the greased pan. Arrange the plum halves on top of the batter, cut side facing up. Bake for 30–40 minutes or until done. Serve with butter caramel sauce.

BUTTER CARAMEL SAUCE
Heat the sugar and butter over low heat in a saucepan, stirring until the sugar has dissolved. Slowly add the cream, bubble for a few minutes and serve with the cake.

Serves 6.

Phyllo pastry roly-poly

Gently simmer dried fruit in a spicy syrup until soft and roll them up in phyllo pastry along with nuts. An easy-to-make, rustic dessert.

500 g mixed dried fruit, chopped
2 apples, peeled and grated (optional)
1 piece stick cinnamon
250 ml (1 c) water
30 ml (2 T) port
a little sugar
12–13 sheets phyllo pastry
melted butter
20 ml (4 t) ground cinnamon
100 g (1 packet) mixed nuts,
   roughly chopped

TO SERVE
cream or ice cream

Preheat the oven to 180 °C. Grease a large baking sheet with butter, margarine or nonstick food spray.
   Bring the dried fruit, apples, stick cinnamon and water to the boil. Simmer gently until soft, drain and set aside. Add the port and a little sugar to taste. Brush 5 phyllo pastry sheets with melted butter and arrange on top of each other. Sprinkle half the dried fruit mixture, cinnamon and nuts on top of the sheets. Brush another 5 sheets of phyllo pastry with melted butter and lay on top of the fruit mixture. Sprinkle the remaining ingredients on top of the pastry and cover with 2–3 more sheets of phyllo pastry that have been brushed with melted butter. Roll up the pastry, starting from the wide end. Put the roll on the prepared baking sheet and bake for 40 minutes or until golden brown. Leave to cool and cut into thick slices. Serve with cream or ice cream.

Serves 8–10.

Tip
Cut down on kilojoules by greasing the phyllo pastry sheets with food spray instead of melted butter.

Sticky lime pudding

This recipe for this pudding was devised by Australian food writer Jill Dupleix. The dessert separates into two layers while baking: a soft sponge on top and a sticky lime sauce at the bottom.

30 ml (2 T) butter
250 ml (1 c) sugar
60 ml (¼ c) cake flour, sifted
juice and grated rind of 4 limes
(or 2 lemons)
500 ml (2 c) milk
4 eggs, separated (the eggs must be fresh)

Preheat the oven to 180 °C and grease an ovenproof dish with butter, margarine or nonstick food spray.

Cream together the butter and sugar. Add the flour, lime juice and rind, milk and egg yolks and mix. Whisk the egg whites until stiff peaks form and fold them into the mixture. Turn the batter into the prepared dish and bake for 30–50 minutes or until the top is golden. Serve with frozen yoghurt.

Serves 4.

Orange pot pudding

Chantelle Liebenberg of Jeffreys Bay makes this dessert in a pot on top of the stove.

SYRUP
1 litre (4 c) water
250 ml (1 c) orange juice
500 ml (2 c) sugar
10 ml (2 t) ground cinnamon
½ thin-peel orange, sliced skin and all
and pips removed

BATTER
45 ml (3 T) butter
30 ml (2 T) golden syrup
250 ml (1 c) pitted dates, finely chopped
500 ml (2 c) cake flour
1 ml (pinch) salt
10 ml (2 t) bicarbonate of soda
125 ml (½ c) lukewarm milk

SYRUP
Slowly bring the water, orange juice, sugar and cinnamon to the boil in a large saucepan. Evenly layer the orange slices in the saucepan and simmer slowly for 5 minutes. Remove from the heat and set aside.

BATTER
Melt the butter and golden syrup and add the dates, mixing well. Stir in the cake flour and salt. Dissolve the bicarbonate of soda in the milk and add to the batter. Bring the syrup to the boil once more and spoon the batter on top of the boiling syrup. Cover and simmer slowly for about 1 hour. Halfway through the cooking process break the pudding into serving sizes with a spoon. Serve with cream or custard.

Serves 8.

Hot chocolate cups

Made from basic ingredients but deliciously decadent. The batter forms a chocolate sauce at the bottom and a soft chocolate cake on top.

300 ml self-raising flour
150 ml caster sugar
100 ml cocoa powder
1 ml (pinch) salt
1 egg
125 ml (½ c) milk
50 g butter, melted
3 ml (generous ½ t) vanilla extract or
    5 ml (1 t) vanilla essence
90 ml (6 T) soft brown sugar
250 ml (1 c) boiling water

Preheat the oven to 180 °C and grease 4 x 250–275 ml ovenproof cups or ramekins with butter, margarine or nonstick food spray.

Sift together the flour, caster sugar, half the cocoa powder and salt. Make a well in the mixture. Lightly whisk together the egg, milk, butter and vanilla essence and pour the mixture into the well. Beat slowly to make a smooth, thick batter. Spoon the batter into the cups or ramekins, spreading the mixture evenly with a spoon. Mix the remaining cocoa powder with the sugar, ensuring there are no lumps.

Spoon the mixture evenly over the batter in the 4 containers. Divide the boiling water among the containers, pouring it slowly on top of the batter until the containers are three-quarters full. Bake for 20–25 minutes or until well risen and firm to the touch. Serve with ice cream if desired.

Serves 4.

Moist chocolate pudding

This recipe comes from Cape Town restaurant Ginga's award-winning chef Mike Basset. The chocolate pudding is made with real chocolate and ground almonds.

250 ml (1 c) sifted icing sugar
150 ml ground almonds
110 ml cake flour
6 extra-large egg whites
150 ml melted butter
50 g chocolate, melted
125 ml (½ c) brown sugar
30 ml (2 T) cocoa powder
2 ml (½ t) instant coffee powder
    (optional)
125 ml (½ c) boiling water

Preheat the oven to 180 °C and grease 4–6 cups or ramekins with butter, margarine or nonstick food spray. Alternatively use a muffin tin with deep hollows.

Combine the icing sugar, almonds and cake flour. Whisk the egg whites until soft peaks form and fold in a third of the flour mixture until just mixed. Fold in the remaining flour mixture. Mix the melted butter and chocolate and fold in. Spoon the mixture into the prepared ramekins, filling them three-quarters of the way. Bake for 12 minutes or until done. Mix the brown sugar, cocoa powder, coffee powder and boiling water and spoon over the puddings as soon as they come out of the oven. Cool slightly and serve with a scoop of vanilla ice cream.

Makes 4 large or 6 small puddings.

HOW TO MELT CHOCOLATE
The easiest way is in the microwave oven. Break or cut a 100 g slab of chocolate into uniform pieces or squares or grate it coarsely in a glass bowl and microwave on high for 1 minute. Stir occasionally and microwave for another 30 seconds. Stir until completely melted. If there are still lumps microwave for another 20 seconds and stir. Do not add any water to the chocolate.

Hot chocolate cups

Peppermint chocolate pudding

Mercia Kruger of Pretoria West adds grated peppermint chocolate to the batter for this simply divine dessert.

BATTER
250 ml (1 c) cake flour
25 ml (5 t) cocoa powder
15 ml (1 T) baking powder
1 ml (pinch) salt
½ slab (50 g) peppermint chocolate, grated
60 ml (¼ c) softened butter
    or margarine
200 ml soft brown sugar
1 extra-large egg
180 ml (¾ c) milk

SAUCE
250 ml (1 c) water
250 ml (1 c) soft brown sugar
½ slab (50 g) peppermint chocolate

Preheat the oven to 180 °C and grease a medium-sized ovenproof dish with butter, margarine or nonstick food spray.

BATTER
Sift together the flour, cocoa powder, baking powder and salt. Add the chocolate and mix. Cream together the butter and brown sugar and beat in the egg and milk. Add the flour mixture and mix well. Turn the batter into the prepared dish.

SAUCE
Bring the ingredients for the sauce to the boil, stirring until the sugar has dissolved. Pour the boiling syrup over the batter and bake for 30 minutes or until done. Serve with ice cream.

Serves 6.

Mocha crème brûlée

Irresistibly delicious.

1 litre (4 c) cream
250 ml (1 c) white sugar
15 ml (1 T) instant coffee powder
1 piece stick cinnamon
10 ml (2 t) vanilla essence
6 extra-large egg yolks
1 extra-large egg
extra white sugar to sprinkle on top

Tips
Chill the baked custards after sprinkling the sugar on top. The sugar will become syrupy, making it easier to caramelise. Reserve the egg whites for making a pavlova. Egg whites will keep well in the fridge for 1 week and also freeze well.

Preheat the oven to 170 °C. Put a tea towel in the bottom of a roasting tin and put 10–12 ovenproof ramekins on top. Add enough boiling water to the tin to cover the bottom. Heat the cream, sugar, instant coffee powder and cinnamon stick over low heat until the sugar has dissolved. Remove the cinnamon and add the vanilla essence. Cool slightly. Whisk together the egg yolks and 1 egg until light and gradually beat in the cream mixture. Pour the mixture into the ramekins and bake for about 55 minutes or until the custard has just set. Remove the ramekins from the roasting tin and chill. When cold, sprinkle the baked custards with a layer of sugar, ensuring the entire surface is covered. Chill for at least 4 hours but preferably overnight.

Preheat the oven grill. Put the ramekins on a baking sheet and heat under the grill until the sugar caramelises, taking care that the topping doesn't burn or that the custards don't become too hot.

Chill for about 1 hour before serving.

Makes 10–12.

Panna cotta

Panna cotta literally means 'cooked cream'. A delectable dessert with a velvety texture.

500 ml (2 c) cream
125 ml (½ c) sugar
finely grated rind of 1 lemon
10 ml (2 t) gelatine
30 ml (2 T) sherry
125 ml (½ c) fruitcake mix, soaked in
  a little sherry
10 glacé cherries, chopped

Slowly heat together the cream and sugar, stirring until the sugar has dissolved. Do not bring the mixture to the boil. Add the lemon rind. Sponge the gelatine in the sherry and heat slowly until melted. Mix the gelatine with a little of the cream mixture and add to the remaining cream mixture. Leave to thicken slightly. Add the fruit and mix. Grease 10 ramekins with nonstick food spray and divide the cream mixture among them. Chill, preferably overnight. Unmould the desserts on plates just before serving and serve with berry sauce (see recipe p. 248).

Serves 10.

> **Variations**
> Melt 250 g dark chocolate with the cream and omit the fruit. Increase the gelatine to 15 ml (1 T).
>
> Substitute buttermilk for half the cream; this will give the desserts a slightly sour taste and make them less rich.

Chocolate mousse

The recipe for this dessert flavoured with a hint of chilli, originally comes from Sydney. It's flop-proof and perfect for entertaining a large number of guests: simply double the quantities. Serve in glass cups.

2 red chillies
30 ml (2 T) brandy
500 g dark chocolate, chopped
3 egg, whisked
3 egg yolks
5 ml (1 t) instant coffee powder
5 ml (1 t) vanilla essence
500 ml (2 c) cream, chilled
stiffly whipped cream and mint leaves
  to decorate

Soak the chillies in the brandy overnight. Remove the chillies and put the flavoured brandy and remaining ingredients, except the cream and mint, in a double boiler. Heat over boiling water, stirring continuously until the mixture is smooth. Remove from the heat and leave to cool. Stir occasionally. Whip the cream until soft peaks form and fold into the cooled chocolate mixture. Put in the fridge and chill until firm. Using an ice-cream spoon put 2–3 scoops into a bowl or glass cup. Serve with whipped cream and fresh mint.

Serves 8.

> **Tip**
> Add 15–30 ml (1–2 T) coffee powder to the chocolate mixture to give it a wonderful cappuccino flavour.

> **Chilli tip**
> Chilli and chocolate are a winning combination. Next time you make chocolate truffles soak 1 chilli in 20 ml (4 t) vodka per 100 g chocolate.

Nutty apple pudding

It's hard to believe such a simple recipe can produce such a delicious result. Jenny Morris, also known as the Giggling Gourmet, simply stir-fries apples, honey and nuts to make this scrumptious dessert.

100 g butter
125 ml (½ c) honey
4 Granny Smith or Braeburn apples,
   cut into thick rings, peel and all
50 g hazelnuts
50 g flaked almonds
50 g pecan nuts
vanilla ice cream to serve

Heat the butter in a saucepan over low heat until it just begins to foam. Add the honey and when the mixture starts bubbling add the apples and nuts. Cook uncovered over medium heat until a syrup just begins to form. Serve in bowls with a scoop of vanilla ice cream.

Serves 4.

Fruit roulade

The meringue for this roulade is so soft it can be rolled. Fill it with yoghurt and a variety of fruit and serve as a light dessert.

ROULADE
3 large egg whites
1 ml (pinch) salt
175 g caster sugar
5 ml (1 t) cornflour
5 ml (1 t) balsamic vinegar
5 ml (1 t) vanilla essence
60 ml (¼ c) flaked almonds
icing sugar

FILLING
250 ml (1 c) fat-free plain yoghurt
1 large ripe peach OR ¼ spanspek,
   peeled, seeds removed and diced
pulp of 4 granadillas

Preheat the oven to 150 °C. Line a 33 cm x 23 cm swiss roll tin with baking paper and grease with butter, margarine or nonstick food spray.

ROULADE
Whisk the egg whites until foamy. Add the salt and whisk until double in volume. Gradually beat in the caster sugar until the mixture is thick and shiny. Sift over the cornflour and beat into the egg whites. Using a metal spoon, fold in the vinegar and vanilla essence.

Spoon the mixture into the tin and spread evenly, taking care not to let any air escape. Scatter the almond flakes on top. Bake for 30 minutes or until the surface is just firm to the touch. Remove from the oven, cover with damp wax paper and leave for 10 minutes.

FILLING
Dust another sheet of wax paper with icing sugar. Remove the damp paper and turn out the meringue on the sugar-coated paper. Remove the paper lining.

Spread the meringue with the yoghurt and scatter the fruit on top. Spoon the granadilla pulp on top. Using the paper as a guide, roll up the roulade from one of the short ends. Cut into slices and serve.

Serves 4–6.

Nutty apple pudding

Spring Pavlova

Summer fruit such as strawberries and berries impart colour to a Pavlova but you can use any available fruit. Fill the Pavlova just before serving or else it will become soggy.

MERINGUE
6 extra-large egg whites,
     at room temperature
2 ml (½ t) salt
450 ml caster sugar
20 ml (4 t) white wine vinegar
25 ml (5 t) cornflour

FILLING
250 ml (1 c) fresh cream, chilled
80 ml (⅓ c) caster sugar
10 ml (2 t) vanilla essence
250 ml (1 c) thick Greek yoghurt
45 ml (3 T) instant vanilla pudding powder
375 ml (1½ c) fruit such as strawberries
     and kumquats, rinsed and halved
1 packet frozen summer berries, drained

Preheat the oven to 140 °C and line 2 large baking sheets with baking paper. Dust with cornflour.

MERINGUE
Whisk the egg whites and salt in a large clean glass bowl until soft peaks form. Add the caster sugar by the spoonful, beating continuously until the mixture is stiff and shiny and retains its shape. Using a metal spoon, carefully fold in the vinegar and cornflour. Divide the mixture in half and shape into 2 x 22 cm circles (1 on each baking sheet). Make a slight hollow in the middle of each circle with the back of a spoon. Bake each meringue base for 1 hour (do not open the oven door during the baking time) and switch off the oven. Cool the meringues in the oven (keep the oven door shut) until completely cool. Remove from the baking sheets and store in an airtight container until needed.

FILLING
Whip together the cream, caster sugar and vanilla essence until stiff. Using the same beater, whisk together the yoghurt and instant pudding powder for 1 minute. Fold into the cream mixture. Chill for at least 1 hour. Spread half the filling on one of the meringue bases and scatter some of the fruit on top. Cover with the other meringue base, spread with the remaining filling and scatter the remaining fruit on top.

Makes 1 double Pavlova.

Variations
Sustitute 250 ml (1 c) stiffly whipped cream mixed with 60 ml (¼ c) lemon curd for the filling.

Pavlova with caramel and banana: Beat together 1 can (397 g) caramel condensed milk, 250 ml (1 c) cream, 60 ml (¼ c) milk and 60 ml (¼ c) instant caramel pudding. Fold in 125 ml (½ c) thick yoghurt and chill until needed. Spoon the filling on top of the meringue base. Slice 6 ripe bananas and arrange on top.

Tips for making a perfect Pavlova
Never fill the meringue with a hot filling.
A Pavlova base will keep well in an airtight container for about 3 weeks.
The meringue base freezes well.
The outside of the meringue base has tiny cracks and it's soft inside.
When making a Pavlova the meringue circle is formed with a spoon and not piped.

Oranges in spicy red wine sauce

This dessert is reminiscent of pears in red wine sauce but more fragrant.

250 ml (1 c) sugar
180 ml (¾ c) water
180 ml (¾ c) red wine
4 whole cloves
2 pieces stick cinnamon, broken into
    pieces
1 piece dried ginger
1 star anise
4 small unpeeled oranges, quartered
200 ml Bulgarian yoghurt

Heat the sugar and water in a saucepan, stirring continuously until the sugar has dissolved. Add the red wine, cloves, cinnamon, ginger and star anise and simmer the mixture for 5–10 minutes or until fragrant. Add the orange quarters and simmer for another 30–50 minutes or until the sauce is syrupy and the orange peel is soft. Baste the oranges continually with the sauce while cooking. Spoon into glasses and serve with a scoop of Bulgarian yoghurt.

Serves 2–4.

Pears in white wine stuffed with dried apricots

6 firm pears
750 ml (3 c) white wine
150 g white sugar
1 ml (pinch) saffron
6 whole cloves
1 piece stick cinnamon
peel of 1 orange, cut into thick strips
peel of 1 lemon, cut into thick strips
15 ml (1 T) whole star anise seeds
100 g dried apricots, chopped

Carefully peel and core the pears. Put all the ingredients except the apricots in a saucepan, cover and slowly bring them to the boil. Simmer gently until the pears are just soft.
    Remove from the heat, add the apricots, cover and leave overnight. Stuff the hollowed out pears with the apricots and serve with plain yoghurt and biscotti or ricotta and blue cheese ice cream (see recipe).

Serves 6.

RICOTTA AND BLUE CHEESE ICE CREAM
Mix 45 ml (3 T) fresh ricotta with 15–30 ml (1–2 T) crumbled blue cheese and fold in 30 ml (2 T) plain fat-free yoghurt. Freeze for 1–2 hours and serve a spoonful or two with the pears.

Pineapple and mango in ginger syrup

A deliciously refreshing dessert. Also serve it with a little plain yoghurt for breakfast, in which case use less sugar for the syrup.

500 ml (2 c) caster sugar
500 ml (2 c) water
10 cm piece fresh ginger, thinly sliced
60 ml (¼ c) rum
60 ml (¼ c) lime juice
1 large pineapple, peeled and cut into
    large chunks
2 large mangoes, peeled and cut into
    large chunks
oil for shallow-frying

Heat the sugar, water and ginger over medium heat, stirring until the sugar has dissolved. Bring to the boil and simmer for about 5 minutes or until the syrup thickens slightly. Stir in the rum and lime juice and leave to chill. Fry the pineapple and mango pieces in an oiled griddle pan or over the coals until brown on both sides. Put the fruit in a large bowl, pour over the syrup and chill overnight. Remove the fruit from the syrup and bring 500 ml (2 c) of the syrup to the boil in a saucepan. Simmer uncovered until reduced by half. Serve the syrup with the fruit and plain yoghurt or ice cream.

Serves 8.

Ice cream bombe with berry sauce

The bombe can be made with a variety of fruit and nuts. Prepare the day before so it can freeze overnight.

BOMBE

2 ready-made swiss rolls, sliced

1 litre (4 c) vanilla ice cream

1 litre (4 c) chocolate ice cream

2 green figs in syrup, drained and sliced

75 g chocolate splinters OR roughly chopped dark chocolate

50 g almond splinters, toasted

75 g glacé cherries, quartered OR mixed citrus peel

BERRY SAUCE

300 g frozen mixed berries, defrosted

30 ml (2 T) water

60–75 ml (4–5 T) caster sugar (or to taste)

30 ml (2 T) port

BOMBE

Line the bottom and sides of a 1,5–2 litre glass bowl with clingfilm, ensuring it overlaps the sides sufficiently so you can cover the bombe before freezing it. Line the bottom and sides of the bowl with the swiss roll slices, packing them tightly so there are no openings. Put the vanilla and chocolate ice creams in separate bowls and stir to soften slightly. Stir the figs and chocolate splinters into the vanilla ice cream and the nuts and cherries into the chocolate ice cream.

Working rapidly to prevent the ice cream from melting, fill the lined bowl with the ice cream in layers, spreading it evenly. Arrange a layer of swiss roll slices on top of the ice cream and cover with the overlapping clingfilm. Cover with another layer of clingfilm and freeze overnight.

TO SERVE

Put a large serving platter in the freezer 30 minutes before serving the bombe. Turn out on the cold platter and remove the clingfilm.

SAUCE

Purée the berries in a food processor until smooth. Add the water, caster sugar and port and mix well. Cut the bombe with a large knife dipped in boiling water and wiped lightly. Serve with the berry sauce.

Serves 10–12.

Variations
Instead of plain swiss roll use chocolate swiss roll or Madeira or sponge cake slices spread with a thin layer of jam or caramelised condensed milk. Sprinkle a little sherry or port over the cake if desired.

Tips
Use peppermint chocolate for an interesting variation.

If using dried fruit such as raisins or apricots soak them in brandy or sherry beforehand.

Serve the bombe with a chocolate sauce.

Ice cream bombe with berry sauce

INDEX